INTRODUCTION TO
WEB TECHNOLOGY
& INTERNET

INTRODUCTION TO WEB TECHNOLOGY & INTERNET

BANKIM PATEL
LAL BIHARI BARIK

Acme Learning
Private Limited
Where quality, innovation and commitment matters

ISBN: 978-81-907104-3-5

First Edition: New Delhi 2009

Published by
Acme Learning Private Limited
2/8, Ansari Road, Darya Ganj
New Delhi-110 002

Printed at
Rajiv Book Binding House
Delhi

This book is dedicated in loving memory of our parents.

Brief Contents

Detailed Contents

Preface

"The biggest growth in the Internet, and the area that will prove to be one of the biggest agents of change, will be e-Learning.

Education of the Internet is going to make e-mail usage like a rounding error in terms of the Internet capacity it will consume"

— JOHN CHAMBERS
CEO, Cisco Systems

Information is the nucleus of today's interconnected world. We need to be able to exchange and retrieve our information quickly, efficiently and securely at any time at any location.

To make such new technology work, Berners-Lee proposed that it would make extensive use of Hypertext to link information across the web. The original proposal noted the importance of working within heterogeneous environments, emphasizing shared information by users of various systems using different browsers. In his conclusion he noted that "We should work toward a universal linked information system, in which generality and portability are more important than fancy graphics techniques and complex extra facilities."

The World Wide Web has changed the way millions of people work and play. The Hyper Text Markup Language (HTML) is at the heart of the web. HTML is a language that is easy to write, easy to understand and highly portable.

The pages that follow in this book contain examples and description of the elements that can be used to build web page. The examples show how to get the syntax right, but they also show how to make a great professional page.

This book helps you to understand the elements that are in your web pages. In addition, to giving examples of the many elements that can be used in an HTML file, sample programs for the web are included. There are illustrations that show how to set up comment form, how to set up a simple search tool for your site and how to update, add or delete files though the Web interface.

The goal of this book is to help you design a professional web page. A professional page will make use of enough standards to make development simple across multiple web pages on your site, while taking into consideration the existent older browsers that do not properly support the latest standards.

We will focus on using HTML and using Cascading Style Sheets to handle certain aspects of design, aspects that stop short of page layouts. We encourage you to use styles for layouts; it is a better choice in the long run. However, our goal here, in keeping with the original intent of the Web, is to link information and allow users to access that information.

BANKIM PATEL
LAL BIHARI BARIK

Acknowledgements

We had a unique opportunity to work on several projects in the area of Internet and Web Designing that helped us to gain and broaden our experience. Without that we could not have written this book. We would like to thank the International Business Machines Corporation and, in particular, it's Academic Initiative Division for having provided us with that opportunity.

Numerous people furnished us with in-depth reviews of the book, supported us and provided us with their valuable expertise. We are indebted to Vikas Manoria, Devkant Aggarwal, Devesh Jinwala, D.R. Shah, J.G. Parmar, K. B. Sukhadia, H.R. Vishwakarma, P. Thrimurthy, R.P. Soni, P. V. Virparia, D. B. Chauksy, Bipin Mehta, Himansu Samal, Gladston Raj S, Prasant Pokarnaa, Jaydeep Chaudhari, Vikram Gaur, N.M. Patel, S.V. Patel, C. K. Bhensdadiya, Kamlendu Pandey, Kiran Trivedi, Paritosh Shukla, Ravi Satpathy, Radha Rani, Sanjib Kumar Sahu, Poonam Mittal, Rekha Chaudhari, Nitin Patel, Mehul S. Rawal, Bhushan Trivedi, Pawanesh Abrol, Sanchita Pal and Mohan Nair.

We would specially like to thank Mamta, Zeel, Nagen, Gagan, Ankita, Akash, Anushree and Kartik for the borrowed time.

Finally, we wish to thank the team of Acme Learning for their help in the final stages of preparing this book.

About the Authors

Dr. Bankim Patel - Director, SRIMCA, Ph.D: Dr. Bankim Patel has over 19 years of experience in academics and has worked in various capacities in the university system. He has taken a lead for starting various computer science and application courses. He has 3 books and 19 research papers under his belt. His area of interest and expertise is Intelligent Information Systems. One M.Phil. and five Ph.D. students have already completed their research work under his guidance. He has been honored with many national level awards.

Lal Bihari Barik - Assistant Professor, SRIMCA, Pursuing Ph.D: He has over eight years industry & teaching experience in the field of Java Technologies and Web development. He has worked on various web driven projects such as HKDA System, Alumni E-mail System and so on. His interactive e-governance portal of Bardoli Nagarpalika was adjudged as the best portal amongst 147 Nagarpalikas by Gujarat Government. His Web Portal on Sardar Sarovar Punravas Yojana got second rank by Gujarat Government. He is also serving as the coordinator of BISAG (Gujarat Government) for various activities of the Industries - Institute Linkage Program. He has served as a Resource Person for many workshops in the area of Java Technologies, DB2, Open Source, etc. He has published and presented several research papers in National and International Conferences & Journals. His primary interest areas are Artificial Intelligence and Goal-Driven Service Oriented Architecture (GD-SOA). For his doctoral thesis, he is working in the area of Artificial Intelligence, where by attempting to develop adaptive intelligent web-based educational system in a multi-agent environment.

CHAPTER 1

Basic Concepts of Internet

CHAPTER OBJECTIVES

In this chapter, you will learn basic concepts of the Internet, how it facilitates communication among all the smaller networks and individual computer systems. We explain the paradigms and principles of Internet and its various connection types and their benefits. We extensively focused on the most important features of e-mail, LISTSERV, NEWSGROUPS, Telnet, GOPHER, VERONICA, WAIS and Electronic Journals.

CHAPTER OUTLINES

1.1 INTRODUCTION

In 1969, the Department of Defense (DOD) of the United States (US) started a network called the ARPAnet (Advanced Research Projects Administration Network). It began in a modest way, with one computer in California and another in Utah. It was an experiment carried out to see whether networking could be reliable, and prevent communications breakdown during the possible war. Also, the DOD wanted to maintain contacts with military research contractors and universities doing military-funded research. These institutes could also share hardware and software resources, which they otherwise could not have afforded. Later, the military allowed other universities to join the network. Students at these universities caught on and then developed much of the software that gave the Internet and its present shape.

ARPAnet quickly grew to encompass the entire American continent and became a big success. In order to manage the size and the complexity of the network were broken into two parts: MILNET for managing military sites and a new smaller ARPAnet for non-military sites. During the 1970s, other networks, like the BITNET and the USENET also came into being. Around the 1980s, a network called the NSFNET (National Science Foundation Network) was created.

The NSFNET allowed universities and research agencies to link up with its super computers. Using the modern technology, it permitted any computer in the system to link up with any other computer connected to the system.

By the 1990s, many leading networks shut down, and the remaining hooked onto the NSFNET. This growing web was the birth of the Internet.

The unique thing about the Internet is that it facilitates communication among all the smaller networks and individual computer systems that connect to it. With the dramatic increases in a bandwidth, decreases in the communication cost and an ever-increasing number of firms using it, the Internet has ushered in a revolution. This is amply borne out by the fact that the worldwide Internet backbone connectivity has grown in 5-6 countries, from Dec. 1987 to 90 and other countries in Dec. 95.

Of late, the Internet phenomenon has also attracted huge media attention, because of stratospheric market caps accorded to Internet companies. This has come in the time of an unprecedented bull-run in corporate America. A question, we all get asked is whether this is for real? The Internet is a technology paradigm change, which has impacted our lives. It is the equivalent of the steam engine, telephone, dynamite, electric bulb and other inventions, which changed human lives for better (or worse?).

The net, which began as a messaging, and a recreational tool has emerged as a powerful media. Experts regard the net as a "new media" business that facilitates e-commerce. The Internet is the closest; you can get to the world of perfect competition, where information on buyers and sellers is available. For some items like software, data and information, it reduces the distribution costs to zero. Both these features have impacted the real world in a dramatic fashion.

According to the recent estimates, the Internet is now, a set of around 10,000,000 million computers seamlessly integrated more than 100,000 networks and the numbers continue to grow.

1.2 HOW THE INTERNET WORKS?

All the computers and networks connected by the Internet work, because they follow a simple rule, TCP/IP (A Communication Protocol) TCP/IP breaks all data into small packets, and the first part of each packet has the address, where the packet is meant to go. There is no central computer or authority. For transmission hardware, the Internet is dependent on the existing infrastructure developed by the telephone companies and other telecommunications companies. Internet service providers lease data circuits from the telephone networks and have dedicated computers at the ends points or nodes. These rely on the distributed intelligence of the networking equipment known as "routers", thus bypassing the telephone company's expensive switching computers, while using their transmission lines. Computers known as the "servers" hold all the content of the Internet, and the servers are owned by organizations and companies who want to distribute information.

For example, if a message is sent from Mumbai to California to a server named california.org, the message will be broken up into packets. Some may travel from VSNL to the MCI router in the US, some may travel to Chennai and then to the MCI router, and so forth. There is no predetermined path and even individual packets of the same message may follow different paths. It all depends upon the traffic at that node, at that moment in time. As the packets reach california.org, they are all put together as in the original message and delivered to the given address.

In order to accomplish the task of the messaging across a network, computers use a networking protocol. This enables different types of computers running different types of operating system to communicate effectively. The de-facto standard today is TCP/IP.

1.3 ROLE OF AN ISP IN THE INTERNET

Suppose you as a user want to access the Internet and see a website called, www.vsnl.com. Then you will have to log onto the net using a telephone and a modem, and use a browser to access the site. Any entity that provides you with means to do so is called an Internet Service Provider (ISP).

The main components of providing access to the Internet consists of:

- International connectivity, which allows you to connect to the amorphous Internet.
- Domestic connectivity, which allows you to connect to the domestic gateway.

There are three ways; an ISP can connect to the Internet cloud, which includes VSNL/DoT, STPI or through private operators. STPI is a semi-government organization that has authorized to sell international gateway services to companies involved in developing software for exporting. It has now been permitted to sell international connectivity to ISPs and is presently providing this service in 10 cities and planning to increase, its presence in other cities throughout India.

Before any Internet Service Provider (ISP) can start operating, he needs the bandwidth, which is the channel for global connectivity. Currently in India, the bandwidth can be obtained from either VSNL or STPI (Software Technology Park India), or the DoT. The government has granted permission to private players for setting-up their own gateways. As per Satyam's estimation this could cost anywhere between Rs. 80 crore to Rs. 100 crore.

The private gateway providers are responsible for connecting routers above 2 mbps with monitoring agencies like the Intelligence Bureau and the RAW. The DoT is responsible for issuing the security clearances. A committee comprising representatives from DoT, Department of Electronics, Ministry of Defence, Space and Home, National Informatics Centre and NASSCOM decides over clearing projects.

Under the new Internet Policy, ISPs were allowed to set up their own gateways, but the absence of any security guidelines precluded this, and they had to lease capacities from VSNL. Like VSNL, they would be allowed to lease surplus capacities to other ISPs. The present policy permits an ISP to utilize the infrastructure of DoT, Railways or Power Grid, etc., for their backbone and lease-line connectivity. The ISP is not permitted to build its own backbone. This policy affects only the nationwide ISPs. Presently, only DoT is able to provide the leased-lines while Power Grid and Railways are yet to build and come out with commercial availability of these lines. The Symmetric bandwidth, (i.e., the bandwidth for both unlinking and downlinking) is same, which is a waste of resource and cost. Buying the bandwidth is an expensive option, but also the most preferred option currently. The disadvantage is that the bandwidth obtained is symmetric. This means, it has equal capability of unlinking as well as downlinking. The unlinking forms a very small part of the data transfer, there is a lot of wastages.

The government has brought some relief to ISPs, by reducing the rent; they had to pay for a telephone line. ISPs will now have to pay the normal costs. In the earlier circular, it was notified that for every telephone line that an ISP took from the DoT, it was supposed to pay an annual rental of Rs. 15,000, which is significantly higher than the rate for normal users. The ISP or Internet Service Provider can be viewed as a new media center. It allows a number of people to interact around it (what experts call as community creation) and can exploit this crowd to get advertising and push e-commerce. There are two aspects of facilitating this interaction:

Uplinking and Downlinking

Downlinking is the transfer of data from the servers located elsewhere, to the one located where the user is. Uplinking is the opposite. It is observed and proven that in case of Internet, uplinking forms is a very small part of the data transfer. Majority of the transfer involves downloading from various servers, which are mostly located outside India. Compare this with a television, where the transfer only involves downlinking from the satellite. There is no uplinking at all.

1.4 INTERNET CONNECTION TYPES

There are various options available to connect to the Internet. To setup an Internet connection you must have an Internet Service Provider (ISP). An ISP (such as BSNL, Sify, Reliance, Data Infosis, GTL, BG Broad India, HCL Infinet, CMC,Guj Info Petro, Rogers, Sprint, Verizon, etc.) provides users with an Internet connection. In India, there are more than 183 operating ISPs available. The commonly used ones are explained below.

1.4.1 Dial-up Access

Dial-up pertains to a telephone connection in a system of many lines shared by many users. A dial-up connection is established and maintained for limited time duration. Dial-up lines are sometimes called switched lines. A dial-up connection can be initiated manually or automatically by your computer's modem or other device.

The most common way to access the Internet from home is with a modem and a phone call to the ISP. The call to the ISP is through the regular MTNL or DoT lines. This option is best suited for small time users, students, etc. This is the most viable option for people using the Internet for 5-6 hours a day.

How to configure and use Dial-up Connections in Windows XP?

Configuring Dial-up Connections

1. Click Start, click Control Panel and then click Network and Internet Connections.
2. Click Create a connection to the network at your office.
3. In the Location Information dialog box, enter the appropriate information. Click OK and then click OK to close the Phone and Modem Options dialog box and start the New Connection Wizard.
4. In the New Connection Wizard, click Dial-up connection, and then click Next.
5. Type a name for the network to which you are connecting (such as "My Office Network") and then click Next.

6. Type the phone number for the network to which you are connecting, including, if necessary, the area code and "1" prefix.
7. Specify whether you want this connection to be available for anyone's use, meaning for any user on this computer, or for your use only, meaning only for the user who is now logged on.
8. Specify whether you want a shortcut to the connection on your desktop.
9. Then Click Finish.

Using Dial-up Connections

1. Click Start, Click Connect To, and the click the connection that you want to use.
2. In the User Name box, type your user name.
3. In the Password box, type your password.
4. Choose one of the following options:
   - To save the user name and password so that you will not have to type them in the future, select the Save this user name and password for the following users check box.
   - If you want only the current user to have access to the saved user name and password, select the me only check box.
   - If you want all users to have access to the user name and password, select the anyone who uses this computer check box.
5. Click Dial.

1.4.2 ISDN (Integrated Services Digital Network)

ISDN network is a very fast, highly reliable medium that brings voice, data and video together on one digital line. The hardware cost for setting up ISDN services is higher. It has two channels, hence it can support up to two voice-grade signals per `ISDN wire'.

An International Standard is for the switched, digital dial-up telephone service for the voice and the data. Analog telephones and the fax machines are used over ISDN lines, but their signals are converted into digital by the ISDN terminal adapter.

Although announced in the early 1980s, it took more than a decade before ISDN became widely available. It enjoyed a surge of growth in the early days of the Internet, because it provided the only higher-speed alternative to analog modems in many areas. Still working in many behind-the-scenes applications, ISDN is rarely used for Internet access.

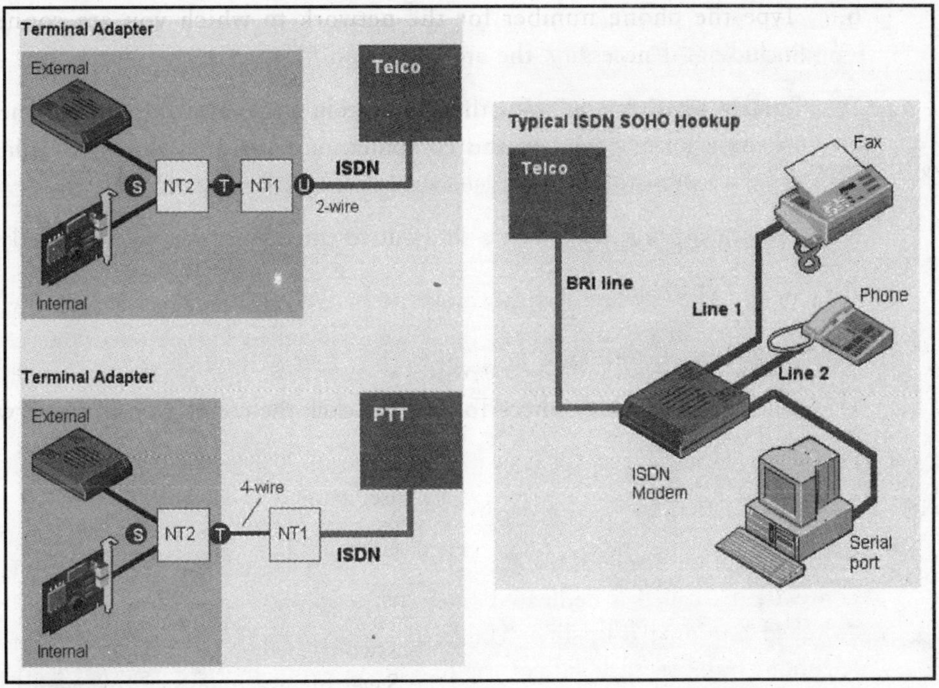

Channels

ISDN uses 64 kbps "B" (bearer) channels to carry the voice and the data. A separate "D" (delta) channel is used for control. The D channel signals the carrier's voice switch to make calls, put them on hold and activate features such as conference calling and call forwarding. It also receives caller ID data. Because the D channel connects directly to the telephone system's SS7 signaling network, ISDN calls are dialed much faster than regular telephone calls.

Basic Service

ISDN BRI (Basic Rate Interface) uses one wire pair to carry two 64 kbps B channels and one 16 kbps D channel (2B + D). Both B channels are often "bonded" into one, providing a total data rate of 128 kbps.

High-Speed Service

ISDN PRI (Primary Rate Interface) uses four wire pairs to provide 23 B channels and one 64 kbps D channel (23B + D). A PRI line is equivalent to a 24-channel T1 line. Bonding channels is common; for example, six channels provide 384 kbps for high-quality videoconferencing. In Europe, PRI includes 30 B channels and one D channel, equivalent to an E1 line. See SS7 and T1.

Connecting to ISDN

ISDN requires a network terminator (NT1) and a terminal adapter (TA). The NT1 plugs into the two-wire line from the telephone company and provides four-wire output to the terminal adapter. In the U.S., the NT1 and TA are typically combined in one unit, but are separate in Europe and Japan.

The terminal adapter is called an "ISDN modem", if it has a built-in analog modem to hook up regular telephones and fax machines. If the ISP supports the Multilink PPP (MPPP) protocol, the TA can bond channels for faster Internet access.

The Terminal Adapter

TAs in the U.S. generally has a built-in NT1 and attaches via a two-wire "U" interface. In Europe and Japan, the NT1 is installed by the telephone company and attaches to the TA via a four-wire "T" interface. The NT2 component, which is built into most devices, is a logical interface for multiple access and attaches via the "S" interface.

1.4.3 Leased Lines

A leased line is a telephone line that has been leased for private use. In some contexts, it's called a dedicated line. A leased line is usually contrasted with a switched line or dial-up line. Unlike traditional PSTN lines, it does not have a telephone number, each side of the line being permanently connected to the other.

Usually, large companies rent leased lines from the telephone message carriers (such as AT&T) to interconnect different geographic locations in their company. The alternative is to buy and maintain their own private lines or increasingly perhaps, to use the public switched lines with secure message protocols. (This is called tunneling.)

Leased lines are dedicated lines directly from the ISP to the subscriber. The speeds available are in the range of 9.6 kbps to 2 mbps. The efficiency of the leased line connection is 2-2.5 times better than the dial-up access. The cost is more than that of the dial up access.

1.4.4 Cable Internet

Nowadays, in addition to the traditional cable services, most of the cable TV companies also provide Internet services. Cable internet technology is a high-bandwidth internet service for homes and small offices. The high-bandwidth is transmitted over the existing cable TV lines. In other words, the internet is accessed over the same line as the cable TV. Although, the cable and the TV signal are transmitted on the same media, there is not interference with the two different signals. The cable TV providers are most likely the ones that also offer the high-bandwidth cable internet. The cable TV lines are coax cables. Cable internet is a continuous connection; therefore, you are always connected to the internet.

For example, with dial-up internet you have to connect with a username and password, but with cable there is no need to do that because it is setup with the cable modem. In order to be connected to cable internet, a computer is needed with a cable modem. This modem does the same thing that the dial-up and the DSL modem does, which is converting analog signal to digital and digital signal to analog signal. The cable provider provides the modem to the customer. The cable internet transmission date rate ranges between 1.5 Mbps and 6.0 Mbps. The cost of cable service ranges from $30 to $50 a month. This cost includes will cover the following services: unlimited inter net access, cable modem rental fee, and internet application software. An installation fee is required when installing cable.

Advantages of Cable Internet

For one thing, cable internet is faster than dialup internet. Another advantage is that cable internet is always on and will not interfere with the cable TV. Cable internet user the existing cable TV lines for data transmission. The distance between the cable customer and the cable internet provide does not affect the speed of the cable. The monthly fee for cable internet is fix regardless of the usage. The cable company provides the cable modem. Also cable internet is able to take advantage in providing VOIP telephone to customers, which is a very cost effective technology.

Disadvantages of Cable Internet

Some areas are unable to get cable internet service. The bandwidth is shared with everyone in your neighborhood who is on the same segment. Cable internet transmission is asymmetric. The upload speed is slower than the download speed.

You could contact your local cable provider to get more information on services provided by them.

1.5 WEB HOSTING

The Internet has unleashed a number of business opportunities, the basic of which is, what is known as web hosting. Web hosting ISPs will provide the servers, where the sites are hosted, For example, when you type www.hotline.com, your request goes to the server on which the site is residing. Some of the smaller entities cannot afford to buy their own servers, so they lease server space. This has resulted in the web hosting opportunity.

1.6 VIRTUAL PRIVATE NETWORK (VPN)

A virtual private network is a group of computer systems, typically connected to a private network (a network built and maintained by an organization solely for its own use) with limited public-network access that communicates "securely" over a public network. VPNs may exist between an individual machine and a private network (client-to-server) or a remote LAN and a private network (server-to-server). Security features differ from product to product, but most security experts agree that VPNs include encryption, strong authentication of remote users or hosts, and mechanisms for hiding or masking information about the private network topology from potential attackers on the public network. As networks get more and more complicated, many corporates may just want to outsource the entire service to a provider who offers managed data network services. That means creating and running the whole network — including the Intranet, extranet and the VPN — for a corporate client.

1.7 VOICE OVER INTERNET

Internet telephony is the new technology, where phone calls can be made in any part of the world through the Internet. There are various web sites offering Net Telephony services like Net2phone (www.Net2Phone.com), Vocal Tec (www.vocaltec.com), NetMeeting (www.netmeeting.com). The voice quality is not comparable to that of the normal telephone call. According to a survey, it has been found that price is a more favored feature than quality. Currently, Internet telephony is banned in India. If it is detected an ISP can lose its operating license.

1.8 E-MAIL

Electronic mail or e-mail is a method of transferring information by electronic means from one location to another. This information can be in the form of the text file or a binary file. It can also be used to retrieve Web pages and files from FTP sites.

The transmission of electronic mail is perhaps one of the most used tools of the Internet. It permits fast, cheap and convenient communication among all the users of the net. Conceptually it is similar to normal mail. An electronic mail program defines a "mailbox" similar to a postal mailbox, which contains the files where the messages that arrive are stored until the owner of the mailbox decides to open his mail. Just as with ordinary mail, there is a sender or author of the message and a receiver or addressee of the same. The difference is that in electronic mail, we use only a computer, a modem and a telephone line, with nothing more is needed than to key in the message and send it automatically and instantaneously to the addressee.

The key to the whole process is in the specification of the address of the user. The messages are directed to the addressee by means of the specification of the name of the file, which the addressee has in a remote computer, and the location of this computer. The address to which you send the information is separated by full stops.

Advantages of e-mail

- *Speed:* A few seconds are enough for the message to get to the mailbox of the addressee. It makes no difference at what distance the receiver is, as the messages arrive with great speed, whether they are within the same town, country or continent.

- *Economy:* The transmission of messages is very cheap. Moreover, the price does not depend on the distance the message travels. The concept of the global village, a world without distances, where communication with a neighbor or somebody on the other side of the planet has the same cost, is changing the world. Frontiers disappear and the entire world is equidistant from the computer.

- *Efficiency:* Automatic transmission of the same message to hundreds of addressees, the possibility of answering messages automatically, the encoding of information in order to maintain the confidentiality of our conversation and the electronic storage in files of the documents sent and received, all make the system an efficient one.

- *Versatility:* Electronic mail is not limited to the transmission of the text. It can also be used for sending and receiving sound, graphics, images or any file with multimedia format, in order to be a member of a discussion group or a newsgroup, to receive electronic journals, to obtain a free copy of software or to interact with any kind of files that can be stored in a computer.

Limitations of e-mail

- *Emptying the mailbox:* If you have a dial-up connection to the Internet, you may not routinely empty your mailbox by dialing into your Internet provider. Internet providers will only hold mail for a certain period. After this, any mail that has not been collected is returned to the sender.

- *Absence of privacy:* The transmission of electronic information gives access to your messages to other people. Therefore, it is not an appropriate system for sending confidential information. However, there are systems, which minimize this problem. There are encryption programs, which encode the information making it unreadable to those users who do not have the software to decode the message. One of the most famous programs for this purpose is PGP (Pretty Good Privacy), which is freely available from numerous FTP servers on the net.

Structure of e-mail Message

This includes important data for the correct transmission of the message. The data includes the following elements, the first three of which are the only indispensable data for correct transmission:

- The address of the addressee.

- The address of the sender.

- The subject of the message.

The others are:

Date: The date and time of the transmission of the message.

Reply to: The address to which the sender wishes a possible reply to be sent. This is used when the sender does not want the correspondence to be sent to the address from which he sent the message, or when he wants the reply be sent to another person.

Cc: This corresponds to the initials of carbon copy. It is used when the sender wants to establish more than one addressee for the message, he is sending. In this way, the message will be sent to the principal addressee and a copy will be sent to all addressees, who figure under Cc.

Bcc: This corresponds to the initials of blind carbon copy. It is used to send a copy of the message to another addressee without his knowing who the principal addressee is or the addressee who figures under Cc.

Keywords: This is to specify keywords to the message sent, to enable carrying out searches among the messages.

Encrypted (Software keyhelp): It gives an idea of the software used to encode the message and of the appropriate manner of decoding.

Received: It informs about details of the path followed by the message to reach its destination.

The Message: The content of the letter.

E-mail Management Software

To be able to compose, send and receive e-mail, you must either use a dedicated e-mail client or have a mail facility within your Web browser. The vast majority of e-mail management programs are capable of connecting automatically with your mail server, the place where your mailbox is located, to import the new message to your computer. It is enough to select from the menu the "Check mail" option. These messages are stored in a mailbox, which normally has the name of "IN", where all the messages you receive are classified.

With the function "New Message", you can simply write the new message to be sent, placing in the appropriate spaces the address of the addressee and the subject of the message. It is enough to select by means of the mouse the options "send" for the message to be sent to the addressee, without any further complication for you. These messages that you send are stored in a mailbox, which usually has the name of "OUT". You can make new mailboxes for whatever subject you choose, in which you can store the messages in whatever way you choose.

One of the most important features you must demand of a good mail manager is the possibility of working while not connected to the Internet, that is to say offline, so that you can write your messages without using connection time. This feature implies that when you are writing and sending messages offline, these are stored in a sort of queue, so that when you connect to the Internet, all your messages present in the queue are sent to their addressees. When carrying out this task, the computer gives a report, which informs that the queue messages are being sent.

Another feature is the ability of the program to send other files related to the message, which may be images, sound, etc. This is known as MIME (Multipurpose Internet Mail Extensions) protocol. In this way, you can send, apart from letters, images, sounds, related files or programs, among many other possibilities.

Other features include the following

- *Text editing features:* These allow you to cut and paste text.
- *"Reply" and "forward" options:* On hitting the "Reply" button, the software automatically creates a new message with the addressee details completed. The original message may also be copied to this file to facilitate the composition of comments and answers. Forwarding mail to other colleagues is achieved by using the "Forward" function.
- *Easy addressing facilities:* As e-mail addresses tend to be long and instantly forgettable, it is important that your software has an address book function, where frequently used e-mail addresses can be stored and accessed. If you have a list of users whom you mail frequently, then the option to create a distribution list is also useful.
- *Support Web addresses:* Increasingly, e-mail messages contain references to various Web sites. If your software can translate a Web address into the clickable link, you can jump directly to that Web page from your e-mail software. The software that can perform this task is said to be HTTP enabled.

Addresses on the Internet

The Internet has a system of addressing information, which is used for navigating on the system and for the transmission of messages by means of electronic mail. In this address, you specify the name of the addressee (user identification), and the location of the computer at which that addressee can be found (domain). The data of the address is separated by the full stops and symbols. The typical structure is:

Syntax

```
userid@domain
```

Both sides of the address can be expanded by means of separation by full stops, such as:

Syntax

```
mpotter@nlm.nih.gov
```

Where the part located furthest to the right reference to the most general or highest-level identification, and as we move toward the left, more concrete or lower-level identification appears. In this particular case, mpolter is to be found at the computer nlm (National Library of Medicine), which in turn is included in nih (National Institutes of Health), while the high-level domain govt. indicates that the nih is a governmental institution.

Free e-mail Accounts

Even if you do not have a personal Internet account, you can still have your own e-mail account. Companies like HotMail and Yahoo! Mail allow anyone to create his own mail account, free of charge. Apart form being free, this type of mail account has other useful benefits including:

- Using a standard Web browser, e-mail can be collected from any Internet-connected computer anywhere in the world.
- As these e-mail services are independent of any Internet Service Provider (ISP), your e-mail address will remain the same, irrespective of how many times you change providers or move jobs.
- If you have multiple e-mail accounts, you can check all of them through one Web-based e-mail account.

For more on how to create a free e-mail account, visit either of the following sites:

HotMail http://www.hotmail.com/ Yahoo! Mail http://mail.yahoo.com/

1.9 INTERNET RELAY CHAT (IRC)

Internet Relay Chat (IRC) is a system for chatting that involves a set of rules and conventions and client/server software. It is a service that allows users to communicate in real time by typing text in a special window. The IRC uses software that allows users to type a message into a particular field and then submit the entry. The entry will then appear on a screen that is also simultaneously accepting input from multiple individuals at one time. That information is sent to all users about every 20 seconds, so everyone can see what everyone also is saying.

Like news, there are hundreds of IRC "channels," each devoted to a subject or user group. It allows for instance communication versus delay responses. It helps; companies can avoid fees from long distance and conference calls. The disadvantages of IRC are consuming bandwidth, spreading worms, susceptible to flooding. The conversations can tend to get very confusing as users try to keep up with streaming information. Again, it may difficult to tell, which comments are being directed to you. The nature of confusing atmosphere may cause users to break away from the group into smaller chat rooms. On the Web, certain sites such as Talk City or IRC networks such as the under net provide servers and help you download an IRC client to your PC. Talk City also offers an IRC client applet that it downloads for you as part of their home page so that you can start chatting right away.

Popular ongoing IRC channels are #hottub and #riskybus. A number of channels are set up and conducted in foreign languages. The most common IRC networks are IRCnet (mostly European), EFnet (mostly North American), Undernet, and Dalnet. Popular IRC clients include mIRC for Windows, IRCle for Mac OS, and irc2 (the original client) for UNIX-base operating systems.

1.10 FILE TRANSFER PROTOCOL (FTP)

The File Transfer Protocol (FTP) was one of the first efforts to create a standard means of exchanging files over a TCP/IP network, so the FTP has been around since the 1970s. The FTP was designed with as much flexibility as possible, so it could be used over networks other than TCP/IP, as well as being engineered to have the capability with exchanging files with a broad variety of machines.

FTP (file transfer protocol) programs are the simplest and most secure way to exchange files from one computer to another. The computers on which you run FTP are referred to as the local computer and the computer from which you receive or to which you send a file is referred to as the remote computer. In order for files to be received and sent, FTP programs must be available on both the local and remote computers. The local FTP is often referred to as the client program, and the FTP running on the remote computer is often referred to as the server program. The operating systems on the local and remote computers need not be the same.

What is an FTP Site?

An FTP site is like a large filing cabinet. With a traditional filing cabinet, the person who does the filing has the option to label and organize the files, however, they see fit. They also decide which files to keep locked and which remain public. It is the same with an FTP site. ftp://ftp.domain.com

The virtual 'key' to get into an FTP site is the UserID and the Password. If the creator of the FTP site is willing to give everyone access to the files, the UserID is 'anonymous' and the Password is your e-mail address (e.g. name@domain.com). If the FTP site is not public, there will be a unique UserID and the Password for each person who is granted access.

When connecting to an FTP site that allows anonymous logins, you're frequently not prompted for a name and the password. Hence, when downloading from the Internet, you most likely are using an anonymous FTP login and you don't even know it.

To make an FTP connection, you can use a standard Web browser (Internet Explorer, Netscape, etc.) or a dedicated FTP software program, referred to as an FTP 'Client'.

When using a Web browser for an FTP connection, FTP uploads are difficult, or sometimes impossible, and downloads are not protected (not recommended for uploading or downloading large files).

When connecting with an FTP Client, uploads and downloads couldn't be easier, and you have added security and additional features. For one, you're able to resume a download that do not successfully finish, which is a very nice feature for people using dial-up connections who frequently loose their Internet connection.

What is an FTP Client?

An FTP Client is software that is designed to transfer files back-and-forth between two computers over the Internet. It needs to be installed on your computer and can only be used with a live connection to the Internet.

The classic FTP Client look is a two-pane design. The pane on the left displays the files on your computer and the pane on the right displays the files on the remote computer.

File transfers are as easy as dragging-and-dropping files from one pane to the other or by highlighting a file and clicking one of the direction arrows located between the panes.

Additional features of the FTP Client include: multiple file transfer; the auto re-get or resuming features; a queuing utility; the scheduling feature; an FTP find utility; a synchronized utility; and for the advanced user, a scripting utility.

Various FTP Clients are: WS_FTP LE, AUTO FTP, WAR FTP, W3FILTER, FREEFTP, FUNFTP, SMARTFTP, CUTEFTP.

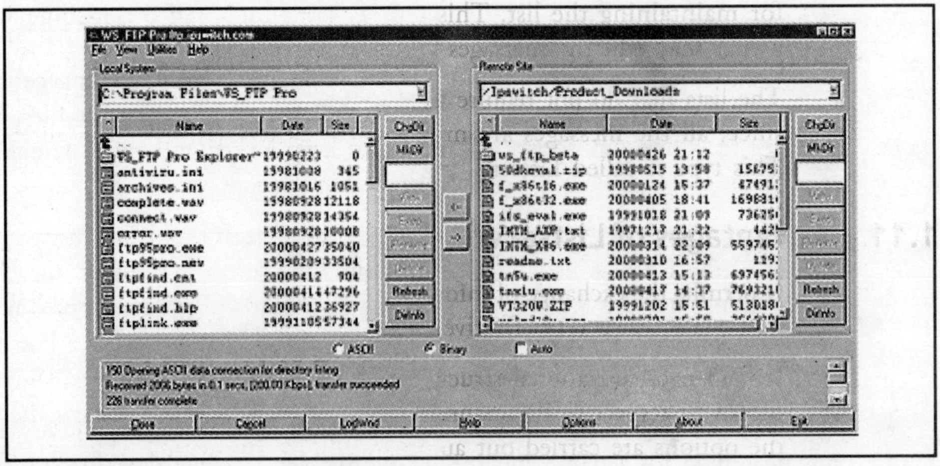

Usenet News is a set of international bulletin boards that allows people to discuss topics of interest with others, who share those interests regardless of time and location. Within Usenet News, the bulletin boards are referred to as Newsgroups.

Usenet Newsgroups share some similarities with electronic mailing lists; that is, both allow people to communicate with others who share an interest, both allow people to subscribe and unsubscribe. However, there are some fundamental differences.

You need to use a program other than your favorite e-mail program to look at the articles in a newsgroup. They are not delivered to your electronic mailbox.

Only one copy of each newsgroup article is sent to each site.

Newsgroups allow you to track the course of a discussion.

1.11 LISTSERV

Listserv (also called "distribution lists" or "discussion forums") is lists of users who, by means of electronic mail, hold a discussion about a particular subject. Once they are members of one of these lists, they receive copies of all the messages sent to the list.

Distribution lists are free and are a very satisfactory way of coordinating the activities of the people who are interested in a subject. All participants of a list can supply to the others the results of their work; ask relevant question or request help on subjects, which must be resolved in common. This system is one of those with easiest access via the Internet, since it only requires the ability to send e-mail. It is not necessary to have full access to the Internet or great knowledge about it on the part of the user.

There are basically two types of distribution lists:

- The lists maintained by a single person, whose active participation is necessary for maintaining the list. This type is sometimes called a mailing list. The owner may edit the messages in this type.
- The lists that do not require the intervention of anybody, to be maintained, since, all the messages are managed by software, which does all the work. This type is called Listserv.

1.11.1 Advantages of Listserv

- It permits the exchange of information among professionals, who are interested in a subject in a very effective way.
- It has an organizational structure, which permits great independence to the user with respect to the manner of the subscription to or leaving the list. All the options are carried out automatically by a program, which manages the necessary steps.
- Its use does not require full access to the Internet.
- Recently new methods of subscription and data reception have been developed. Some Listservs are capable of sending the information in magazine form - a

single message with all the new contributions of the users - instead of sending each message separately.

To use Listserv appropriately you need to be aware of the number of distribution lists you subscribe to, because the volume of information generated is sometimes too great. You should always keep a list of the Listservs that you have subscribed to, including the method of canceling the subscription. If the supplier levies charges, it is sensible to subscribe to lists in the form of a digest to reduce the costs.

1.11.2 Finding the List

Four of the major listservers - Listserv, Listprocessor, Majordomo and Mailbase - contain more than 85,000 discussion lists. Visit the Listserver database at http://www.listzt.com.

Methods of bringing the list of distribution lists up-to-date are:

- There is a listserv called NEW-LIST, specifically devoted to information about existing listservs and those which have appeared recently. Its address is vml.nodak.edu, and the most frequent method of the use consists of sending a message asking for information. In this list, there is an analysis of newly appearing lists on the Internet, together with advice and utilities for its use.
- The Internet provides a multitude of directories about the medical resources on the Internet. In these, it is possible to find, using TEL-NET, FTP, Gopher, WWW, etc, and all the information about the existence of a particular type of listserv. In those lists, which are prepared for it, the Command LIST GLOBAL may be used. This command provides a complete list of the listservs, which exist at the time.

1.12 NEWSGROUPS

Newsgroups are a worldwide system for the electronic exchange of news and views on a particular topic. It is also referred to as Usenet News. In a way, Usenet is a discussion forum similar to distribution lists. However, on the Usenet the messages are stored on a notice board to which you must go to have a look, rather than being automatically distributed to the members of a distribution list. You do not formally subscribe to a newsgroup. Not subscribing means that if, on a particular day, you wish to read postings made to a given newsgroup, and you merely indicate this via your newsgroup client. There is no newsgroup equivalent of the list server. To participate in this global distributed discussion system you must have the following facilities:

- Your Internet provider must offer a "news feed" service. Messages sent to newsgroups are propagated around the Internet by a protocol called NNTP (network news transport protocol). If your provider does not have an NNTP server, you can use a public news server such as the WReN (Web Reading News) interface, hosted by Supernews (http://wren.supernews.com/

- You must have a client on your computer that can interpret data sent from an NNTP server. Typically, this will take the form of a dedicated newsreader, or your Web browser if it has been "news enabled".

  The choice of a newsreader client will depend on your operating system and what is currently, available. Whatever the client you choose, it should support the following:

  - Message threading
  - An offline facility

  Message threading sorts messages by the heading, so that replies are shown next to the original message. Offline reading allows you to collect your messages from the NNTP server but read them once your connection to your Internet provider is severed.

In order to give structure to the world of Usenet and to facilitate its systematic use, a classification of large generic groups has been established. These groups are identified by means of initials, which head the name of the particular Newsgroups. After these initials, is the name of the subject dealt with by the Newsgroup, which may in turn be divided into narrower subjects? Normally these names have two or three levels of specifications, although there are Newsgroups with five or six specifications.

The following list gives examples of generic groups:

Group	Topic
Alt	Alternative
Bionet	Biology
Biz	Business
Comp	Computers
Misc	Miscellaneous
News	Topics on Newnet Newsgroups
Rec	Recreational
Sci	Sciences
Soc	Social Issues
Talk	Debate-Oriented Groups

The following is an example of subdividing:

sci.med	Scientific Newsgroup devoted to general medicine
sci.med.radiol	Scientific Newsgroup devoted to general medicine, dealing with radiology
bionet.genome.chr22	Biological Newsgroup dealing with chromosome 22

There is a version of Newsgroup equivalent to a moderated distribution list. Moderated Newsgroups do not allow publication of comments unless they have previously been reviewed and accepted by the editors of the Newsgroup.

Participation in already existing debates is not the only option. It is also possible to create your own discussion forum after what is called a call for votes. If there are a sufficient number of people interested in the subject for debate, the group is created and is added to a list of existing Newsgroups. There are various Newsgroups, which are specifically designed to discuss the necessary aspects for the creation of new News-groups, such as news.groups or news.announce.newuser.

1.12.1 News Management Software

News management programs are usually divided into three types of information windows:

- ***Windows of Newsgroups available for connection:*** This window shows all the newsgroups, which your software recognizes as existing on the Internet. The latest list can be imported so that all the Newsgroups, which interest you at a given time, are up-to-date. By selecting one of the Newsgroups on the list, you gain access to the window, which deals with the articles, which can be read, in that Newsgroup.

- ***Window of articles in a Newsgroup:*** This window shows the articles of the Newsgroup you have chosen, presented in a list with data including the size, date of publication, author and subject. From this window you can decide to send a new article to the Newsgroup. The selection of one article takes you to the third window.

- ***Window of reading an article:*** Here you can read the articles, which other Usenet users send to the Newsgroup. From this window, you may decide to answer an article, sending a new article in response to the one you are reading. At any time, you can choose either to send a new article to the News group, normally by means of the option "New Message", or to reply to the author of an article you have read, normally by means of the option "Reply". The original articles normally have a title connected with the subject they are dealing with, while articles in reply have the original title of the article, which gave, rise to the reply, preceded by "Re:".

1.13 TELNET (TELETYPE NETWORK)

Telnet is a network protocol that is most commonly used to log into a remote computer. It is also the single most powerful hacking tool on the planet. With just a telnet client program, you can:

- Send email.
- Download source code from web sites.

- Send unexpected input to web servers that can give you amazing and sometimes illegal results.
- Give arbitrary input to many other services on Internet host computers.
- Probe the services offered by servers, routers and even people's home computers.

The Telnet environment is based on text, as it does not support the graphical interface. Telnet corresponds to an emulation of the remote terminal. Normally, the remote connection gives a presentation of the information in menu form, so you can select the various options by means of the keyboard. It is possible to get access via Telnet to many other Gopher applications although you will only have a text interface.

To get access via Telnet, you need an access code. However, on many occasions, access is free and does not require a code, or, alternatively, it will be enough to key in "new user" or "guest" when the computer asks for the code.

1.13.1 Using Telnet

There are two ways of using the Telnet tool: the input mode, and the command mode. The input mode allows you to establish the connection and use the remote computer. It is initiated by keying in the sequence TELNET<address>. The command mode is used to set the parameters to Telnet, and is very infrequently used.

After introducing the order TELNET and the appropriate address, your computer locates the remote computer by means of its IP address and establishes a direct connection. From this moment, the access process depends on the configuration of the remote computer, and therefore varies from case to case, that is whether there is a need for access code. Once you provide the code, if necessary, you have access to all the information in the remote control by means of the menu, which is presented to you. From this moment on, you work in the remote computer as if it were a local computer. You key in the appropriate orders. Once you have reached the database itself, you select information search by key words. Immediately you are informed of the possible sources available on the database. When you select one of them, you receive the information you are looking for. On closing the connection, a message reading "connection closed" appears.

1.14 GOPHER

Gopher is a hierarchical menu-based system for exploring the Internet. It was developed at the University of Minnesota, where its first server is available by Telnet and by special MS-DOS, Windows 3.1 and Macintosh client programs. The software for MS-DOS and Macintosh is distributed by boombox.micro. umn.edu. Gopher clients for Windows are available from NOTIS Inc., and as shareware from several popular FTP sites.

There are some speculations about the origin of the name Gopher. Some ascribe it to the mascot of the University (gopher in American English). Others insist that it comes from the words "GO FOR". It does allow you to go for information in a very direct fashion. Among its basic characteristics are:

- Great eases of use with a user interface based on menus. Selection of options is carried out by moving the cursor on the menu, by keying in the number of the option, or by selecting the desired option.
- It offers the possibility of discovering sources of information on the Internet without needing to know their location. Gopher server automatically directs the search to the address, where what you want to see is stored.

Originally, Gopher had a text-based interface. Then it has evolved greatly, becoming a tool for obtaining multimedia data. New servers provide the ability to retrieve plain text, formatted text, images, sound and full motions video. You can access Gopher by means of Telnet, although the menu options cannot be selected with the mouse. However, it is used more powerfully if you use a client Gopher program. This is a program on your computer, which connects you to a Gopher server, managing the data transmission. This program allows you to select the information displayed to you on the menus. Client programs are becoming popular to the extent that practically all-public and private entities offering connections to the Internet have the possibilities of using Gopher directly.

1.14.1 Access via Gopher Client

The best way of learning how to use Gopher is to navigate with it. There are no special rules of use. Normally, having opened the Gopher icon on your computer, you are automatically connected to a preset Gopher server. In order to change to a particular server, use the option on the program, which allows you to connect to the Gopher server in question.

After making the connection by means of a client Gopher with a Gopher server on the Internet, you will find an environment similar to the following:

- At first, you are shown a menu with various options. Each option has an identification letter at the beginning, or an icon, depending on which client you have. The identifying letters make reference to:
  - *(D) Directory:* A new menu from which you have to select another option.
  - *(F) File:* Normally a text file. It informs you of the end of the search when you select this option. No further menus appear in relation to the selection.
  - *(I) Image:* An image you can import to your computer.
  - *(S) Search:* On choosing this option, some relevant data should be keyed in to initiate a search on the Internet.

- There are other references, which may vary according to the browser to indicate access to resource directories, access to Tel-net, WAIS searches, etc.
- You can interact with the menu by means of the mouse. If you double-click one of the options, the information search is redirected and you are taken to where you want to go.
- If you want to obtain information about a specific subject, the first step is to select the option, which refers to the information about the field of that specific subject. You get a multitude of options for the search. After briefly interacting with one of them, you get a menu on which, there is a reference to the information, and you are interested in.
- Backtracking, when the selected option is not what you are interested in, can be carried out by selecting the icon in the top left-hand corner of the window. Some client Gophers have an icon designed for this purpose.
- After selecting the specific subject option (by the identifying F of the final file at the beginning of the selection) you will get a text with the desired information. It is also possible to carry out searches by means of keywords related to the information. For example, after connecting to a database, you choose the option of consulting the contents of the files referring to a keyword, which you key in to start the search.
- You can get more than just text via Gopher, as you can also import other types of documents such as images, in the same manner of search for text.

1.14.2 Access via Telnet

The majority of Gopher addresses on the Internet allow access via Telnet. The required password is mostly "gopher". This is useful for those who do not have a client Gopher and want to find out what these resources can offer. However, it is advisable to get a client for more access that is convenient.

After connecting to a Gopher server, you see that it is not possible via Telnet to use the mouse for selecting the options. In this case, you have to either key in the number of the option or use the cursor.

For using Gopher via Telnet:

- Connect to the address via Telnet.
- Key in the password "gopher" and get access to the initial menu.
- Select one option and pass to a new menu.
- Go to the specified topic and select one to get the full text.

The system of menus offered by Gopher has a number of signals adopted by convention, which help you to decide the best for obtaining what you want:

- When there is a full stop at the end of the text of a menu option, selecting that option will take you to a file, and there are no menus beyond that option.
- When you find a slash at the end of the text, selecting that option will take you to another menu, which will allow you to continue selecting options.
- The presence of a question mark (?) after the text of an option indicates that after choosing that option you will be asked for information. The information, in such cases, is usually a keyword, which will help you to find what you are looking for.
- The word <picture> indicates a picture after the selection.
- The word <cso> indicates the presence of a directory in the style of the yellow pages.
- The presence of <tel> indicates that after the selection a Telnet type connection will be established.

Normally, at anytime in the course of a search carried by Gopher and independently of the screen you are on, there are various options:

- To return to the previous menu
- To get online help
- To terminate the connection

There are other options, which vary from one Gopher server to another. All of these options appear on the screen at the bottom of each page so that you are permanently reminded of their existence. When you are faced with enormous menu options, use the command "/" to go to the area of the menu, which you are interested in. However, this is not necessary in the case of most modern client Gopher programs, which perform all selections by the mouse and scroll bars.

Before starting to browse, you should decide to which Gopher server you have to connect. So you should have a method for finding and updating the Gophers you need. These can be found in various ways:

- Using the tool called VERONICA, which is discussed below?
- Using Telnet, WWW, FTP, WAIS or any other tool, you can obtain a list of the medical Gopher servers.

1.15 VERONICA

Veronica is a tool, which simplifies the search for resources in Gopher. The name Veronica comes from "Very Easy Rodent Oriented Networked Index of Computerized Archives". Veronica starts the search on the Gopher menus, from which you select "GOPHER-space search" or the name veronica, by keying in a keyword. It gives you Gopher addresses with the keyword on their menus. You can choose which of these sources interest you in order to enter them. You have to bear in mind the following characteristics:

- The search is not case-sensitive, which means that capital and lower cases are the same.
- Veronica does not carry out searches in the complete text of the resources available on the Internet. It simply looks for the key word you have given in on the menus of the Gopher on the network.

Access to Veronica is achieved via a client Gopher. Connection is achieved to a Gopher server. The main center of the search via Veronica is found at "gopher.unr.edu". After connecting to the server, you select the option of using Veronica (or GOPHERspace), and a menu is displayed which offers you various Veronica servers to initiate the search. The possibilities are various:

- Access to information on how to use Veronica.
- Selecting the most appropriate Veronica server. Any of them will in principal, offer you the same information. However, it is advisable to use the geographically closest one. However, not all servers bring their search indexes up-to-date at the same time, so the results may vary depending on which server you consult.

1.15.1 Different types of search using VERONICA

- Searching GOPHER space by keywords in titles. This type locates all types of resources that have title containing the keyword (ASCII files, images, binary files, Gopher directories, etc.)
- Searching Gopher directories only for keywords in titles. It searches only for the directories in which the keyword is contained in the title.
- Simplified Veronica. When you select the option, Veronica asks you for the keyword or words you want, together with additional information to control the search:

  (a) *Simple search:* This only requires one keyword to be keyed in. The result is displayed and you select one, and you can accede directly to the information it contains. It should be pointed out that the number of addresses Veronica gives is set at a default value of 200.

  (b) *Search by more than one keyword:* Logical operators (Boolean logic) are used here. The use of parentheses modifies the logical order of the operators.

  (c) *Search for word roots:* Veronica allows the use of "*", a symbol which permits search for word roots, such as "neuro*".

(d) *Search by types of Gopher:* It is possible to define a type of resource to which you want to accede in order to simplify your searches. A number of types of Gopher have been arbitrarily defined, each of which is classified as a number or letter, which permit this type of the search:

0. File
1. Directory
2. CSO Phonebook Server
3. ERROR
4. BinHexed MAC File
5. DOS Binary Archive
6. UNIX uuencoded File
7. Index-search server
8. Pointer to a Telnet Session
9. Binary File

I. Image

S. Sound

The search is executed by adding to the keyword the extension -t, then (without leaving space) the number, which defines the different types of the search. More than one number may be added after -t without leaving spaces.

(e) Specification of the number of resources analyzed. The number of addresses Veronica can give is 200 by default. However, if you need to broaden the search, use the extension -m followed by the number of responses you want Veronica to give. If you want to get all references on a keyword key in:

keyword-m

without any number.

Veronica can also be accessed via WWW. Its use is not managed by the Web browser, but by means of a connection with a Gopher session.

1.16 WAIS

WAIS (Wide Area Information Servers) is a tool designed to search for information on the Internet by means of the keyword, and provide as a result a list of the resources related to the keyword, ordering them according to the number of times the keyword appears in the document. WAIS gives the first document on the list a score of 1000, the maximum, and gives points in descending order to the remaining documents in the list.

In contrast with Gopher, which finds information as a result of selections made on successive menus, WAIS searches for keywords, selected by the user in the text of the files stored on the network. Therefore, It is a system of searching in the complete text, not just on the menus or in the names of files. One of the characteristics, which differentiate WAIS from other search tools, is the use of the so-called Natural Query Language. In this way, the query is put into the system in natural language and WAIS discounts the irrelevant words and starts to search for the keywords.

WAIS can be used by means of a client program in your computer, which runs the search. Alternatively, it can be used by means of a connection via Telnet, Gopher or WWW to a server with a client WAIS installed. The majority of WAIS servers that you can connect to are free.

1.16.1 Searching for Documents with WAIS

As mentioned earlier, you can gain access to WAIS in various ways:

- Using a client program, which is the most appropriate way.
- Making a connection with quake.think.com and login as wais.
- Entering WAIS via WWW. There are several documents, which permit access to WAIS. They are entry points to WAIS - WAIS-GATES.

When you initiate a WAIS session, you have first to select the WAIS database in which you are going to carry out the search, when you are presented with the names of these databases on the screen. One of the WAIS databases called directory-of-servers and managed at quake.think.com informs you about the characteristics of each WAIS database. If you do not know the most appropriate database, initiate the search in directory-of-servers. This is done by keying in a keyword and the directory-of-servers will locate the WAIS databases, which are most appropriate for your search.

After you have chosen the database, the tool permits you to key in new keywords to commence the search. However, there are some limitations to the types of keywords permitted:

- Stop Words may not be used. Stop words are very common words in every day usage, such as "a", "the", "about", "he", etc.
- Buzzwords may not be used. Buzzwords are words that refer to particular subjects, but are of too frequent use in documents. Examples are "account", "address", "able", etc. Each WAIS server has its own buzzwords, classified according to the number of their occurrences in the database.
- Search for word roots is not permitted. WAIS searches for the precise keyword it is given.
- It is not possible to use logical operators. In WAIS, it is only possible to search for a single keyword or several keywords with a no modifiable logical

relationship between them. For example, with keywords "hepatic tumour" WAIS will search for all documents with the word "Hepatic" and all the documents with the word "tumour". Of course, those documents, which have both words, will score higher on the relevance scale WAIS creates. In this way, it is possible to decrease the proportion of irrelevant documents by adding more keywords for the search.

After introducing the keyword, the search commences on pressing <re-turn>. The result of the search has a structure similar to the following:

- *Score:* The indication of the relevance of the document taking into account that the maximum score is 1,000.
- *Bytes:* Size of the File.
- *Title:* Title of the Article.
- *Type:* Type of File.

Furthermore, by means of WWW, access via hypertext to the selected resource is permitted.

Access to WAIS by means of Telnet does not offer the graphic capabilities of WWW, but can be an acceptable solution for those who do not have full access to the Internet. To use WAIS on a Telnet, connect to quake.think.com, and key login "wais" to get access to a screen on which the available WAIS databases are listed. Select your database and proceed to the keyword search. Once you have entered the database, you can formulate any search using Natural Query Language.

In order to make the use of WAIS via Telnet easier, there are a number of simple commands, which give access to different options. You can obtain online help about these commands by pressing "?" or "h".

These commands are:

<space>	Selects
W	Keywords
Arrows	Move
<return>	Searches
q	Quits
↓, down arrow, ^n	move down one source
k, up arrow. ^p	move up one source
j, ^v, ^d	move down one screen
k, <esc>v, ^u	move up one screen
# # #	position to source number # #
Isss	search for source sss

Contd....

<space>, <period>	select current source
=	deselect all sources
V, <comma>	view current source inf
<ret>	perform search
S	select new sources (refresh source list)
w	select new keyword
X, “	remove current source permanently
•	set and show wais options
h, ?	show this help display
H	display program history
Q	leave the program

Once WAIS presents to you the lists of documents found, you can view them directly online or, request the program to send them to an e-mail address. If you press the letter "m", you will be asked for the e-mail address to send them to. If the located documents are not of interest to you, you can go back and redefine the search in other WAIS databases or with other keywords.

1.17 ELECTRONIC JOURNALS

An electronic journal may be defined as the journal that may take two different forms:

- The journal that is otherwise published in print form, available in digital form.
- Electronic-only journal, which is produced, published and distributed via an electronic medium. It may not necessarily need a publisher, and it can be managed by an editor or a scholarly community.

The electronic journal has many advantages including the following:

- Instant access.
- Issues can be unbundled. You only need to obtain those articles that you want.
- Issues are directly loadable into an electronic database. Copyright has to be observed in such cases.
- Proofreading can be done by authors.
- Electronic storage is more efficient than that for print volumes.
- Paperless, but it has to be recognized that readers may want a printout of the articles they are interested in.

But the electronic journal has some disadvantages such as:

- Hardware and software are required. With this, the question of standardization has to be answered.
- Training. The user has to be trained on the utilization of modern information technology. You have to be aware that some users suffer from the computer phobia.
- Peer review is less common. Most of the peer-reviewed journals are still in print form, although some of them have electronic parallel.
- Graphics are problematic because of the size of their files and the slowness of transmission although the situation has improved since WWW was introduced.
- Copyright is uncertain.
- Archives are hard to maintain.

1.17.1 Types of Electronic Journals

The types of electronic journals may be classified in various ways such as:

- ***By Location***: This answers the question: Where is the publication physically situated? It may be:
  - *Centralized:* meaning that the full text journals are stored on a remote computer with access via dialup or leased line. An example of this is Current Clinical Trials.
  - *Decentralized:* meaning that the information is sold in packages. CD-ROMs and electronic journals distributed via the Internet are examples.
  - *Hybrid:* meaning that information is stored in a medium such as the videodisc, while the bibliographic description is sought in a bibliographic database from which the text and drawings are sought from the medium.
- ***By Products:*** There are two products:
  - Primary journals, which contain source or full text material.
  - Secondary journals, which contain only the references or citations.
- ***By Availability of Print Products:*** The electronic journals in this case may be:
  - Parallel journals
  - Fully electronic journals.
- ***By Types of Technology Applied:*** Electronic journals come in a variety of technologies: CD-ROM, online, or disk.
- ***By Price:*** Electronic journals may be acquired by: subscription, license, payment for single articles, or free.

- *By Peer Review*: Electronic journals may be refereed or not.

Some of the examples include Elsevier Science Direct and some society publishers such as the American Chemical Society, Johns Hopkins University Project (MUSE) and the American Medical Association.

1.17.2 Characteristics of Electronic Journals

Electronic journals have the following characteristics:

- *Limited Cost:* This factor is reduced due to the absence of printing on paper, binding and transport.
- *Global Distribution*: The present access to the journals makes the place of the journal production irrelevant. Frontiers disappear and the international scientific community tightens its links.
- *Very Satisfactory Quality of Reproduction of Images:* The quality of this reproduction on the screen is equal or even superior to the quality of reproduction on paper, although many print journals are notable to publish images in color, generally for economic reasons. The reproduction in color or black and white has the same cost in electronic journals. Multimedia technology allows the transmission of sound and video.
- *Electronic Subscription and Sending in of Articles:* It will be sufficient to send the details of your bank account to the server of the journal in order to have an immediate subscription. The sending of articles is direct via e-mail whether text or images.
- *Personalized Subscription:* You will be able to create a profile of the information you need and receive only those articles which interest you, paying a certain amount per article. You will be permitted to receive these articles in your computer.
- *The Possibility of Reliable Analysis of Readership:* It will be possible to know the number of times that an article has been requested or even the number of times an article has been mentioned in the bibliography.
- *The Use of Hypertext:* Hypertext offers the possibility of jumping from one computer to another in search of the information you require without worrying about locating the information.
- *Digital Storage:* Electronic storage makes physical storage unnecessary.
- *Good Communication between the Author and the Reader:* This communication will make it possible to give additional explanations on the subject of an article, or for the reader to send his own results for consideration by the author. Letters to the editor will be interactive, and will be read by the general public almost immediately after the publication of the article.

- *Commercial Independence:* Costs will be reduced so that advertising will become unnecessary. This will permit greater stability with less effort put into financing the publication.

Moreover, the miniaturization of computer components will lead in the near future to the development of the so-called "personal assistants": small computers connected to the Internet by mobile phone.

EXERCISE

Objective Type Questions

1. TCP and UDP are respectively
   (A) Connection oriented and connection less
   (B) Unreliable and reliable
   (C) To avoid relocation
   (D) Neither (a) nor (b)
2. The Internet is a world wide collection of computer______.
   (A) Interfaces (B) Users
   (C) Networks (D) All of the above
3. The world's largest Network is______.
   (A) Microsoft (B) Google
   (C) Internet (D) Netscape Browser
4. A widely used communication device is a______.
   (A) Modem (B) CD drive
   (C) Monitor (D) Microphone
5. Transmission permitting data to move both directions but only one way at a time______.
   (A) Half-duplex (B) Full-duplex
   (C) Simplex (D) Start/stop
6. ______is the protocol that governs communications on the Internet.
   (A) EFT (B) MAN
   (C) EDI (D) TCP/IP
7. What types of company provides people with access to the Internet?
   (A) PSI (B) SPI
   (C) ISP (D) IPS
8. JARING and TMNet are examples of
   (A) Internet Service Provider (B) Web browser
   (C) Search engine (D) Portal
9. E- mail means
   (A) Electronic mail (B) Effortless mail
   (C) Enhanced mail (D) Easy mail

10. The creator of the Web was

(A) Rand Corporation (B) Tim Berners-Lee

(C) ARPANET (D) Marc Andreessen

11. A message to be sent to another computer over the Internet is divided into

(A) URLs (B) Domain

(C) Packets (D) Frames

12. The software on a user's computer that provides a graphical interface to access the Internet is called a(n)

(A) URL (B) TP

(C) ISP (D) Browser

13. The World Wide Web is

(A) a network of computer networks

(B) a domain

(C) a web of linked documents

(D) primarily for military use

14. The first network that linked four universities was known as

(A) TCP/IP (B) NSFnet

(C) BBS (D) ARPAnet

15. When you are on the Internet, you can

(A) send and receive e-mail (B) shop with your credit card

(C) do research (D) all these answers

16. An example of browser software is

(A) Gopher (B) ARPAnet

(C) Netscape Navigator (D) Hypertext

17. The header of an e-mail message always includes

(A) a subject (B) a body

(C) a signature (D) an attachment

18. Browsers

(A) are software

(B) are needed to find and process the hypertext links

(C) have changed from being only text based to include graphics

(D) all the above

19. HTTP

(A) is a programming language

(B) stands for HyperTelnet Transfer Protocol

(C) stands for Hypertext Transfer Protocol

(D) is used to transfer sound

20. URLs

(A) are Internet protocol (B) are Web page addresses

(C) list recently visited sites (D) none of the above

21. What helps you organize URLs for frequently visited sites by allowing you to create topic folders?

(A) caches (B) favorites

(C) history lists (D) plug-in

22. What is an example of a search engine?

(A) Yahoo! (B) Netcape Navigator

(C) Icab (D) Internet Explorer

23. Because you can't see body language in electronic communication, people use

(A) netiquette (B) emoticons

(C) signatures (D) a watch list

24. Rules of proper electronic communication are known as

(A) spam (B) flames

(C) netiquette (D) moderating

25. To have an access to a newsgroup, you need a

(A) browser (B) word processor

(C) newsreader (D) spreadsheet

26. The World Wide Web is

(A) A network of computer (B) An internet service

(C) A protocol (D) A network telephone lines

27. The software on a user's computer that provides a graphical interface to access the Internet is called a(n)

(A) URL (B) FTP

(C) ISP (D) Browser

28. A newsreader is

(A) A person who reads a newspaper

(B) Software that used for newsgroup

(C) A device used by the visually impaired

(D) None of above

29. The header of an e-mail messages always includes

(A) subjects (B) body

(C) signature (D) filter

30. In the e-mail address, lalbihari@hotmail.com, the user ID is

(A) lalbihari (B) mouse

(C) hotmail.com (D) @

31. Email used to

(A) Send a single message to many recipients

(B) Send a message that includes text, voice, video, or graphics

(C) Send a message to user on a network outside the internet

(D) All the above

32. To have access to a newsgroup, you need a

(A) browser (B) word processor

(C) newsreader (D) spreadsheet

33. A message that an individual posts to a newsgroup is known as

(A) Newsgroup name (B) Articles

(C) Thread (D) Newsreader

34. Rules of proper electronic communication are known as

(A) spam's (B) netiquette

(C) newsgroups (D) FAQs

35. Who is making the Web standards?

(A) The World Wide Web Consortium

(B) Netscape

(C) Microsoft

(D) Google

36. What is the correct HTML for making a hyperlink?

(A) <a name="http://www.srimca.com">srimca.com</a>

(B) <a href="http://www.srimca.com">srimca</a>

(C) <a>http://www.srimca.com</a>

(D) <a url="http://www.srimca.com">srimca.com</a>

37. How can you make an e-mail link?

(A) <a href="xxx@yyy">

(B) <mail href="xxx@yyy">

(C) <a href="mailto:xxx@yyy">

(D) <mail>xxx@yyy</mail>

38. In email address______ character is essential.

(A) _ (B) %

(C) @ (D) *

39. LAN stands for______.

(A) Local Area Network (B) Linear Area Network

(C) Link Area Network (D) None of these

40. MAN stands for______.

(A) Main Area Network

(B) Middle Area Network

(C) Metropolitan Area Network

(D) Mix Area Network

41. WAN stands for______.

(A) Wide Area Network (B) Web Area Network

(C) World Area Network (D) Width Area Network

42. FTP Stands for______.

(A) Field Transfer Protocol (B) File Transfer Protocol

(C) Fix Transfer Protocol (D) Flexible Transfer Protocol

43. Primary aspects of Web design are content, Technology, economics &______.

(A) visuals (B) site

(C) person (D) graphics

44. The word internet stands for______.

(A) Internation Network (B) Internal Network

(C) Intermediate Network (D) none of these

45. Internet is

(A) a local computer network

(B) a world wide network of computers

(C) an interconnected network of computers

(D) world wide interconnected network of computers which use a common protocol to communicate with one another

46. The facilities available in the internet are

(i) electronic mail (ii) remote login

(iii) file transfer (iv) word processing

(A) i, ii (B) i, ii, iii

(C) i, ii, iv (D) ii, iii and iv

47. Internet requires

(A) an international agreement to connect computers

(B) a local area network

(C) a commonly agreed set of rules to communicate between computers

(D) a World Wide Web

48. Internet uses

(A) Packet switching (B) Circuit switching

(C) Telephone switching (D) Telex switching

49. Internet data is broken up as

(A) fixed length packets (B) variable length packets

(C) not packetized (D) 64 bytes packets

50. Internet packet data structure consists of

(i) source address (ii) destination address

(iii) serial number of packets (iv) message bytes

(v) Control bits for error checking (vi) Path identification bits

(A) i, ii, iii (B) i, ii, iii, iv

(C) i, ii, iii, iv, v (D) i, ii, iii, iv, v, vi

51. The packets of an internet message

(A) take a predetermined path

(B) take a path based on packet priority

(C) go along different paths based on path availability

(D) take the shortest path from source to destination

52. The time taken by internet packets

(A) can be predetermined before transmission

(B) may be different for different packets

(C) is irrelevant for audio packets

53. Mail routing involves

(i) Finding a path (ii) Error checking

(iii) Speed optimization (iv) Cost optimization

(A) all of the above (B) only (i) & (ii)

(C) only (i), (ii) & (iii) (D) only (i) & (iii)

54. On the Internet the mailing route is

(A) specified by the user (B) done by IP

(C) done by TCP (D) all of the above

55. Smart-host routing is a technique used in

(A) UUCP (B) WWW

(C) Dial-up PPP (D) Internet

56. The following is not a Windows e-mail programme

(A) Outlook (B) Pegasus

(C) Eudora (D) Pine

(E) None of the above

57. Which of the following protocols is used by Internet mail ?

(A) HTTP (B) FTP

(C) TCP /IP (D) PPP

(E) None of the above

58. What are messages posted to news groups called?

(A) Archie (B) Articles

(C) Listserv (D) Bitnet

59. What is X.400 about?

(A) A directory server

(B) Procedure for bootstrapping diskless clients

(C) Mail addressing system

(D) Mapping of IP addresses

60. What does Internet Control Message Protocol (ICMP) do?

(A) Map IP addresses onto Ethernet addresses

(B) Communicate error messages

(C) Send single packets to destination

(D) Compress IP headers

61. What is bandwidth?

(A) The speed of data flow through modem

(B) The capacity of an ISDN connection

(C) Data capacity of a channel

(D) Nope of the above

62. What is Usenet?

(A) It is used to forward jobs and files through several hosts

(B) It is a low-cost dial-up network

(C) It is a provider of news

(D) None of the above

63. Which of the following was a precursor to the Internet?

(A) Gopher (B) ARPANET

(C) World Wide Web (D) IETF

64. By an intranet we mean

(A) a LAN of an organization

(B) a Wide Area Network connecting all branches of an organization

(C) a corporate computer network

(D) a network connecting all computers of an organization and using the internet protocol

65. By an extranet we mean

(A) an extra fast computer network

(B) the intranets of two co-operating organizations interconnected via a secure leased line

(C) an extra network used by an organization for higher reliability

(D) an extra connection to internet provided to co-operating organization

66. A search engine is a program to search

(A) for information

(B) web pages

(C) web pages for specified index terms

(D) web pages for information using specified search terms

67. Which is true?

(A) Web surfing is a client-server application, but email is not

(B) Email is a client-server application, but Web surfing is not

(C) Neither are client-server applications, they are networked applications

(D) Neither are client-server applications, they are collaborative applications

(E) Both are client server applications

68. Google provides support resources and tools for

(A) Docs developers

(B) Docs users

(C) Both Docs users and developers

(D) Neither - Docs is an application suite

69. One could subscribe to the RSS feed of a blog using

(A) email, but not an RSS reader

(B) an RSS reader, but not email

(C) email or an RSS reader

(D) neither email nor an RSS reader can be used to subscribe to a blog feed

70. If you do both VOIP and FTP on your computer, how many of the following statements are true?

(A) VOIP and FTP use the same application layer protocol

(B) VOIP and FTP use the same transport layer protocol

(C) VOIP and FTP use the same Internet layer protocol

(D) VOIP and FTP use the same data link layer protocol

(E) VOIP and FTP use the same physical layer protocol

71. Which is not central goal of Gopher from following option?

(A) A file-like hierarchical arrangement that would be familiar to users

(B) A simple syntax

(C) A system that can be created quickly and inexpensively

(D) Bridges the last kilometer or mile from the internet provider to the subscriber

72. The following is not a part of header field in a mail message

(A) Subject (B) From

(C) Message-id (D) None of the above

73. E-mail address consists of

(A) Name of the machine handling title mail

(B) User identification

(C) Both

(D) None of the above

74. What is a spider?

(A) a new internet game (B) a new game for Mac enthusiasts

(C) an Internet search engine (D) a spy programme

75. Usenet is mainly a provider of

(A) news (B) mail

(C) utilities (D) help services

76. The protocol used by packet radio or ham radio is called

(A) X.2S (B) AX.2S

(C) X.400 (D) X.SOO

Review & Discussion Questions

1. What are the two main requirements for web hosting?
2. What is ISP? Name one ISP in India.
3. Define Search Engines. Name any two search engines.
4. What is a Local Area Network (LAN)? What are its advantages?
5. Briefly explain a Wide Area Network (WAN).
6. Define a firewall and what are its benefits?
7. What is the main purpose of Telnet? What model does Telnet follow? Write a short note how does it operate?
8. What is a Proxy Server? What are the advantages of a Proxy Server?
9. Justify the term for the Internet "Network of Networks". How the Internet is differing from World Wide Web (WWW)?
10. What do you understand by E-mail? What are the advantages of it over conventional mailing system?
11. What is the difference between FTP and Telnet?
12. What are the uses of search engines? Write name of two famous search engines.
13. How to create your E-mail account and how to send or receive E-mail?
14. What is HTML and why it is use in the Internet?
15. What is Internet? List different uses of Internet.
16. Explain the features of Internet.
17. Write a step to create email account.
18. List the steps to read and send an email.
19. List the steps to send email with attachment.
20. What are the advantages of Email over Traditional mail system?
21. Explain Newsgroups in details.
22. Differentiate LAN with MAN.
23. Differentiate LAN and WAN
24. How to create email account?
25. Write a step to search information about cricket using search engine.
26. What is messenger? Steps down to send the message.
27. Differentiate intranet and extranet.

28. Write advantages of messenger services.
29. Write educational applications of internet.
30. Discuss different commercial applications of internet.
31. List the applications of Internet.
32. Explain in brief the history of internet.
33. What is Search Engine? Write steps to search using google.com.
34. How we design a good web site? List the criterion to define a better web.

CHAPTER 2

Mobile Internet Connectivity

CHAPTER OBJECTIVES

In this chapter, you will able to know about the access of Internet while away from the Local Area Network (LAN). You will get the idea of different types of mobile internet connectivity and how it works. This chapter identifies the technologies used for mobile internet connectivity and any associated connectivity issues.

CHAPTER OUTLINES

2.1 INTRODUCTION

One of the next major steps forward in internet access is to enable users to access the Internet while away from the Local Area Network (LAN). This access is referred to in this document as 'mobile internet connectivity', although there is no commonly accepted term. While mobile internet connectivity has been, until comparatively recently, limited to relatively slow data rates or to very short access ranges, technology is being introduced that will allow users to connect to the Internet with data rates that are theoretically in excess of home-use broadband connections, and with far greater range than is currently available. This chapter identifies the technologies used for mobile internet connectivity and any associated connectivity issues.

2.2 TYPES OF MOBILE INTERNET CONNECTIVITY

- *Global systems for mobile communication (GSM):* designed for voice communications, but adapted for small amounts of data transfer.
- *High speed circuit switched data (HSCSD):* designed to allow GSM to transfer data at rates of up to four times the original network data rates.
- *General packet radio services (GPRS):* designed to give increased data rates as well as charging based on the amount of data transferred rather than the time spent transferring the data.
- *Third generation (3G) mobile:* designed to offer a consistent set of services to mobile computer and phone users. Increased data rates (up to a theoretical maximum of 2Mbps) should allow a far wider range of services, including video conferencing.
- *Enhanced data GSM environment (EDGE):* designed to co-exist with GSM. It should allow GSM operators who don't have licences for the 3G spectrum to provide users with data rates that would, in some cases, challenge 3G data rates (up to a theoretical maximum of 554Kbps).
- *Public access WLAN:* designed to enable users to access the Internet in localised 'hotspots' via a wireless local area network (WLAN) access card and a personal digital assistant (PDA) or laptop. While data speeds are relatively fast compared with mobile telecommunication technology data rates, their range is short.
- *Linked public access WLANs:* designed to link a number of public access WLANs to give high speed access in, for example, the centre of a town.
- *Public access WLAN and mobile telecommunication convergence:* access technology that allows users/devices to swap between a telecommunications technology (e.g., GPRS, 3G) and public access WLAN to gain the highest available data rate, depending on their geographical location. This is now

being discussed and it is likely that devices will become available that allow seamless roaming between technologies.

2.3 MOBILE INTERNET CONNECTIVITY WORKS

Mobile internet connectivity is a fast-moving area of technology that can be divided into two broad areas; Mobile telecommunications and public access WLANs.

Mobile Telecommunications: There are three mobile telephony technologies that currently allow internet access on the move in the India: GSM, HSCSD and GPRS. Each technology is at a different stage of growth. While some services for the user may be available with all three technologies, other services are only available (in practical terms at least) for users of GPRS. It should be noted that, even though all of the technologies use the GSM network as their starting points, users will have to purchase a separate handset in order to upgrade from GSM. For example, a standard GSM handset will not access HSCSD services or GPRS services. There are some handsets and laptop adapters, however, that allow access to all three technologies.

- GSM is the most widely used mobile telecommunications technology. It is a circuit switched-based technology that is mainly used for voice, but over recent years has also been used to carry data such as text messages. It is possible to use GSM to access email and the Internet, but data rates are limited to 9.6Kbps. GSM phones and services are now mature - with most phones and operators it is possible to roam whilst abroad for voice calls; opportunities to roam whilst abroad for data calls are also relatively widespread. Services over GSM are limited by the data-transfer rates, and commercial take up of internet access using GSM has been slow. The introduction of Wireless Application Protocol (WAP) in 1997 provided users with an interface that was suited to small mobile devices, but it was limited by a slow uptake of users and of websites, which had to be written in a different web language.

- High-speed Circuit Switched Data (HSCSD) is a newer technology. It is based on GSM and was created to address some of the data-transfer rate limitations of GSM. Using several GSM frequencies or radio channels, HSCSD can achieve maximum data-transfer speeds of 38.4Kbps, although this is dependent on the network operator - the more capacity an operator makes available for transmitting data, the less remains for voice telephony. As this technology is still a circuit switched-based technology, users will normally be charged for the time that data takes to download, rather than the amount of data.

- GPRS uses a packet switched-based technology over GSM networks. In terms of service, GPRS allows users to access the same content on the Internet as they can from fixed networks with internet access. WAP can still be used to access web pages that are specifically written for devices with smaller screens, such as mobile phones, but GPRS is not limited to WAP. While much of the

GPRS architecture is the same as for GSM, GPRS has the advantage of being able to gain, in theory, much higher data-transfer rates than GSM or HSCSD. As GPRS is a packet switched-based technology as opposed to a circuit switched-based technology, users can be charged by the amount of data sent or received, regardless of the time taken to achieve this. This leads to the 'always-connected' concept where users can stay on line for extended periods and only be charged for the actual data transferred. GPRS can, in theory, achieve data-transfer rates of up to 115Kbps. However, the actual data rates achieved will normally be significantly lower and will be influenced by a number of factors:

- ❖ Most importantly, as GPRS shares radio resources with GSM, operators give priority to circuit switched calls (usually voice) and thus the resources for GPRS are limited.
- ❖ Many of today's mobile devices that are GPRS-enabled are limited to data rates of less than the theoretical maximum network data rates. At present, the maximum downloading rate for GPRS is limited by many devices to 52Kbps.
- ❖ The data rates can also be limited by the data compression techniques used by the operator.

GPRS should, in theory, have the same coverage as an operator's GSM network. However, this is dependent on each operator allocating resources for GPRS from their GSM frequencies.

Mobile devices for GPRS are classed in two ways. These can be referred to as the 'mode' class of the device and the 'speed' class.

- ❖ *Mode class:* Class A devices support GPRS and other GSM services, such as SMS and voice, simultaneously. As such, a Class A device can make or receive calls on two services simultaneously. Class B devices can monitor GSM and GPRS channels simultaneously, but can support only one of these services at a time. Thus, users can make or receive calls on either a packet call or a switched call type sequentially, but not simultaneously. With Class C devices, the user must select which service to connect to.
- ❖ *Speed class:* This class refers to the speed of data transfer that is possible in the upwards (upload) and downwards (download) directions. In general, the higher the class, the faster the upload capabilities of a device. For example, a Class 12 device can upload at up to 52 Kbps, whereas a Class 8 device can only upload at 13 Kbps. Most modern GPRS devices have download capabilities of up to 52 Kbps.

There are two further mobile telephony technologies that should eventually allow internet access on the move: 3G and EDGE. Access to the Internet has not been implemented in the India using either technology although some services using 3G technology are now available.

- 3G Mobile is a set of standards that allows mobile internet connectivity roaming worldwide at greatly enhanced speeds. 3G is a packet mode technology that allows voice, text and multimedia services on one device at theoretical speeds ranging from ~64 Kbps when a user is travelling at speed (for example, on a train) to 384 kbps/2 Mbps (depending on the implementation of 3G) when a user is very close to a base station. It is likely that higher data rates will only be achieved in those areas that have a high density of base stations.

  3G services and networks have already started to be introduced into the India by the operator '3'. Other operators will introduce their 3G networks and services gradually to their legacy GSM/GPRS systems, but the introduction of these networks in Europe is, in many cases, behind the planned schedule. This is mostly due to the costs of introducing the highly expensive infrastructure (such as masts and network nodes) and the vast sums that operators spent to buy 3G radio spectrum licences from many European governments.

- EDGE enhances GSM networks to enable near-3G data rates to be delivered over existing GSM networks using existing frequency bands. EDGE provides theoretical user data rates of up to 384 Kbps in the wide area and up to 554 Kbps in the local area. However, this maximum rate can only be offered over a very short range. One of the main reasons for the introduction of EDGE was to give GSM operators who were not awarded licences for the 3G radio spectrum the chance to offer higher data rate services. Interest in EDGE technology is high amongst European mobile telecom operators but has yet to be commercially deployed.

Public Access WLANs: Public access WLANs are typically connected to the Internet via a wired technology connection. This allows members of the general public to use the WLAN for internet connectivity. At around 100 metres, the range of this technology is far less than mobile telecommunication-based technologies used for mobile internet connectivity, but the potential data rates are much greater - more than four times as fast as a 3G network. A network card needs to be used in conjunction with an access device (a laptop or PDA, for example) and users gain internet connectivity via the public access WLAN upon user authentication. At present, this type of technology can be found at some larger hotels, airports, train stations and various stores.

By linking public access WLANs (by overlapping the WLAN cells), larger WLANs can be built up. For the user, this means that mobile internet connectivity could be achieved over a whole town centre, for example. (NB Some towns already have linked WLANs but these tend to be provided by local communities or societies.)

Discussions about combining public access WLAN and mobile telecommunications are in their infancy. It is already possible to buy a device (such as a laptop) with a

WLAN and a mobile telecommunications SIM card but the technology for seamless switching between the two is not yet commercially available.

Table 2.1 ♦ Data Rates, Coverage and Range for Mobile Internet Connectivity

Network/ Technology	Absolute maximum data rates	Present realistic maximum data rates	Future realistic maximum data rates	Range
Mobile Telecommunications				
Fixed LANs	100/1000 Mbps	70/700Mbps	7Gbps	~100m
GSM900/ 1800	9.6 Kbps	9.6 Kbps	9.6 Kbps	Only limited by adoption of technology by the operator
HSCSD	57.6 Kbps using GSM 1800, 38.4 Kbps with GSM900	~9.6 Kbps– 38.4 Kbps for GSM900	~9.6 Kbps– 38.4 Kbps for GSM900	Only limited by adoption of technology by the operator
GPRS	171.2 Kbps	52 Kbps*	85.6 Kbps* (estimated)	Only limited by adoption of technology by the operator
EDGE	554 Kbps	n/a	~128 Kbps– 344 Kbps*	Only limited by adoption of technology by the operator
3G	384 Kbps -2Mbps (depending on network implementation)	128 Kbps* (estimated	144 Kbits- ~512Kbps* (estimated)	Only limited by adoption of technology by the operator
Public Access WLANs				
Public Access WLANs (802.11b)	11 Mbps	7 Mbps	7 Mbps	~100m
Linked public access WLANs	11 Mbps	n/a	7 Mbs or 27 Mbps- 30 Mbps (dependant on standard implemented)	City centre, for example

* Contended by number of users

2.4 CONTENT/APPLICATIONS FOR MOBILE INTERNET CONNECTIVITY

Potentially, mobile internet connectivity can provide access to a wide range of services, content and applications. In many cases these will be accessed from free or commercial services on the Internet. However, users may also wish to access content, applications or services from their organization's LAN. In this case, it is important to note that access may be limited by the organization's network remote access policy and network security configuration settings.

2.5 CURRENT USE OF MOBILE INTERNET CONNECTIVITY

At present, accessing data via mobile internet connectivity can be limited by network data rates, in the case of mobile telecommunication technologies, and by user range, in the case of public access WLANs.

- GSM, HSCSD and GPRS allow voice and basic internet services (such as e-mail and web pages) at a range of data rates but, presently, the data rates are normally insufficient for accessing more than a small amount of data.

  The 3G services that have been launched by '3' in the India are a limited subset of what we may see in the future. Whilst connection to the Internet is not currently available, services do include news and weather reports in addition to email, video calling and video downloading.

  It is worthwhile noting that Gartner analysts have several reservations concerning the available current 3G services. One of their main concerns is the lack of high bandwidth available. Without high bandwidth, the users' experience of accessing the large amounts of data or large video clips and high quality video calls for example, will be limited. This lack of available bandwidth could also limit a user's experiences of downloading large amounts of data once Internet connectivity is made available.

  There are commercial 3G networks in several European countries including Austria, Spain, Italy, Germany and Sweden but service and subscriber information is not readily available. In Japan and the Far East where subscribers of 3G services are highest, Internet and more advanced location based services are available.

- Aside from issues concerning remote access, public access WLAN users should be able to gain access to the same services as are available on their organization's LAN.

2.6 FUTURE USE OF MOBILE INTERNET CONNECTIVITY

In the next few years, advancements in technology will allow users to access a wider range of services than is available at present via mobile internet connectivity. For example, services such as online gaming are likely to become available. It is also likely that certain services will be bundled into packages to which users will be able to subscribe for a discounted fee. In areas of linked public access WLANs, the range of services is likely to be even greater as faster transfer rates will allow more complex multimedia services to be exploited further than in slower mobile telecommunication technologies.

Advantages and Disadvantages of Mobile Internet Connectivity Compared with Fixed-line Internet Connectivity

2.7 ADVANTAGES

- The greatest advantage of the technologies described above is that of portability of devices and services and the ability to access the internet while away from the organization's LAN.
- Mobile internet connectivity builds on both the mobile voice and fixed data networks. It therefore offers a high degree of compatibility and inter-operability with the services offered over these networks.
- Users could potentially gain access to their intranet and mail services when away from their organization's LAN, as well as to content and services provided by their organization's LAN (see later comments regarding remote access and security issues).
- In future, infrequent users of the Internet may be able to use these technologies as their sole means of accessing the Internet.

2.8 DISADVANTAGES

There are several disadvantages of mobile connectivity when compared with fixed access networks. Some are inherent in the technology and others are due to the immaturity of mobile connectivity systems.

- To remain portable, devices for mobile internet connectivity usually have smaller screens than their fixed access equivalents, meaning that less information can be viewed on a screen.
- In terms of downloading and uploading data rates, mobile internet connectivity technology can be considerably slower than fixed network connectivity (see Table 2.1).
- Data rates will decrease in many access technologies as the distance from the base station increases, or indeed as the speed that the user is travelling at increases.
- Reliability of access can be an issue in rural and mountainous regions.
- Security of devices themselves and the data that they contain is a much greater area for concern than in fixed networks.
- Network security is an issue, especially concerning public access WLAN.
- Mobile internet connectivity equipment is often more expensive than fixed network equipment.
- Mobile internet connectivity is likely to be more expensive than fixed network internet connectivity. At present, a user will often have to pay a monthly

subscription for commercially provided public access WLAN internet connectivity, or pay for use at an hourly or daily rate. Telecommunication operators have a range of tariffs for connecting to the Internet depending on the technology used for internet access. In some cases, a further subscription is needed in addition to the Internet access subscription. For example, for mobile internet connectivity access via GPRS, a subscription to both GSM and GPRS networks is sometimes needed.

- Mobile internet connectivity devices are not always compatible with devices using a different mobile internet connectivity technology.

2.9 WHERE IS MOBILE INTERNET CONNECTIVITY BEING USED?

Mobile internet connectivity is already being used in the commercial sector, although the services are often limited due to remote access difficulties, security issues and low data rates via mobile telecommunication technologies.

In the UK, the first 3G operator '3' launched its service on 3 March, 2003. Current GSM operators who have a 3G licence have yet to fix dates as to their 3G release but it is anticipated that no other 3G operators will deploy 3G services before at least the end of the first quarter of 2004. In some cases this may be quite a bit later than this date, but operators' licence agreements with the UK government state that their initial 3G services must be made available to 80% of the UK population by the end of 2007. This means that 3G networks and services will most likely be gradually made available during the next few years.

State-owned MTNL will become the first Indian service provider to commercially launch 3G services when it unveils the services 11 December coinciding with the India Telecom 2008 event organized by FICCI and DoT. Services available from different operators using other mobile telecommunications technologies tend to be limited, often because of the relatively slow data speeds of current mobile telecommunication networks. As network data rates improve, it is likely that telecommunication devices will allow any internet service to be available via a mobile telecommunications technology.

Public access WLANs are now being deployed at selected airports, train stations, hotels, service stations and shops. Both community and commercial providers are planning to dramatically increase the number of public access WLANs over the next few years.

2.9.1 Issues to Consider when Buying Mobile Internet Connectivity Contracts and Equipment

There are four main issues that need to be considered before purchasing mobile internet access equipment.

- Mobile internet connectivity is not mainstream at present. In practical terms, most of the technologies available work independently of each other and are relatively immature in terms of mobile internet connectivity. Thus, it is too early to conclude which technologies will prevail or indeed what level of technology convergence will take place.

- Users who need regular access to the Internet while on the move are currently limited to slow data rates using mobile telecommunication technologies and isolated instances of public WLAN access.
- Many of the technologies mentioned in this document are relatively expensive in terms of access devices and subscriptions and have a set of fairly immature services.

Other considerations are:

- *Network Data Rates:* Consider what data rates are actually needed for the services required. For example, real-time video services will require a technology with much faster data rates than a service that simply sends back text results from a field trip. Most of the technologies mentioned advertise the maximum theoretical network speeds. In most cases this speed will not be achievable. For example, the advertised maximum data rate for GPRS of 52kbps is unlikely to be achieved as users have to share this bandwidth with other GPRS users in close proximity. In addition, as GPRS traffic shares network resources with GSM traffic, data rates could potentially drop to a few kbps per GPRS user.
- *Network Range and Coverage:* The maximum range of each public access WLAN will most likely be in the order of 100m, so both network coverage and range are severely limited when compared with mobile telecommunications technology (see Table 2.1). GSM and GPRS coverage is in the range of 99% of the population for most operators.
- *Devices:* In certain cases, such as older GPRS devices, the devices themselves limit the data rate. Some devices use compression techniques in order to improve data rates. For example, a device using an advanced compression technique over GSM may download a web page in the same period of time as a lower-end GPRS device.
- *Price:* Mobile internet connectivity devices are expensive. Laptops are more expensive than their equivalent desktop PCs, for example, and some PDAs with GPRS capabilities are as expensive as lower-end desktop PCs. Mobile telecommunication operators have traditionally subsidised mobile phone-type devices in return for the user signing a fixed-term contract and, for GPRS and 3G devices, this subsidy is continuing.

For GPRS, users normally have to sign a fixed-term contract with an associated tariff. As data is charged per packet use as opposed to time use (as with GSM) it is difficult for the user to know the cost of a particular service in advance. Currently, no two operators/suppliers use the same price plans although many are similar. In addition, several operators currently require users to have a GSM contract and a

GPRS contract in order to access GPRS services. It remains to be seen whether price plans and call/data costs will be simplified in the future.

For current 3G use, '3' offer users a fixed-term contract with an associated tariff or a non monthly subscription based tariff. Services are currently charged at a range of set rates although it is anticipated that as Internet access becomes available Internet data will be charged per packet use and thus it will be more difficult for the user to know the cost of a particular download in advance.

In the case of public access WLANs, users can buy access for a period of time ranging from one hour to a monthly subscription. There is typically no extra charge for the amount of data that is downloaded or uploaded.

- *Network Service Providers – Mobile Telecommunication Technologies:* In the India, all GSM operators offer extensive coverage for their services and have a range of roaming agreements with other operators. However, one operator may have a better reception in some areas of the country or have a greater range of services. In many cases, users could choose the same network provider for GPRS services as their current GSM supplier. It is anticipated that this choice will continue when GSM operators who own a 3G license launch their services. It should be noted, however, that some operators will have greater network coverage than others. This is likely to be especially true with regards to 3G coverage and services which operators plan to introduce over a period of time.

  Public access WLAN: It would be useful to note which providers have reciprocal agreements with other providers of public access WLAN.

  Public access WLAN and mobile telecommunication convergence: In the future there is likely to be some degree of convergence between mobile internet connectivity technologies. Thus, network providers who have agreements with providers of other access technologies may be a better choice for users who need access from a variety of places.

- *Security:* The main security concerns with mobile internet connectivity are likely to be around remote access to the user's intranet or extranet. To protect a device such as a laptop computer, personal firewalls are now available that can monitor data that enters and exits the device. This means that unauthorised attempts to gain access to data on that device are stopped and the user is alerted that an unauthorised access attempt has been made.

- *Compatibility Issues:* As previously mentioned, a new device will have to be purchased for each stage in mobile telephony development. The technology does ensure backwards compatibility in the network and changes to the network should not affect the user, at least in the short term, once a device is purchased. However, 3G and EDGE technologies are likely to follow the same path as GSM and GPRS, with new services only being available to the most advanced user devices.

At present, devices that work with both WLAN cards and Subscriber Identity Module (SIM) cards (to access the mobile phone networks) are available. However, it remains to be seen whether network enhancements will be backwards compatible with present-day devices.

A further compatibility consideration concerns whether a device connects to or synchronises well with presently owned devices and networks. For example, some GPRS devices are in the form of PDAs. It may be important for the users of these types of devices to be able to synchronise the data on their PDAs with the data on their networked desktop PCs. To enable this, the applications on the mobile internet devices and on the organization's LAN need to be compatible.

- *Remote Access:* If access is needed to an organization's LAN there may be some remote access issues. Trialling mobile internet connectivity technologies is advised if remote access is likely to be required.
- *Support:* Support for present-day mobile telecommunication technologies is provided through telephone helplines or email. Public access WLANs are a relatively recent concept in the India and support for the near future is likely to be limited to a helpline and email support and occasionally to a local helpdesk.
- *Training:* Access to various networks may need specific initial training, although mobile internet connectivity is simply a way of accessing internet services while away from a fixed network. Therefore, once access to a network is made, further training should be limited to training on the use of a specific device or a specific program running on that device.
- *Battery Life:* There have been recent advancements in lower power consumption devices, but the periods between battery recharging are still relatively short especially when using colour displays and accessing or manipulating graphics.
- *Health and Safety Issues:* There is still a degree of public concern surrounding the safety of wireless devices. For further information, contact the National Radiological Protection Board or the Radiocommunications Agency.

2.10 IMPLEMENTATION ISSUES FOR MOBILE INTERNET CONNECTIVITY

In general terms, users have little influence on how mobile networks are implemented. Nevertheless, there are implementation issues regarding the devices and use of services for mobile internet connectivity that need to be considered, depending on whether the user needs individual access to the Internet or is responsible for an organization's mobile internet connectivity.

Common to both types of user is the choice of device. Users should be aware, as mentioned above, that for mobile telecommunication and wireless technologies, a new device or at least a new network card will have to be acquired for each new technology introduced. Consider connecting to a PDA or laptop using a mobile phone. In this way, as new mobile telecommunication technologies are made available for faster access to the Internet, only the mobile handsets themselves need updating as long as the connection to the PDA or laptop can still be maintained by the new device. Some devices may need some initial data inputting into the device to gain access to the network, but this is specific to each device and network and is steadily becoming a dynamic process that is seamlessly carried out when the device is first turned on.

Issues for the Individual: Some research is needed to find the appropriate tariff for the user's needs and select the appropriate access device. At a basic level the user needs only to acquire a network device and network card for the appropriate operator's network.

Issues for the Organization: Organizations have several concerns when implementing mobile internet connectivity.

- ***Network choice:*** If all users in the organization need the same type of connectivity, implementation issues are eased - one network operator can be chosen and each user issued with the same type of device. However, in larger organizations it may be that different users need different types of connectivity and levels of service. This may mean separate network providers and associated tariffs. If public access WLAN is used then several accounts from different providers may be needed.

- ***Compatibility:*** Each different device will need to be checked to see if it is compatible with the organization's fixed network. For example, checking whether a mobile device can synchronise with the user's computer on the organization's LAN. If a mobile phone is used to connect to a laptop or PDA for mobile internet connectivity then it will be useful if all the organization's laptops and PDAs are connected to the mobile phone in the same way.

- ***Remote access:*** If access is needed to the organization's network while a user is roaming, there are likely to be some authorisation issues regarding the organization's firewall. There may be occasions when a user will have different levels of access to the organization's network depending upon whether the user is using mobile internet connectivity or accessing from the organization's network. This may mean that an organization needs to implement a further level of security on its network in order to ensure the level of security required.

EXERCISE

Objective Type Questions

1. Which of the following is not relevant to marketing via the Internet?

   (A) Click-and-mortar marketing (B) Viral marketing

   (C) Brick-and-mortar marketing (D) Mobile marketing

2. Connectivity is a concept related to

   (A) transmitting information, either by computer or by phone

   (B) the interconnections within a computer

   (C) using computer networks to link people and resources

   (D) being in an active session with your computer

3. One of the most dramatic changes in connectivity and communications in the past five years or so has been _____.

   (A) mobile or wireless telephones

   (B) public and private discussion

   (C) satellite uplinks

   (D) running programs on remote computers

4. Most Web-enabled devices follow a standard known as FireWire

   (A) Bluetooth (B) TCP/IP

   (C) Wi-FI

5. This wireless standard is widely used to connect computers to each other and to the Internet.

   (A) 802.11 (B) RJ45

   (C) Blueband (D) Broadband

6. Bluetooth is a type of radio wave information transmission system that is good for about

   (A) 30 feet (B) 30 yards

   (C) 30 miles (D) 300 miles

7. Which of the statements are correct?

   (A) Class A devices support GPRS and other GSM services

   (B) Class B devices can monitor GSM and GPRS channels simultaneously

(C) With Class C devices, the user must select which service to connect to

(D) All of the above

8. Most modern GPRS devices have download capabilities of up to

(A) 52Kbps (B) 100Kbps

(C) 112Kbps (D) 2Mbps

9. A term relating to sending data to a satellite is

(A) Uplink (B) downlink

(C) Modulate (D) demodulate

10. A wireless LAN found in a train or bus station is an example of a(n)

(A) public wireless LAN

(B) ad-hoc wireless LAN

(C) infrastructure wireless LAN

11. Which of the following statements is true of a wireless LAN?

(A) Communication between devices may only occur in ad-hoc mode

(B) Communication between devices may only occur via an access point

(C) Communication between devices may occur via an access point, or in ad-hoc mode

12. This technology will replace existing standards in 2006-2010 and offer fully end-to-end IP networks.

(A) GPS (B) 2.5G

(C) 3G (D) 4G

13. This technology has been in existence since 1991 and is the global wireless communication specification.

(A) GPS (B) 4G

(C) SMS (D) WAP

14. EDGE stands for

(A) Enhanced Data GSM Environment

(B) Embedded Data GSM Environment

(C) Embedded Download Group Environment

(D) Enhanced Data Group Environment

(E) None of the above

Review & Discussion Questions

1. List out the different types of mobile internet connectivity available now days.
2. Write a short note on Public Access WLANs.
3. What is the main difference between GSM & CDMA?
4. Write a short note on Global systems for mobile communication.
5. What is Telecom regulatory body of India?
6. Write a short note on High speed circuit switched data.
7. Write a short note on General packet radio services.
8. Write a short note on Enhanced data GSM environment.
9. Write a short note on Global systems for mobile communication.
10. What content/applications can mobile internet connectivity deliver?
11. What are the advantages and disadvantages of mobile internet connectivity compared with fixed-line internet connectivity?
12. Where is mobile internet connectivity being used?
13. What are the issues to consider when buying mobile internet connectivity contracts and equipment?
14. List out the network service provider for mobile telecommunication technologies.
15. What are the implementation issues for mobile internet connectivity?

CHAPTER 3

Domain Name Services (DNS)

CHAPTER OBJECTIVES

In this chapter, you will able to know about DNS, underlying network topology and IP addresses. This provides stability at the application level while enabling network applications to find and communicate with each other using the Internet protocol no matter how the underlying physical network changes. We cover the most commonly used top level domains, Country-Code Top-Level Domains (ccTLDs), Information about the IANA's Procedures Concerning ccTLDs, Generic Top-Level Domains and Infrastructure Top-Level Domain.

CHAPTER OUTLINES

3.1 INTRODUCTION

The Domain Name System (DNS) was originally developed to support the growth of email communications on the ARPANET, and now supports the Internet on a global scale. The Domain Name System (DNS) as a whole consists of a network of servers that map Internet domain names like www.bpkm.org.in to a local IP addresses.

The DNS enables domain names to stay constant while the underlying network topology and IP addresses change. This provides stability at the application level while enabling network applications to find and communicate with each other using the Internet protocol no matter how the underlying physical network changes. Most Internet services rely on DNS to work. If DNS fails or is too slow, web sites cannot be located and email delivery stalls.

You can look up information on existing Internet domain names with the WHOIS service, and get your own domain name from an accredited registrar.

3.2 TOP-LEVEL DOMAINS

There are two types of top-level domains, generic and country code, plus a special top-level domain (.arpa) for Internet Infrastructure. Generic domains were created for use by the Internet public, while country code, domains were created to be used by individual countries as they deemed necessary. Below you will find links to more information about each type of top-level domain, including contact information or links to their registration services.

- *Country Code Domains* (.uk, .de, .jp, .us, etc.)
- *Generic Domains* (.aero, .biz, .cat, .com, .coop, .edu, .gov, .info, .jobs, .mobi, .int, .mil, .museum, .name, .net, .org, .pro, and .travel)
- *Infrastructure Domain* (.arpa)
- *List of Top Level Domains*

3.2.1 Country-Code Top-Level Domains (ccTLDs)

Information about Existing ccTLDs

Information about the delegation of existing ccTLDs appears in the Internet Access Number Authority IANA ccTLD Database, or it may be obtained at the IANA whois service (port 43 access available at whois.iana.org). This listing contains basic information for the top-level domains for each country, such as the sponsoring organization's name and the technical and administrative contacts. If you desire to register a domain name under one of these top-level domains, you should contact the person(s) listed via E-mail or visit their website if one is listed.

Information about the IANA's Procedures Concerning ccTLDs

The IANA's ccTLD database contains authoritative information about ccTLDs. This information includes sponsoring organization, administrative contact, technical contact, nameserver information, registration URL, and whois server address. The following sections give information about the procedures that the IANA follows in maintaining the ccTLD database.

1. *Establishment of New ccTLDs:* In determining whether new TLDs should be added, the IANA follows the ISO 3166-1 list as published by the ISO 3166 Maintenance Agency. For more information about establishing new ccTLDs, see the IANA's Procedures for establishing ccTLDs.

2. *Redelegation of ccTLDs:* The process of changing the designated manager(s) of a ccTLD is known as redelegation. This process is conducted according to the principles described in ICP-1 and RFC 1591. For a simplified summary of the process that is followed in implementing these principles, see the ccTLD Redelegation Step-by-Step Overview. The "IANA Reports" listed below illustrate many of the considerations made in the decision whether to redelegate.

3. *Requests by ccTLD Managers to Change Nameservers:* The IANA is responsible for receiving and acting on requests by the designated ccTLD managers to change information (name and IP address) about the ccTLD's nameservers in the root zone. Requests should be made by filling out the root-zone modification template and sending it to root-mgmt@iana.org. For more information about the requirements that apply to nameserver-change requests, please see Format and Technical Requirements for Requests to Change TLD Nameservers in the Root Zone. The procedures followed by the IANA in handling these requests (effective 31 March, 2003) are described in Procedures for Handling Requests by ccTLD Managers to Change Nameservers.

4. *Requests by ccTLD Managers to Change Contact Data:* The IANA is also responsible for receiving and acting on requests by the designated ccTLD managers to change contact information about the ccTLD's designated sponsoring organization, administrative contact, and technical contact. Requests should be made by filling out the root-zone modification template and sending it to root-mgmt@iana.org. For more information about how to request changes in contact data, see Format, Content, and Technical Requirements for Requests to Change TLD Contact Information.

3.2.2 Generic Top-Level Domains

- The *.aero* domain is reserved for members of the air-transport industry and is sponsored by Société Internationale de Télécommunications Aéronautiques (SITA).

- The ***.biz*** domain is restricted to businesses and is operated by NeuLevel, Inc.
- The ***.cat*** domain is reserved for the catalan linguistic and cultural community and is sponsored by Fundació puntCat.
- The ***.com*** domain is operated by VeriSign Global Registry Services.
- The ***.coop*** domain is reserved for cooperative associations and is sponsored by Dot Cooperation LLC.
- The ***.info*** domain is operated by Afilias Limited.
- The ***.jobs*** domain is reserved for human resource managers and is sponsored by Employ Media LLC.
- The ***.mobi*** domain is reserved for consumers and providers of mobile products and services and is sponsored by mTLD Top Level Domain, Ltd.
- The ***.museum*** domain is reserved for museums and is sponsored by the Museum Domain Management Association.
- The ***.name*** domain is reserved for individuals and is operated by Global Name Registry.
- The ***.net*** domain is operated by VeriSign Global Registry Services.
- The ***.org*** domain is operated by Public Interest Registry. It is intended to serve the noncommercial community, but all are eligible to register within. org.
- The ***.pro*** domain is restricted to credentialed professionals and related entities and is operated by RegistryPro.
- The ***.travel*** domain is reserved for entities whose primary area of activity is in the travel industry and is sponsored by Tralliance Corporation.

Registrations in the domains listed above may be made through dozens of competitive registrars. For a list of the currently operating accredited registrars, go to the InterNIC site. Information about becoming an accredited registrar is available on the ICANN site.

- The ***.gov*** domain is reserved exclusively for the United States Government. It is operated by the US General Services Administration.
- The ***.edu*** domain is reserved for post secondary institutions accredited by an agency on the U.S. Department of Education's list of Nationally Recognized Accrediting Agencies and is registered only through Educause.
- The ***.mil*** domain is reserved exclusively for the United States Military. It is operated by the US DoD Network Information Center.

The .int domain is used only for registering organizations established by international treaties between governments. It is operated by the IANA .int Domain Registry.

3.2.3 Infrastructure Top-Level Domain

The .arpa domain is the Address and Routing Parameter Area domain and is designated to be used exclusively for Internet-infrastructure purposes. It is administered by the IANA in cooperation with the Internet technical community under the guidance of the Internet Architecture Board. The .arpa domain currently includes the following second-level domains:

.arpa

e164.arpa

in-addr.arpa

ip6.arpa

uri.arpa

urn.arpa

3.2.4 List of Top Level Domains

Domain	Country	Domain	Country
.ac	Ascension Island	.cd	Congo, The Democratic
.ad	Andorra	.cf	Central African Republic
.ae	**United Arab Emirates**	.cg	Congo, Republic of
.af	Afghanistan	.ch	Switzerland
.ag	Antigua and Barbuda	.ci	Cote d'Ivoire
.ai	Anguilla	.ck	Cook Islands
.al	Albania	.cl	Chile
.am	Armenia	.cm	Cameroon
.an	Netherlands Antilles	**.cn**	**China**
.ao	Angola	.co	Colombia
.aq	Antarctica	.cr	Costa Rica
.ar	**Argentina**	.cs	Serbia and Montenegro
.as	American Samoa	.cu	Cuba
.at	Austria	.cv	Cape Verde
.au	**Australia**	.cx	Christmas Island
.aw	Aruba	.cy	Cyprus
.az	Azerbaijan	.cz	Czech Republic
.ax	Aland Islands	**.de**	**Germany**
.ba	Bosnia and Herzegovina	.dj	Djibouti
.bb	Barbados	**.dk**	**Denmark**
.bd	Bangladesh	.dm	Dominica

Contd....

.be	Belgium	.do	Dominican Republic
.bf	Burkina Faso	.dz	Algeria
.bg	Bulgaria	.ec	Ecuador
.bh	Bahrain	.ee	Estonia
.bi	Burundi	**.eg**	**Egypt**
.bm	Bermuda	.eh	Western Sahara
.bn	Brunei Darussalam	.er	Eritrea
.bo	Bolivia	.es	Spain
.br	**Brazil**	.et	Ethiopia
.bs	Bahamas	.eu	European Union
.bt	**Bhutan**	.fi	Finland
.bv	Bouvet Island	.fj	Fiji
.bw	**Botswana**	.fk	Falkland Islands (Malvinas)
.by	Belarus	.fm	Micronesia, Federal State of
.bz	Belize	.fo	Faroe Islands
.ca	**Canada**	**.fr**	**France**
.cc	Cocos (Keeling) Islands	.ga	Gabon
.gb	**United Kingdom**	**.jp**	**Japan**
.gd	Grenada	**.ke**	**Kenya**
.ge	Georgia	.kg	Kyrgyzstan
.gf	French Guiana	.kh	Cambodia
.gg	Guernsey	.ki	Kiribati
.gh	**Ghana**	.km	Comoros
.gi	Gibraltar	.kn	Saint Kitts and Nevis
.gl	Greenland	.kp	Korea, Democratic People's
.gm	Gambia	.kr	Korea, Republic of
.gn	Guinea	**.kw**	**Kuwait**
.gp	Guadeloupe	.ky	Cayman Islands
.gq	Equatorial Guinea	.kz	Kazakhstan
.gr	**Greece**	.la	Lao People's Democratic
.gs	South Georgia and the South Sandwich Islands	**.lb**	**Lebanon**
.gt	Guatemala	.lc	Saint Lucia
.gu	Guam	.li	Liechtenstein
.gw	Guinea-Bissau	**.lk**	**Sri Lanka**
.gy	Guyana	.lr	Liberia
.hk	**Hong Kong**	.ls	Lesotho
.hm	**Heard and McDonald Islands**	.lt	Lithuania

Contd....

.hn	Honduras	.lu	Luxembourg
.hr	Croatia/Hrvatska	.lv	Latvia
.ht	Haiti	.ly	Libyan Arab Jamahiriya
.hu	**Hungary**	.ma	Morocco
.id	**Indonesia**	.mc	Monaco
.ie	Ireland	.md	Moldova, Republic of
.il	Israel	.mg	Madagascar
.im	Isle of Man	.mh	Marshall Islands
.in	**India**	.mk	Macedonia, The Former Yugoslav Republic of
.io	British Indian Ocean Territory	.ml	Mali
.iq	**Iraq**	.mm	Myanmar
.ir	Iran, Islamic Republic of	**.mn**	**Mongolia**
.is	Iceland	.mo	Macau
.it	**Italy**	.mp	Northern Mariana Islands
.je	Jersey	.mq	Martinique
.jm	**Jamaica**	.mr	Mauritania
.jo	Jordan	.ms	Montserrat
.mt	Malta	.rw	Rwanda
.mu	**Mauritius**	.sa	Saudi Arabia
.mv	Maldives	.sb	Solomon Islands
.mw	Malawi	.sc	Seychelles
.mx	**Mexico**	**.sd**	**Sudan**
.my	Malaysia	**.se**	**Sweden**
.mz	Mozambique	**.sg**	**Singapore**
.na	Namibia	.sh	Saint Helena
.nc	New Caledonia	.si	Slovenia
.ne	Niger	.sj	Svalbard and Jan Mayen Islands
.nf	Norfolk Island	.sk	Slovak Republic
.ng	Nigeria	.sl	Sierra Leone
.ni	Nicaragua	.sm	San Marino
.nl	Netherlands	.sn	Senegal
.no	**Norway**	.so	Somalia
.np	**Nepal**	.sr	Suriname
.nr	Nauru	.st	Sao Tome and Principe
.nu	Niue	.sv	El Salvador

Contd....

.nz	New Zealand	.sy	Syrian Arab Republic
.om	**Oman**	.sz	Swaziland
.pa	Panama	.tc	Turks and Caicos Islands
.pe	Peru	.td	Chad
.pf	French Polynesia	.tf	French Southern Territories
.pg	Papua New Guinea	.tg	Togo
.ph	Philippines	**.th**	**Thailand**
.pk	**Pakistan**	.tj	Tajikistan
.pl	Poland	.tk	Tokelau
.pm	Saint Pierre and Miquelon	.tl	Timor-Leste
.pn	Pitcairn Island	.tm	Turkmenistan
.pr	Puerto Rico	.tn	Tunisia
.ps	Palestinian Territories	.to	Tonga
.pt	Portugal	.tp	East Timor
.pw	Palau	.tr	Turkey
.py	Paraguay	.tt	Trinidad and Tobago
.qa	Qatar	.tv	Tuvalu
.re	Reunion Island	.tw	Taiwan
.ro	**Romania**	.tz	Tanzania
.ru	Russian Federation	.ua	Ukraine
.ug	Uganda	.vu	Vanuatu
.uk	**United Kingdom**	.wf	Wallis and Futuna Islands
.um	United States Minor Outlying Islands	.ws	Samoa
.us	**United States**	.ye	Yemen
.uy	Uruguay	.yt	Mayotte
.uz	Uzbekistan	**.yu**	**Yugoslavia**
.va	Holy See (Vatican City State)	**.za**	**South Africa**
.vc	Saint Vincent and the Grenadines	**.zm**	**Zambia**
.ve	**Venezuela**	**.zw**	**Zimbabwe**
.vg	Virgin Islands, British	**.vn**	**Vietnam**
.vi	Virgin Islands, U.S.		

3.3 .IN - INDIA

3.3.1 Sponsoring Organization

National Centre for Software Technology

Gulmohar Cross Road #9, Juhu

Mumbai, Maharashtra 400 049. (INDIA)

3.3.2 Administrative Contact

.IN Registry

National Internet Exchange of India

612-A, Chiranjiv Tower, 43 Nehru Place

New Delhi, Delhi 110019. (INDIA)

Email: info@nixi.in

Voice: +91 11 26424001/02

Fax: +91 11 51608472

3.3.3 Technical Contact

Domain Name: Services Technical Adminitrator

National Internet Exchange of India

C/O STPI Block -IV, 2nd Floor

Ganga Shopping Complex, Sector 29

Noida, DE 201 303. (INDIA)

Email: domaintech@registry.in

Voice: +91 120 2450411 ext. 348

Fax: +91 120 5318082

3.3.4 Domain Servers

ns.ripe.net	193.0.0.193
ns-ext.vix.com	204.152.184.64
tld1.ultradns.net	204.74.112.1 2001:502:d399:0:0:0:0:1
tld2.ultradns.net	204.74.113.1
tld3.ultradns.org	199.7.66.1
tld4.ultradns.org	199.7.67.1 2001:502:100e:0:0:0:0:1
tld5.ultradns.info	192.100.59.11
tld6.ultradns.co.uk	198.133.199.11

URL for registration services: http://www.registry.in

Whois server: whois.inregistry.net

Record last updated - 13-June-2006

Record created - 08-May-1989

EXERCISE

Objective Type Questions

1. The URL http://www.srimca.edu.in/panda/help.htm
   (A) includes a word document
   (B) requires a helper application to be viewed
   (C) contains the domain name srimca.edu.in
   (D) uses the File Transfer Protocol
2. The most used top-level domain is
   (A) .net (B) .edu.
   (C) .com (D) .gov
3. In the URL, http;//www.srimca.eud.in/pr/main.htm, the domain is
   (A) http (B) www.srimca.edu.in
   (C) pr/main.htm (D) www
4. A URL specifies the following
   (i) protocol used
   (ii) domain name of server hosting web page
   (iii) name of folder with required information
   (iv) name of document formatted using HTML
   (v) the name of ISP
   (A) i, ii, iii, iv (B) ii, iii, iv, v
   (C) i, iii, iv (D) i, ii, iii, v
5. The routing scheme inside the domain is
   (A) completely visible to the outside world
   (B) regulated by IETF
   (C) subject to Govt. media policies
   (D) none of the above
6. Protocols in network mean
   (A) Languages for communication between computers
   (B) Rules for exchange of messages between two or more hosts
   (C) Both
   (D) None of the above

7. The arrangement and meaning of Internet mail headers are defined by an Internet standard called

(A) RFC 822 (B) RFC 1597

(C) RFC 920 (D) RFC 782

8. Which of the following is not an example of common top level domain

(A) com (B) org

(C) govt (D) mil

9. Protocols are used to communicate between

(A) similar modules (B) dissimilar modules

(C) both (D) none of the above

10. Which of the following services are not offered by CompuServe?

(A) Electronic mail box (B) BBS

(C) News (D) Information on computer h/w & s/w

(E) None of the above

11. The following is not a domain name

(A) com (B) dev

(C) gov (D) org

12. Which of the following is not one of the uses of repeaters?

(A) Boost signal power

(B) Clean signal pulses

(C) Increase maximum interconnection length

(D) None of the above

(E) None of the above

13. What is a domain?

(A) It is a host that is connected to two networks

(B) It is a collection of sites that are related in some sense

(C) It is a precursor to the WWW

(D) None of the above

Review & Discussion Questions

1. What are the two main requirements for web hoisting?
2. What are the top level domains used for Internet?
3. What is the use of Generic Domains? List out some of the Generic domains that are used for public.
4. What is ccTLDs? How IANA's ccTLDs Database works?
5. Which domain is used for air-transport industry? Mention the sponsoring authority for such domain.
6. Who operates .info domain? What is the use of .mobi domain?
7. What is the use of Global Name Registry?
8. What is the use of Public Interest Registry?
9. What is the use of .gov, .edu and .mil domains? List out the operating body for each domain.
10. What is .arpa domain? List out its second level domains.
11. What are the top level domain for countries like Brazil, United Arab Emirates, China, Germany, Bhutan and India?
12. Who is the authority for .IN Registry? For technical help to whom one can contact?

CHAPTER 4

IP Address

CHAPTER OBJECTIVES

In this chapter, you will take a brief look at the IPv4 and IPv6 addresses and get glimpse of their allocation assigned in a delegated manner. You will also examine the fundamental difference between Network part and host part of IP address. In addition, you will get idea about IP address classes and their formats. This chapter emphasis on Internet Security Alliance (ISAlliance) and need to deploy IPV6 protocol as a replacement for the current implementation of Internet Protocol (IPV4).

CHAPTER OUTLINES

4.1 INTRODUCTION

Currently there are two types of Internet Protocol (IP) addresses in active use: IP version 4 (IPv4) and IP version 6 (IPv6). IPv4 was initially deployed on 1st January, 1983 and is still the most commonly used version. IPv4 addresses are 32-bit numbers often expressed as 4 octets in "dotted decimal" notation (for example, 192.0.32.67). Deployment of the IPv6 protocol began in 1999. IPv6 addresses are 128-bit numbers and are conventionally expressed using hexadecimal strings (for example, 1080:0:0:0:8:800:200C: 417A).

Both IPv4 and IPv6 addresses are assigned in a delegated manner. Users are assigned IP addresses by Internet Service Providers (ISPs). ISPs obtain allocations of IP addresses from a Local Internet Registry (LIR) or National Internet Registry (NIR), or from their appropriate Regional Internet Registry (RIR):

http://www.ip2location.com

http://www.whatismyip.com

In the most widely installed level of the Internet Protocol (IP) today, an IP address is a 32-bit number that identifies each sender or receiver of information that is sent in packets across the Internet. When you request the HTML page or send e-mail. The Internet Protocol part of TCP/IP includes your IP address in the message (actually, in each of the packets, if more than one is required) and sends it to the IP address that is obtained by looking up the domain name in the Uniform Resource Locator, you requested or in the e-mail address you're sending a note to. At the other end, the recipient can see the IP address of the Web page requestor or the e-mail sender and can respond by sending another message using the IP address it received.

An IP address has two parts: the identifier of a particular network on the Internet and an identifier of the particular device (which can be a server or a workstation) within that network. On the Internet itself - that is, between the router that moves packets from one point to another along the route i.e. only the network part of the address is looked at.

4.2 THE NETWORK PART OF THE IP ADDRESS

The Internet is really the interconnection of many individual networks (it's sometimes referred to as an internet work). So the Internet Protocol (IP) is basically the set of rules for one network communicating with any other (or occasionally, for broadcast messages, all other networks). Each network must know its own address on the Internet and that of any other networks with which it communicates. To be part of the Internet, an organization needs an Internet network number, which it can request from the Network Information Center (NIC). This unique network number is included in any packet sent out of the network onto the Internet.

4.3 THE LOCAL OR HOST PART OF THE IP ADDRESS

In addition to the network address or number, information is needed about which specific machine or host in a network is sending or receiving a message. Therefore, the IP address needs both the unique network number and a host number (which is unique within the network). (The host number is sometimes called a local or machine address.)

Part of the local address can identify a subnetwork or subnet address, which makes it easier for a network that, is divided into several physical subnetworks (for examples, several different local area networks) or to handle many devices.

4.4 IP ADDRESS CLASSES AND THEIR FORMATS

Since networks vary in size, there are four different address formats or classes to consider when applying to NIC for a network number:

Class A addresses are for large networks with many devices.

Class B addresses are for medium-sized networks.

Class C addresses are for small networks (fewer than 256 devices).

Class D addresses are multicast addresses.

The first few bits of each IP address indicate which of the address class formats, it is using. The address structures look like this:

Class A 0 Network (7 bits) Local address (24 bits)

Class B 10 Network (14 bits) Local address (16 bits)

Class C 110 Network (21 bits) Local address (8 bits)

Class D 1110 Multicast address (28 bits)

Class	Address Range	Supports
Class A	1.0.0.1 to 126.255.255.254	Supports 16 million hosts on each of 127 networks.
Class B	128.1.0.1 to 191.255.255.254	Supports 65,000 hosts on each of 16,000 networks.
Class C	192.0.1.1 to 223.255.254.254	Supports 254 hosts on each of 2 million networks.
Class D	224.0.0.0 to 239.255.255.255	Reserved for multicast groups.
Class E	240.0.0.0 to 254.255.255.254	Reserved.

Ranges 127.x.x.x are reserved for loop back tests, for example, 127.0.0.1. Ranges 255.255.255.255 are used to broadcast to all hosts on the local network.

All IP addresses are broken down into 4 sets of octets that break down into binary to represent the actual IP address. The below chart is a basic example of the basic IP 255.255.255.255.

IP:	255.	255.	255.	255.
Binary value:	11111111.	11111111.	11111111.	11111111.
Octet value:	8	8	8	8

If we were to break down the IP "166.70.10.23", which is the IP address of http://bpkm.org.in you would get the below value.

166.	70.	10.	23
10100110.	01000110.	00010010.	00010111
128+32+4+2=166	64+4+2=70	8+2=10	16+4+2+1=23

There are several IP addresses used or automatically assigned on a network. For example:

166.70.10.0	0 is the automatically assigned network address.
166.70.10.1	1 is the commonly used address used as the gateway.
166.70.10.2	2 is also a commonly used address used for a gateway.
166.70.10.255	255 is automatically assigned on most networks as the broadcast address.

Users and/or companies who need to register an IP address or a valid range of IP addresses must register that IP address through InterNIC.

The IP address is usually expressed as four decimal numbers, each representing eight bits, separated by periods. This is sometimes known as the dot address and, more technically, as dotted quad notation. For Class A IP addresses, the numbers would represent "network.local.local.local"; for a Class C IP address, they would represent "network.network.network.local". The number version of the IP address can (and usually is) represented by a name or series of names called the domain name.

The Internet's explosive growth makes it likely that, without some new architecture, the number of possible network addresses using the scheme above would soon be used up (at least, for Class C network addresses). However, a new IP version, IPv6, expands the size of the IP address to 128 bits, which will accommodate a large growth in the number of network addresses. For hosts still using IPv4, the use of subnets in the host or local part of the IP address will help reduce new applications for network numbers. In addition, most sites on today's mostly IPv4 Internet have gotten around the Class C network address limitation by using the Classless Inter-Domain Routing (CIDR) scheme for address notation.

4.5 RELATIONSHIP OF THE IP ADDRESS TO THE PHYSICAL ADDRESS

The machine or physical address used within an organization's local area networks may be different from the Internet's IP address. The most typical example is the 48-bit Ethernet address. TCP/IP includes a facility called the Address Resolution Protocol (ARP) that lets the administrator create a table that maps IP addresses to physical addresses. The table is known as the ARP cache.

4.6 STATIC VERSUS DYNAMIC IP ADDRESSES

The discussion above assumes that IP addresses are assigned on a static basis. In fact, many IP addresses are assigned dynamically from a pool. Many corporate networks and online services economize on the number of IP addresses, they use by sharing a pool of IP addresses among a large number of users. If you're an America Online user, for example, your IP address will vary from one logon session to the next, because AOL is assigning it to you from a pool that is much smaller than AOL's base of subscribers.

4.7 COMMENTS OF INTERNET SECURITY ALLIANCE (ISALLIANCE)

The Internet Security Alliance is pleased to provide its response to the above captioned Notice of Inquiry: Request for Comments on Deployment of Internet Protocol Version 6, as published in the federal Register by NIST and NTIA on 21 January, 2004.

As a trade association focused on improved cyber security and representing more than 50 corporate members serving various sectors of the economy on four continents, we believe that, we have a unique perspective to address the security aspects of this inquiry.

The Internet Security Alliance (ISAlliance) understands the desire, and in many cases, the need to deploy IPV6 protocol as a replacement for the current implementation of Internet Protocol (IPV4) from a network addressability perspective and for the merits that the expanded network feature set provides to the implementer.

IPv6 would be deployed to co-exist with and ultimately replace a set of IPv4 systems and protocols that have 20+ years of implementation and deployment experience. The IS Alliance has concerns regarding the motivation for the deployment of IPv6 from the perspective of network security as outlined in the 3 broad areas below:

- Many security vulnerabilities result from software implementation errors and network configuration errors that continual inspection, due to real, everyday experience in production networks, has largely served to eliminate from the IPv4 code base. That said, after 20 years of IPv4, many implementation errors are found every year. The IPv6 code base will initially not have benefited from this vast degree of close scrutiny and consequently, it is likely that the introduction of IPv6 will manifest many more security vulnerabilities during the early phases of production deployment than are currently seen with IPv4.

  Industry, with assistance from the established security monitoring and alerting services, can and must use the systems established during the development of IPv4 to expedite the security hardening of IPv6 implementations.

- The experience and perspectives gained from running IPv4 networks will certainly help to bring the security of IPv6 networks up to the levels of current IPv4 networks more rapidly, but during the transition, a number of novel network solutions are likely to be required. Networks running IPv4 and IPv6 in parallel and using relatively untried transition mechanism may well suffer from additional unanticipated security vulnerabilities during the initial transition period.

  Again, the overall effect of such vulnerabilities can be minimized by rapid identification and promulgation of revised best practices by the industry assisted by government agencies that are running pilot programs.

- Many of the security weaknesses of IPv4 are inherited by IPv6, at least partially because of the desire to ease the learning curve for network operators during the transition and the desire to reuse the tried and tested tools of IPv4 to the greatest extent possible. Examples are insecure routing protocols, firewall implementations etc. Consequently, there are areas of IPv6 where more secure solutions might theoretically be implemented but have not been. In many instances security will not necessarily be any better than is achieved by IPv4, at least during initial deployment.

  There are areas, where ultimately IPv6 has the capacity to improve on v4, and there are components that have been taken over from IPv4 that should be enhanced in the new more flexible environment that is offered by the IPv6 architecture.

The ISAlliance believes that the experience, expertise and systems put in place to build up the security of IPv4 can be applied to ameliorate the initial shortcomings of IPv6 implementations.

It is of major concern to the ISAlliance membership that organizations considering the deployment of IPV6 understand, very clearly, that implementations of IPV6 are not necessarily more secure than IPv4 despite the addition of IPSec capabilities to the protocol as a standard feature set. We believe that the deployment of IPv6 alongside IPv4 will throw up additional issues in security that has not been experienced in the single protocol environment of existing IPv4 networks. It is very important that all parties work together to deliver solutions and improved practices to overcome these problems.

EXERCISE

Objective Type Questions

1. Each computer connected to the internet must
   (A) be an IBM PC
   (B) have a unique IP address
   (C) be internet compatible
   (D) have a modem connection
2. IP address is currently
   (A) 4 bytes long
   (B) available in plenty
   (C) 6 bytes long
   (D) not assigned as it is all used up
3. IP addresses are converted to
   (A) binary string
   (B) alphanumeric string
   (C) a hierarchy of domain names
   (D) a hexadecimal string
4. For the sites on the internet, the IP address assigned by
   (A) NIC
   (B) IETF
   (C) IEEE
   (D) You are free to choose any 32-bit number
   (E) None of the above
5. How long is IP address in IPv4?
   (A) 4 bytes
   (B) 8 bytes
   (C) 16 bytes
   (D) 6 bytes
6. Internet addresses must always have at least
   (i) a country name or organization type
   (ii) internet service provider's name
   (iii) name of organization
   (iv) name of individual
   (v) type of organization
   (A) i, ii, iii
   (B) ii, iii, iv
   (C) i, iii
   (D) ii, iii, iv, v

7. What does the "IP" in IP Address stand for?

(A) inter peer address

(B) internet protocol address

(C) international private address

(D) international postal address

8. Identify the class of the following IP address: 4.5.6.7.

(A) class A (B) class B

(C) class C (D) none of the above

9. Which of the following networking solution is suitable for networking in a building?

(A) LAN (B) WAN

(C) MAN (D) All of the above

10. You want a firewall if :

(i) You are trying to protect your network from external access

(ii) You are trying to deny access to the world outside from your network

(iii) To protect your network from viruses

(A) (i) & (ii) (B) All

(C) (iii) only (D) (i) & (iii)

11. Which of the following is true about TCP?

(A) It is responsible for reliability of communication

(B) It allows several concurrent logins

(C) It helps in defining an abstract interface through which hardware is addressed

(D) All of the above

(E) None of the above

12. Which of the following is not true about IP?

(A) It turns physically dissimilar networks into one apparently homogenous one

(B) It is hardware independent

(C) It is, by intent, not reliable

(D) It is responsible for reliability of communications

13. Identify the class of the following IP address: 229.1.2.3.

(A) class A (B) class B

(C) class D (D) none of the above

14. Identify the class of the following IP address: 191.1.2.3.

(A) class A (B) class B

C) class C (D) none of the above

15. Which of the following is true of the IP address 231.1.2.3?

(A) The netid is 231 (B) The class is D

(C) The hostid is 1.2.3. (D) None of the above

16. Which of the following is true of the IP address 192.0.0.10?

(A) The netid is 192

(B) The hostid is 0.10.

(C) The network address is 192.0.0.0.

(D) None of the above

17. Using the direct broadcast address, a _______ sends a packet to _______ on the network.

(A) host; all other hosts (B) router; all other hosts

(C) host; a specific host (D) none of the above

18. Using the limited broadcast address, a _______ sends a packet to _______ on the network.

(A) host; all other hosts (B) router; all other hosts

(C) host; a specific host (D) none of the above

19. The loopback address is used to send a packet from the _______ to _______.

(A) host; all other hosts (B) router; all other hosts

(C) host; a specific host (D) none of the above

20. A host can get its IP address from its server by using _______ as the source address and _______ as the destination address.

(A) 255.255.255.255; 0.0.0.0 (B) 127.0.0.0; 255.255.255.255

(C) 0.0.0.0; 255.255.255.255 (D) None of the above

21. A host with an IP address of 142.5.0.1 needs to test internal software. What is the destination address in the packet?

(A) 131.0.0.0 (B) 127.1.1.1

(C) 129.1.127.127 (D) None of the above

22. The number of addresses in a class C block is ______.

(A) 65,534 (B) 16,777,216

(C) 256 (D) None of the above

23. The number of addresses in a class B block is ______.

(A) 65,534 (B) 16,777,216

(C) 256 (D) None of the above

24. The number of addresses in a class A block is ______.

(A) 65,534 (B) 16,777,216

(C) 256 (D) None of the above

25. An organization has been granted a class A address. If the organization has 256 subnets, how many addresses are available in each subnet (including special addresses)?

(A) 65,534 (B) 16,777,216

(C) 256 (D) None of the above

26. An organization has been granted a class B address. If the organization has 64 subnets, how many addresses are available in each subnet (including special addresses)?

(A) 65,534 (B) 1024

(C) 256 (D) None of the above

27. An organization has been granted a class C address. If the organization has 4 subnets, how many addresses are available in each subnet (including special addresses)?

(A) 4 (B) 1024

(C) 256 (D) None of the above

Review & Discussion Questions

1. What is an IP address? What is the use of an IP address?
2. What is a network ID? What is a host ID?
3. What is a unicast IP address?
4. What is a multicast IP address?
5. What is a broadcast IP address?
6. How IP addresses are classified?
7. Can a single network interface have more than one IP address associated with it?
8. What is the use of classifying IP addresses?
9. What are the different classes of IP addresses?
10. How to determine the class of an IP address?
11. How many bytes does each Class of IP address use to represent network and host IDs?
12. What is the format of the various IP address classes?
13. How many numbers of networks and hosts can be represented using the IP address classes?
14. What is the possible range of IP addresses for the different classes?
15. What is Physical Address? Give the relationship of IP address with Physical Address.
16. Write a short note on Internet Security Alliance (ISAlliance).
17. What kind of networks use a Class A or Class B or Class C IP address typically?
18. What is the use of Class D IP addresses?
19. What is the use of Class E IP addresses?
20. How to decide which class of IP address to use for a particular network?
21. Does the maximum number of hosts in a network, restrict the class of IP address that can be used for the network?
22. What are the various special IP addresses?

CHAPTER 5

World Wide Web (www)

CHAPTER OBJECTIVES

This chapter includes the basic principles behind the Web. You will also examine the fundamental difference between the various Web browsers that are currently being used access the Web. In addition, you will take a look at more technical things that need to be done in order to properly plan for a Web site such as server side, client side and various network components. The chapter discusses directory structure, filenames and URLs. The different structure that a Web site can take on is also discussed. The uses of existing and new programming languages have extended the capabilities of the Web. You will also experience a basic guide to a group of the more common languages and functions in use on the Web today.

CHAPTER OUTLINES

5.1 INTRODUCTION

The World Wide Web is an architectural framework for accessing linked documents spread out over thousands of machines all over the Internet. This is a hypertext-based knowledge system of Internet servers that supports hypertext to access several Internet protocols on a single interface. The World Wide Web is often abbreviated as the Web, WWW, or W3.

The World Wide Web was developed in 1989 by Tim Berners-Lee of the European Particle Physics Lab (CERN) in Switzerland. The initial purpose of the Web was to use networked hypertext to facilitate communication among its members, who were located in several countries. Word was soon spread beyond CERN, and a rapid growth in the number of both developers and users ensued. In addition to hypertext, the Web began to incorporate graphics, video, and sound. Over the past few years, the use of the Web has reached global proportions.

Almost every protocol type available on the Internet is accessible on the Web. Internet protocols are sets of rules that allow for inter-machine communication on the Internet.

5.2 THE CLIENT SIDE

From the user's point of view, the Web consists of a vast, worldwide collection of documents, usually just called pages for short. Each page may contain links (pointers) to other, related pages, anywhere in the Internet. Users can follow a link (e.g., by clicking on it), which then takes them to the page pointed to. Pages that point to other pages are said to use hypertext.

Pages are viewed with a program called a browser, of which Internet Explorer (IE) and Netscape Communicator are two popular ones. The browser fetches the page requested, interprets the text and formatting commands that it contains, and displays the page properly formatted on the screen. Strings of text that are links to other pages, called hyperlinks are highlighted, either by underlining, displaying them in a special color, or both. To follow a link, the user places the cursor on the highlighted area and selects it (by clicking the mouse). Voice based browsers are also being developed.

Not all pages are viewable in the conventional way. For example, some pages consist of audio tracks, video clips, or both. When hypertext pages are mixed with other media, the result is called hypermedia. Some browsers can display all kinds of hypermedia, but others cannot. Instead, they check a configuration file to see how to handle the received data. Normally the configuration file gives the name of a program called an external viewer or a helper application to be run with the incoming page as input.

5.2.1 An Overview of the Web Browser

In it's basic form a Web browser is an application that uses information stored at locations around the World Wide Web, in order to perform a local task.

To get the desired information from the Web, a browser uses the client-server paradigm. When given the URL of a document, the browser becomes a client that contacts a Web Server on the computer specified in the URL, to request the document.

When a browser interacts with a Web server, the two programs follow the Hyper Text Transport Protocol (HTTP). HTTP allows a browser to request a specific item, which the server then returns. To ensure that browser and server can inter-operate unambiguously, HTTP defines the exact format of request sent from a browser to a server as well as the format of the servers reply.

While a Web server performs a straightforward task of waiting for a request and sending reply, the browser handles most of the details of document access and display. To be able to perform this tasks the Web browser contains some software components that interact to provide the illusion of seamless service.

The conceptual organisation of a browser is depicted in Figure 5.1.

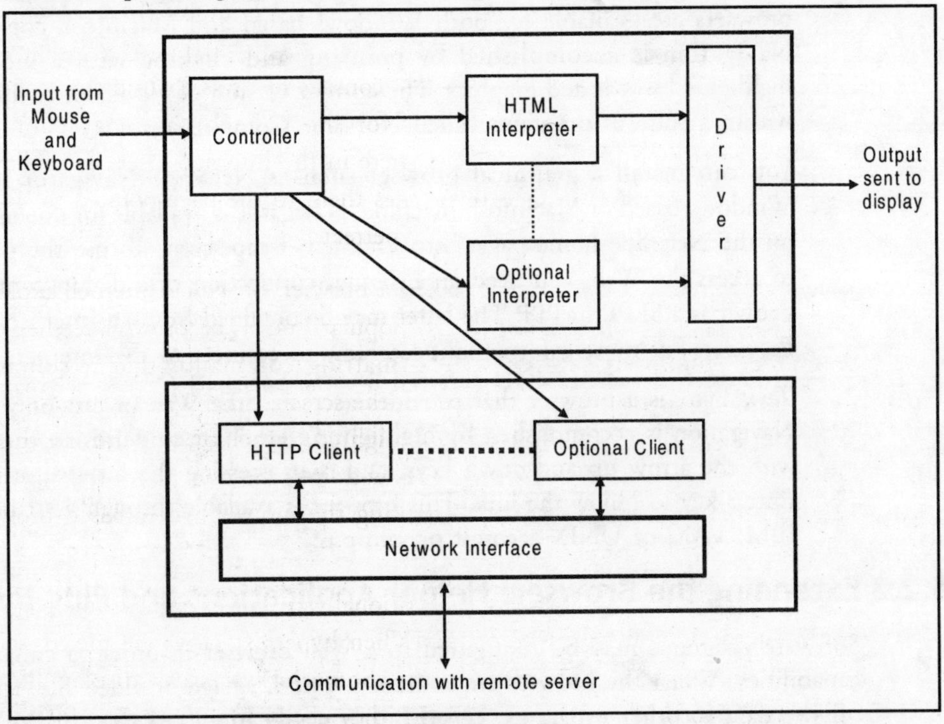

Figure 5.1 ♦ Conceptual Organisation of Web Browser

A browser consists of a set of clients, a set of interpreters and a controller that mange them. The controller forms the central piece of the browser. It interprets both mouse clicks and keyboard inputs, and calls other components to perform operations specified by the user.

Example: When you press a link, the controller will call a client to fetch the requested document from the remote server, and an interpreter to display the document for the user.

Besides an HTTP client and an HTML interpreter a browser can contain components that enable the browser to perform additional tasks. Many browsers include an FTP client that is used to access the file transfer service and an e-mail client that enable the browser to send and receive mail.

The user doesn't invoke such services explicitly; instead, the service is invoked automatically, when it is needed to perform a task. For Example, file transfer can be associated with a selectable object on the screen, when a user selects the item the browser uses the FTP client to obtain a copy of the file.

5.2.2 How to Access the World Wide Web: Web Browsers

There are two types of browsers:

1. *Graphical:* Text, images, audio, and video are retrievable through a graphical software program such as Netscape Navigator and Internet Explorer. These browsers are available for both Windows-based and Macintosh computers. Navigation is accomplished by pointing and clicking with a mouse on highlighted words and graphics. The current version of Navigator is contained within a suite of programs called Netscape Communicator.

   You can install a graphical browser such as Netscape Navigator in your Windows-based or Macintosh machine. Navigator is available for downloading on the Netscape home page: http://home.netscape.com. To use the program to access the Web, you need an Ethernet connection or a dialup connection known as a SLPP or PPP. The latter may be obtained from an Internet Service Provider. For more information, see How to connect to the Internet.

2. *Text:* Lynx is a browser that provides access to the Web in text-only mode. Navigation is accomplished by highlighting emphasized words in the screen with the arrow up and down keys, and then pressing the forward arrow (or Enter) key to follow the link. This browser is available through your personal IBM, VAX, or UNIX account on campus.

5.2.3 Extending the Browser: Helper Applications and Plug-Ins

Software programs may be configured to a Web browser in order to enhance its capabilities. When the browser encounters a sound, image or video file, it hands off the data to other programs, called helper applications, to run or display the file. Working in conjunction with helper applications, browsers can offer a seamless multimedia experience. Many helper applications are available for the free.

File formats requiring helper applications are known as MIME types. MIME stands for the Multimedia Internet Mail Extension, was originally developed to help e-mail software handle a variety of binary (non-ASCII) file attachments. The use of MIME has expanded to the Web. For example, the basic MIME type handled by Web browsers is text/HTML associated with the file extension.HTML.

A common helper application utilized on the Web is the Adobe Acrobat Reader. The Acrobat Reader allows you to view documents created in Adobe's Portable Document Format. These documents are the MIME type application/pdf and are associated with the file extension .pdf. When the Acrobat Reader has been configured to your browser, the program will open and display the file requested when you click on a hyperlinked file name with the suffix .pdf.

Plug-ins are software programs that extend the capabilities of a Web browser in a specific way, such as the ability to play audio files or view video movies from within Navigator. Web browsers are often standardized with a small suite of plug-ins. Additional plug-ins may be obtained at the browser's Web site, at special download sites on the Web, or from the home pages of the companies that created the programs. The number of available plug-ins is increasing rapidly. For example, nearly 200 plug-ins are available for downloading at the Netscape site.

Once a plug-in is configured to your browser, it will automatically launch when you choose to access a file type that it uses.

Netscape Communicator can be downloaded with a variety of helper applications and plug-ins configured to the browser, including:

- Cosmo Player to view 3D sites created with Virtual Reality Modelling Language (VRML) (file suffixes .wrl, .wrz)
- Netscape Media Player for streaming audio metafiles (file suffix .lam)
- Live Audio for sound files (file suffixes .au, .aiff, .wav, .midi, .la, .lma) QuickTime Player for video (file suffix .mov)
- NPAI32 Dynamic Link Library for video in Windows (file suffix .avi)

5.2.4 Beyond Plug-Ins: Active X

ActiveX is a technology developed by Microsoft, which may make plug-ins less necessary. ActiveX offers the opportunity to embed animated objects, data, and computer code on Web pages. A web browser supporting ActiveX can render most items encountered on a Web page. For example, Active X allows users to view three-dimensional VRML worlds in a Web browser without the use of a VRML plug-in. As another example of the power of ActiveX, this technology can allow you to view and edit PowerPoint presentations directly within your Web browser. ActiveX is supported by the Internet Explorer and Netscape Navigator 4.x browsers.

5.2.5 The Experience of The Web

Today's World Wide Web(WWW) presents an ever-diversified experience of multimedia, programming languages, and real-time communication. There is no question that, it is a challenge to keep up with the rapid pace of developments. The following presents a brief description of some of the more important trends to watch.

5.2.6 Multimedia

The Web has become a broadcast medium. It is possible to listen to audio and video over the Web both prerecorded and live. For example, you can visit the sites of various news organisations and view the same videos shown on the nightly television news. Several plug-ins are available for viewing these videos. For example, Apple's Quick Time Player downloads files with the .mov extension and displays these as "movies" in a small window on your computer screen. Quick Time files can be quite large, and it may take patience to wait for the entire movie to download into your computer before you can view it.

The problem of slow downloads times has been answered by a revolutionary development in multimedia capability: streaming data. In this case, audio or video files are played as they are downloading, or streaming, into your computer. Only a small wait, called buffering, is necessary before the file begins to play. The RealPlayer plug-in plays streaming audio and video files. Extensive files such as interviews, speeches and hearings work very well with the RealPlayer. The RealPlayer is also ideal for the broadcast of real-time events. These may include press conferences, live radio and television broadcasts, concerts, etc. A list of sites that make use of the RealPlayer is available at http://www.albany.edu/library/internet/net_info/realaudio.html. The Windows Media Player is another streaming media player. A list of sites that make use of this player is available at http://wmg.netcastnetwork.com/. Many sites offer the option to use one player or the other.

Shockwave presents another multimedia experience. Shockwave allows for the creation and implementation of an entire multimedia display combining graphics, animation and sound.

Sound files, including music, may also be heard on the Web. It is not uncommon to visit a Web page and hear background music. Sound files are also available for downloading independent of Web page visits. Sound files of many types are supported by the Web with the appropriate helper applications.

Live cams are another aspect of the multimedia experience available on the Web. Live cams are video cameras that send their data in real time to a Web server. These cams may appear in all kinds of locations, both serious and whimsical: an office, on top of a building, a scenic locale, a special event, and so on.

5.3 THE SERVER SIDE

Every Web site has a server listening to TCP port 80 for incoming connections from clients (normally browsers). After a connection has been established, the client sends one request and the server sends one reply. Then the connection is released. The protocol that defines the legal requests and replies is called HTTP.

For example, a user clicks on an icon those points to the page whose name (URL) is http://www.timesofindia.com/hypertext/project.html. The steps that are executed between the time that the user clicks and the page being displayed are as follows:

1. The browser determines the URL (by seeing what was selected)
2. The browser asks DNS for the IP address of www.timesofindia.com
3. DNS replies with AAA.BBB.CCC.DDD (say).
4. The browser makes a TCP connection to port 80 on AAA.BBB.CCC.DDD
5. It then sends a GET /hypertext/project.html command.
6. The www.timesofindia.com server sends the file project.html.
7. The TCP connection is released.
8. The browser displays all the text in project.html.
9. The browser fetches and displays all images in project.html.

5.3.1 HTTP (HyperText Transfer Protocol)

The standard Web transfer protocol is HTTP. It transmits hyptertext over networks. The name is somewhat misleading in that HTTP is not a protocol for transferring hypertext; rather, it is a protocol for transferring information with the efficiency necessary for making hypertext jumps. The data transferred by the protocol can be plain text, hypertext, audio, images or any other Internet accessible information.

The HyperText Transport Protocol (HTTP) is an application-level Protocol used by Web client and Web servers to communicate with each other. HTTP has been in use since 1990. The HTTP is a transaction-oriented client/server protocol. To provide reliability, HTTP makes use of TCP. Although the use of TCP for the transport connection is very common, it is not formally required by the standard. As and when ATM networks become commercially available the HTTP requests, replies can be carried in AAL5 just as well.

HTTP is a "*stateless*" protocol. Each transaction is treated independently. Therefore, a typical implementation will create a TCP new connection between client and server for each transaction and then terminate the connection as soon as the transaction is complete. Each interaction consists of one ASCII request, followed by one RFC 822 MIME-like response i.e., Messages are in a format similar to that used by Internet Mail and the Multipurpose Internet Mail Extensions (MIME). HTTP is constantly evolving, several versions are in use and others are under development.

The World Wide Web provides a single interface for accessing all these protocols. This creates a convenient and user-friendly environment. It is no longer necessary to be conversant in these protocols within separate, command-level environments. The Web gathers, together these protocols into a single system. Because of this feature, and because. of the Web's ability to work with multimedia and advanced programming languages, the World Wide Web is the fastest-growing component of the Internet.

5.3.2 Understanding HyperText Transport Protocol (HTTP)

HTTP is a request/response protocol. A web client establishes a connection with a Web server and sends a resource request. The request contains a request method, protocol version, followed by a MIME-like message. The message contains request modifiers, client information, and possible body content.

The Web server responds with a status line, including the message's protocol version and a success or error code. It is followed by a MIME-link message containing server information, entity meta-information, and possible body content. Figure 5.2 shows where the HTTP layer fits into Web client and servers.

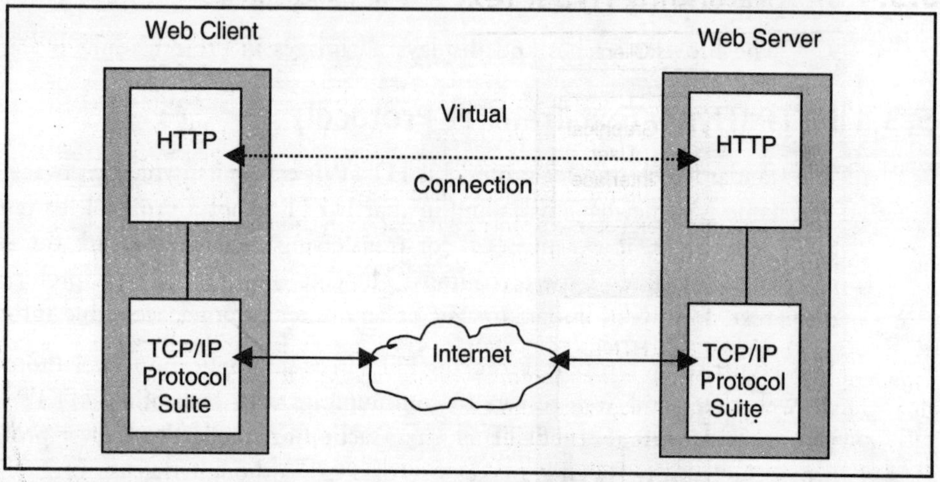

Figure 5.2 ♦ The Web client communicates with the Web server using an HTTP virtual circuit

Details of HTTP can be found in the following Request for comments (RFC):

- HTTP 1.0 specifications are described in RFC 1945:
  http://www.cis.ohio-state.edu/htbin/rfc/rfc1945.html
- MIME specifications are described in RFC 1521:
  http://www.cis.ohio-state.edu/htbin/rfc/rfc1521.html

5.3.3 Hypertext: The Motion of the Web

The operation of the Web relies primarily on hypertext as its means of information retrieval. HyperText is a document containing words that connect to other documents. These words are called links and are selectable by the user. A single hypertext document can contain links to many documents. In the context of the Web, words or graphics may serve as links to other documents, images, video, and sound. Links may or may not follow a logical path, as each connection is programmed by the creator of the source document. Overall, the WWW contains a complex virtual web of connections among a vast number of documents, graphics, videos and sounds.

Producing hypertext for the Web is accomplished by creating documents with a language called Hyper Text Markup Language, or HTML. With HTML, tags are placed within the text to accomplish document formatting, visual features such as font size, italics and bold, and the creation of hypertext links. Graphics may also be incorporated into an HTML document. HTML is an evolving language, with new tags being added as each upgrade of the language is developed and released. The World Wide Web Consortium, led by Tim Berners-Lee, co-ordinates the efforts of standardising HTML.

5.3.4 Understanding HyperText Markup Language (HTML)

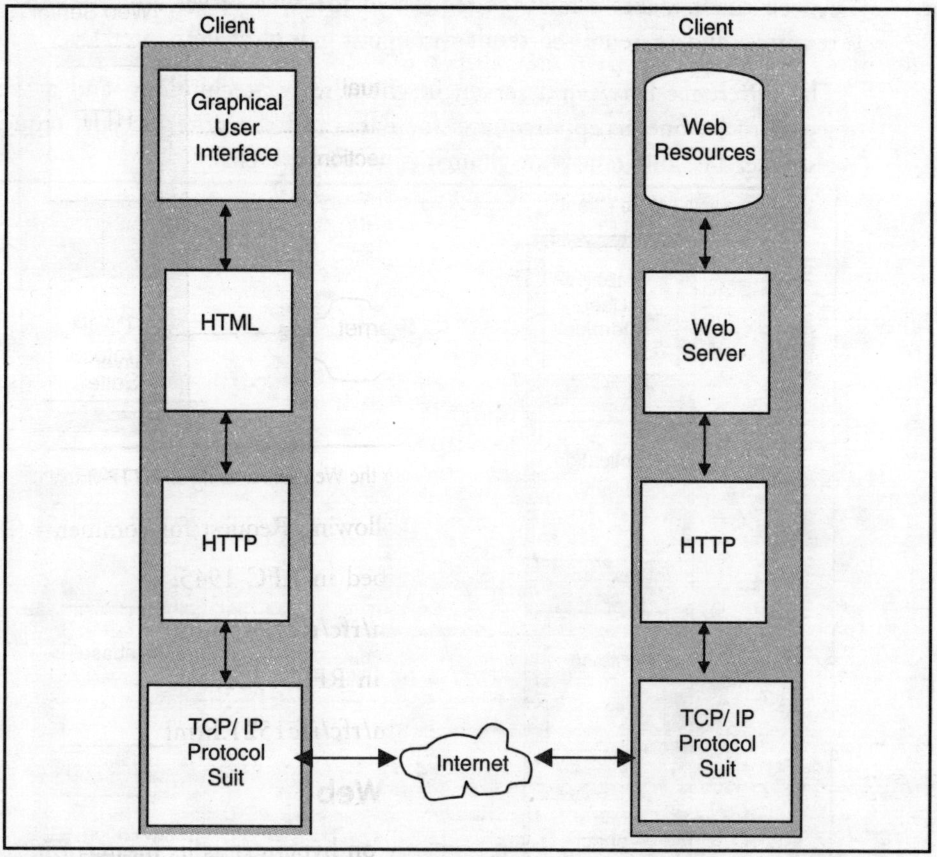

Figure 5.3 ♦ HTML is transported between the web client and web server over the HTTP virtual connection

The HyperText Markup Language is a document-layout, hyperlink specification, and markup language. Web clients use it to generate resource requests for Web servers, and to process output returned by the Web server for presentation. A markup language described what text means and what it is supposed to look like. Figure 5.3 shows where the HTML layer fits into Web clients.

A fundamental property of HTML is that the text it describes can be rendered on most devices. A single HTML Web page on a Web server can be displayed on a PC, Mac, UNIX, and so on. HTML specifications are available online at: http://www.w3c.org/.

5.4 WEB CLIENT/SERVER

A web is similar to the server in client/server technology. The server, in client/server technology, usually connects to a database. The client, in client/server technology, makes a data request to the server, processes the returned data, and presents the result through a graphical user interface.

A web client makes a resource request to the Web server, processes the returned resource, and presents the result through a graphical user interface.

The difference between a server, in client/server technology, and a Web server seems to be one accepts requests for data, and the other accepts requests for a resource. The differences are dramatic, as we look closer.

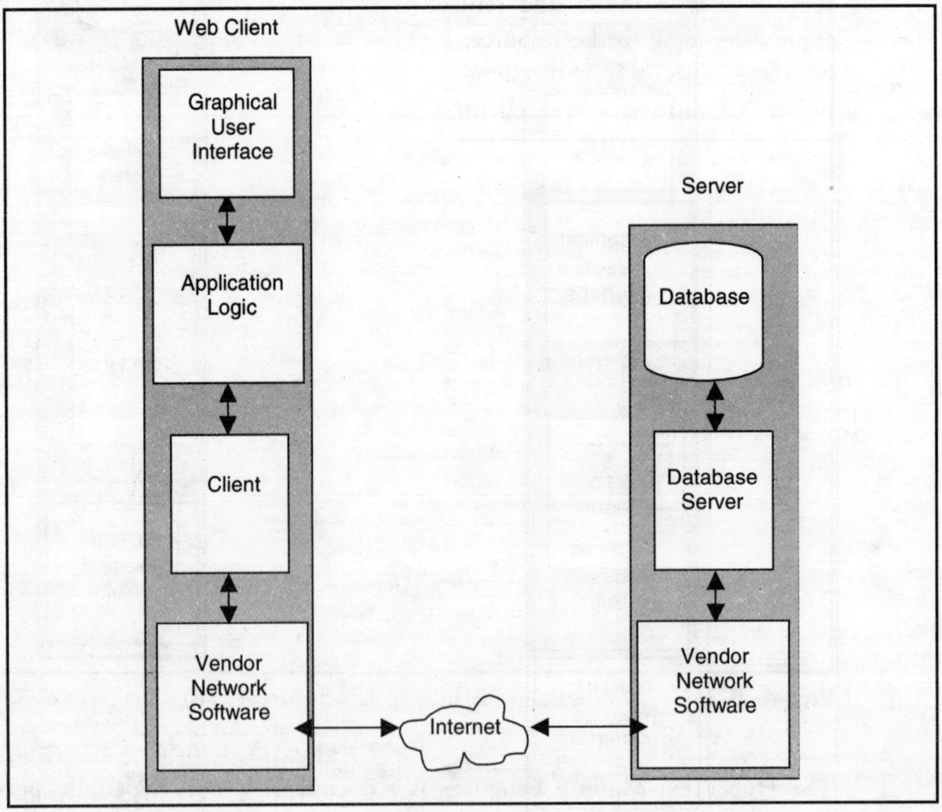

Figure 5.4 ♦ Client/Server concept: A "Fat Client"

The server, in client/server technology, is typically a specialized database server. The Microsoft SQL server product is a good example. A database server receives requests for data from a client through vendor proprietary network software. It locates the data and returns it. The client applies application logic to the data, and presents the result through a graphical user interface. This is a "fat client" because the application logic is in the client. Figure 5.4 illustrates client/server components.

Not just any client in client/server technology can request data from the database server. All clients must run the correct vendor proprietary network software. Likewise, a database server can only locate the return data form the vendor proprietary database, without using a database gateway to another proprietary database.

The network connection between the client and the database server remains until one or the other closes it, or until the network fails. The database server retains state information about the client for the entire lifetime for the connection. This saves the database server time in completing requests for data.

Web servers receive requests for a resource from Web client through the standard TCP/IP protocol Suite. The resource can be a file, or data returned by another process. The Web server locates the file and returns it, or executes another process, supplies it with input, and returns the output. The Web client does not apply application logic to the resource. It presents the resource through a graphical user interface. This is a "thin client" because it does not contain application logic. Figure 5.5 illustrates Web client/server components.

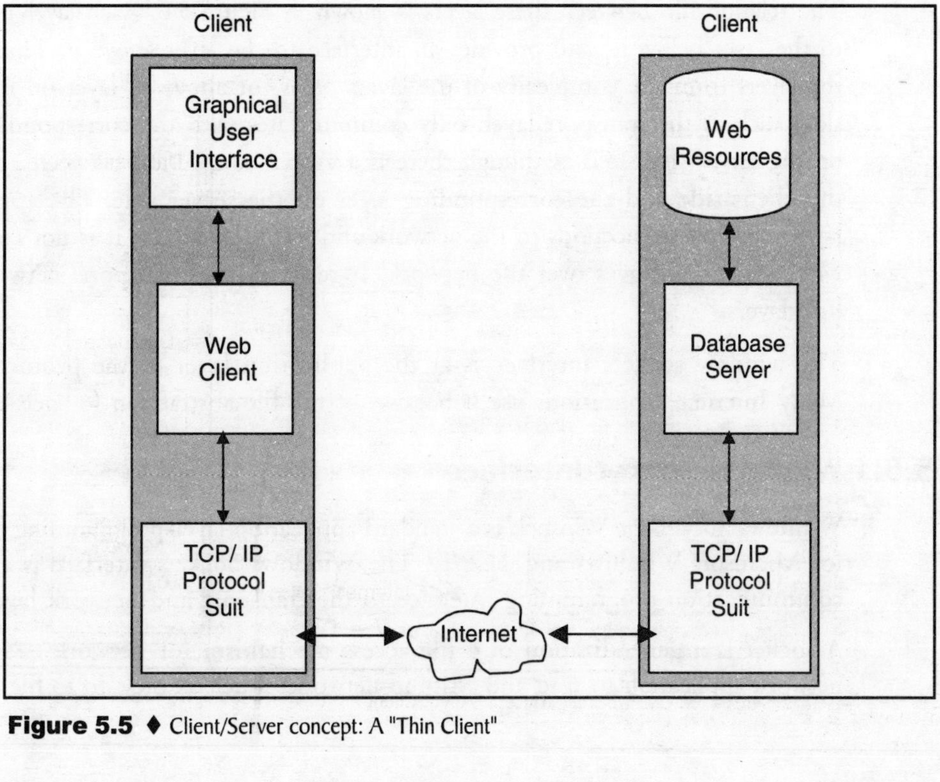

Figure 5.5 ♦ Client/Server concept: A "Thin Client"

Any web client can request a resource from any Web server, and any Web server can request a resource from any other web server. This is possible, because they use the standard TCP/IP Protocol Suite.

The network connection between the Web client and Web server remains only until the Web server has returned the resource. The Web server does not retain any state information about the Web client.

5.5 NETWORK COMPONENTS

Any Web client can request a resource from any Web server, because they use the standard TCP/IP Protocol Suite.

The TCP/IP Protocol Suite has four layers:

- *Link Layer:* The link layer interfaces the operation system to the network interface card.
- *Network Layer:* The network layer manages the movement of packets around the network.
- *Transport Layer:* The transport layer manages the flow of data between the client application and the application layer.
- *Application Layer:* The application layer manages the connections to the network and transport layers.

The relationship between these layers is shown in Figure 5.6. Each layer interfaces to the layer below it, and provides an interface to the layer above it. This isolates the layers from the complexity of the layers below or above. A layer on the client side, such as the transport layer, only communicates with the corresponding layer on the server side. It is as though there is a virtual connection between a layer on the client side and the corresponding layer on the server side. The application layer manages connections to the network and transport layers. It is not concerned with how data moves over the network. It relies on the transport, network, and link layers.

The window sockets interface is at the application layer of the protocol suite. Many Internet applications use it because of the file abstraction for networks.

5.5.1 Windows Socket Interface

Windows Sockets or Winsock is a standard application layer-programming interface for Microsoft Windows and TCP/IP. The Windows Sockets interface is a generic communication-programming interface to the transport and network layers.

A socket is a generalization of a file access mechanism for networks. It enables network application to read and write to networks much as they do to file systems.

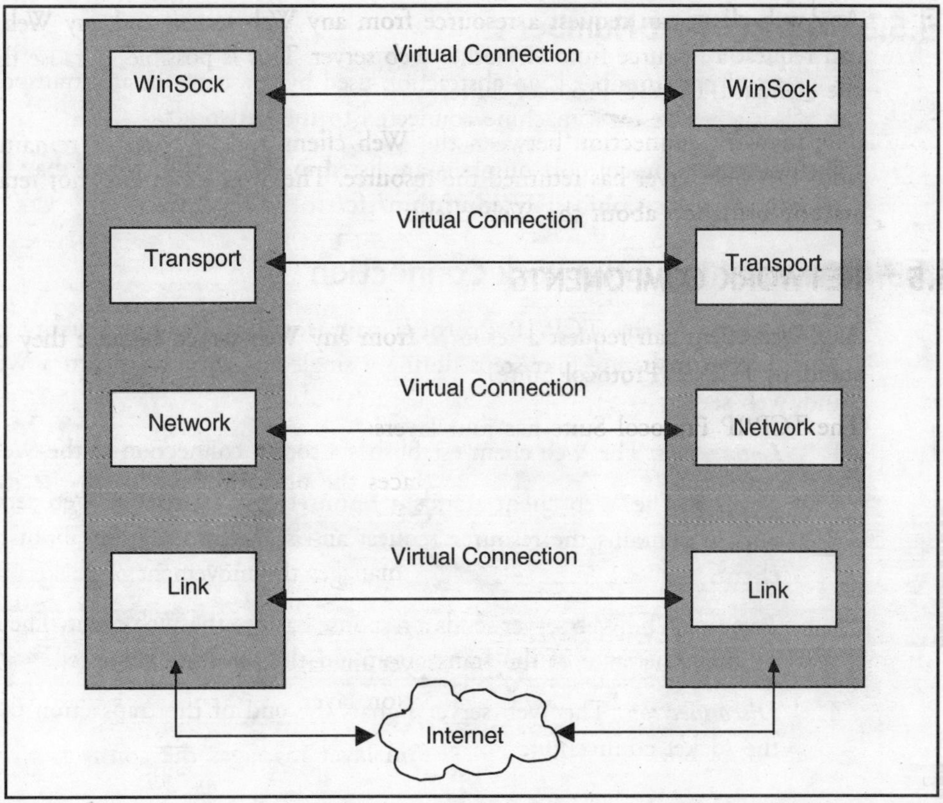

Figure 5.6 ♦ The relationship between the TCP/IP protocol Suite layers

The layers 1 to 4 have been discussed in earlier. But application layer needs some special mention. The network application program makes an operating system request to create a socket. The operating system creates one return a socket descriptor.

This is similar to how an application would make a file system request. The operating system returns a file description instead of a socket descriptor. An application uses the file descriptor to access a file.

A network application must take an additional step before it can access the network. The operating system creates a socket in an unconnected state. The network application must make a request to the Windows NT Server operating system to connect the socket to a network endpoint. The network application can then read and write to the network much like a file system.

Information about Windows Sockets can be found at http://www.stardust.com

5.5.2 Network Endpoint

A network endpoint is an Internet address and a protocol port number. A network client application uses it to uniquely identify a service on a machine connected to the network.

5.5.3 Protocol Port Number

A protocol port number is an abstraction used by the network and transport layers to select a service on a machine connected to the network.

The assigned protocol port numbers are listed in RFC 1700, which may be found at: http://www.cis.ohio-state.edu/htbin/rfc/rfc1700.html.

5.5.4 Establishing a Network Connection

The essence of the TCP/IP Protocol suit is establishing and using network connections. There are four steps during a single translation between a Web client and Web server:

1. *Connection:* The Web client establishes a socket connection to the Web server.
2. *Request:* The Web client stands a resource request to the Web server. The request contains the resource request and some information about the Web client.
3. *Response:* The Web server sends a response back to the Web client. The response contains the state of the transaction and the resource requested.
4. *Disconnection:* The Web server signals the end of the transaction by closing the socket connection.

Connection

A Web browser establishes a network connection to a Web server when the user clicks on a Uniform Resource Locator (URL) such as http://www.informax.com/info.html

The Internet works with numeric addresses. It does not understand symbolic computer names such as www.bpkm.org.in, by calling the gethostbyname (...) socket function. This function takes the symbolic computer name as an argument and returns its numeric IP network address.

The gethostbyname (...) function works with the name resolver on the Web client computer. If the name resolver cannot resolve the name, it calls the Internet Domain Name System (DNS).

Internet DNS is a collection of distributed databases linked together by the Internet Symbolic names are grouped into zones of authority. One or more hosts in a zone of authority have the task for maintaining a database of symbolic names and numeric IP network addresses.

Internet DNS resolves the bpkm.org.in portion of the symbolic computer name. It then contains the bpkm.org.in computer using the IP network address. Internet DNS asks the bpkm.org.in computer to resolve the www portion of the symbolic name, and to return the IP network address of www.bpkm.org.in to the Web client computer.

Name resolution is complex and time-consuming. The Web client resolver and DNS make use of cache storage to expedite name resolution requests.

The Web client computer now has the IP network address of the www.bpkm.org.in Web Server computer. It opens a socket connection with the Web Server by calling the connect (...) socket function. This function sends a SYN packet to the Web Server. The Web Server sends a SYN packet back as a reply. The Web client then sends an ACK packet back to the Web Server. A network connection is now established.

Request

A Web resource request is made of components. The first resource is a GET, PUT, or POST method. A URL is the second component. A set of headers follows. They specify such things as kinds of documents the Web client is willing to accept, and authentication information. The PUT method uses an optional data field.

Response

The Web server parses the Web resource request and invokes the appropriate method. The Web server sends a response back to the Web client. Status codes are sent first, indicating whether the request succeeded or failed.

The Web server then sends a set of object headers, meta-information about the data file, and then the data file.

Disconnection

The Web server signals the end of the transaction by closing the socket connection.

5.5.5 Keep-Alive

A Web client resource request may contain text and graphical images. The resource request may be text in a single file. The text makes references to graphical images by file name. Each graphical image is a separate file.

A Web browser makes a connection to a Web server for each file that is a part of the resource. It makes a connection to the Web server and requests a single graphical image file. The Web server disconnects after sending it. This process repeats for each graphical file.

A resource text file with several graphical image references requires a connection for the text document and one for each graphical image. This overhead increases the latency time from when the user clicks on the URL, to when the resource document is displayed.

The Web client makes a Keep-Alive request in the request header sent to the Web Server. The Web Server keeps the connection alive and informs the Web client in the header it returns. This continues until the Web client does not request a

Keep-Alive, or the Web server has not received a Web client request during a time-out period.

A decrease upwards of 30 percent in latency time using Keep-Alive, is not unusual for resource documents with several graphical images.

5.6 RETRIEVING DOCUMENTS ON THE WEB: THE URL

URL stands for Uniform Resource Locator. The URL specifies the Internet address of a file stored on a host computer connected to the Internet. Every file on the Internet, no matter what its access protocol, has a unique URL. Web software programs use the URL to retrieve the file from the host computer and the directory in which it resides. This file is then displayed on the user's computer monitor.

URLs are translated into numeric addresses using the Internet Domain Name System (DNS). The numeric address is actually the "real" URL. Since numeric strings are difficult for humans to use, alphanumeric addresses are employed by end users. Once the translation is made, the Web server can send the requested page to the user's Web browser.

5.6.1 Anatomy of a URL

A URL contains the following information:

- *Protocol:* Specifies the Internet protocol to access a resource. The abstract encompasses FTP, Gopher, and HTTP Internet Protocols.
- *Network Endpoint:* Internet Addresses of Internet Information Server and Protocol Port Number.
- *Resource Location:* Path information to locate a resource on Internet Information Server URL syntax is {service}: ://{host} [: port]/[path /... /] [file name]

Required parameters are surrounded by { }. Optional parameters are surrounded by [ ]. Other characters are mandatory separators.

Note

Service is a required field. Web server support FTP, Gopher and HTTP services.

Host is a required field. This field is the host name or IP address of the Internet Information Server.

Port is an optional field. This field is an abstraction used by the network and transport layers to select a service on the server. This field is not frequently used. It may be specified if the service is available on a non-standard protocol port number.

Path is an optional field. It specifies URL resource location. A path without a file name following must always end with a /character.

The combination of host and port is a network endpoint.

An example of a URL is: http://www.bpkm.org.in:8080/welcome.htm.

The http: component is the service. The //www.bpkm.org.in: 8080 component is the network endpoint. The /welcome.htm component is the resource location. Uniform Resource Locators are described in RFC 1738 and RFC 1808 which may be found at.

http://www.cis.ohio-state.edu/htbin/rfc/rfc1738.html

http://www.cis.ohio-state.edu/htbin/rfc/rfc1808.html

For example, this is a URL on the home page of the U.S. Census Bureau http://www.census.gov/pubinfo/additional/news.html. This URL is typical of addresses hosted in domains in the United States.

Structure of this URL:

- ***Protocol:*** http
- ***Host computer name:*** www
- ***Second-level domain name:*** census
- ***Top-level domain name:*** gov
- ***Directory name:*** pubinfo
- ***Directory name:*** additional
- ***File name:*** news.html

5.7 WORLD WIDE WEB (WWW) SERVICE

Web browsers processing HTML documents use Internet HTTP protocol to transact with World Wide Web (WWW) Service. Web Server WWW Service knows how to respond to an HTML request by analyzing URL fields.

5.7.1 Static HTML Page

Static pages are those on your site that send exactly the same response to every request. An obvious example of a static page is an old style HTML document; the only way to change a HTML page is to upload a new or updated version in its place. Every time a static file is downloaded, the file contents that are sent to the browser are the same for everyone that accesses that file. Flash and Shockwave presentations are also classed as static content; despite the fact that user interaction can lead to different ways of presenting the same data, everyone will download the same file from the server. WWW Service looks for a file name in the path field. An example is:

http://www.bpkm.org.in/welcome.htm

Most of these advantages and disadvantages apply to normal HTML pages in particular.

Advantages

- Quick and easy to put together, even by someone who doesn't have much experience.
- Ideal for demonstrating how a site will look.
- Cache friendly, one copy can be shown to many people.

Disadvantages

- Difficult to maintain when a site gets large.
- Difficult to keep consistent and up to date.
- Offers little visitor personalization (all would have to be client side).

5.7.2 Understanding Dynamic Web Pages

The popularity of the static, billboard style, Web page is declining. Dynamic pages can customize the response on the server to offer personalization based on cookies and information, it can get from the visitor. Web server content developers are creating dynamic Web pages with data from the databases and other data sources, such as real-time stock market data feeds. Web technology is being used to create new client/server applications because of the ability to dynamically create Web pages on the fly.

Many Web servers do not have database or other data access mechanisms built-in. They rely on the Common Gateway Interface (CGI). Dynamic web pages are typically written in various scripting languages or technologies such as ASP, PHP, Perl or JSP.

Advantages

- Offers highly personalized and customized visitor options.
- Database access improves the personalized experience (as opposed to using just client side cookies).
- Scripts can read in data sources and display it differently depending on how it is run.
- Can create the illusion of being updated regularly using time and date sensitive routines (or even randomizers) to display pre-written text.

Disadvantages

- Personalized pages are not very cache friendly.

- Requires a basic minimum knowledge of the language being used.
- Scripts need more consideration, when uploading and installing, particularly to *nix servers.

5.7.3 Understanding CGI

The Common Gateway Interface (CGI) is a standard way of interfacing external applications with Web servers. A CGI external application executes in real-time and dynamically produces output information. It processes HTTP requests for Web clients and returns an HTML document. CGI external applications usually access information not in HTML form. They act as a gateway between the web client and the information. Figure 5.7 illustrates a Common Gateway Interface.

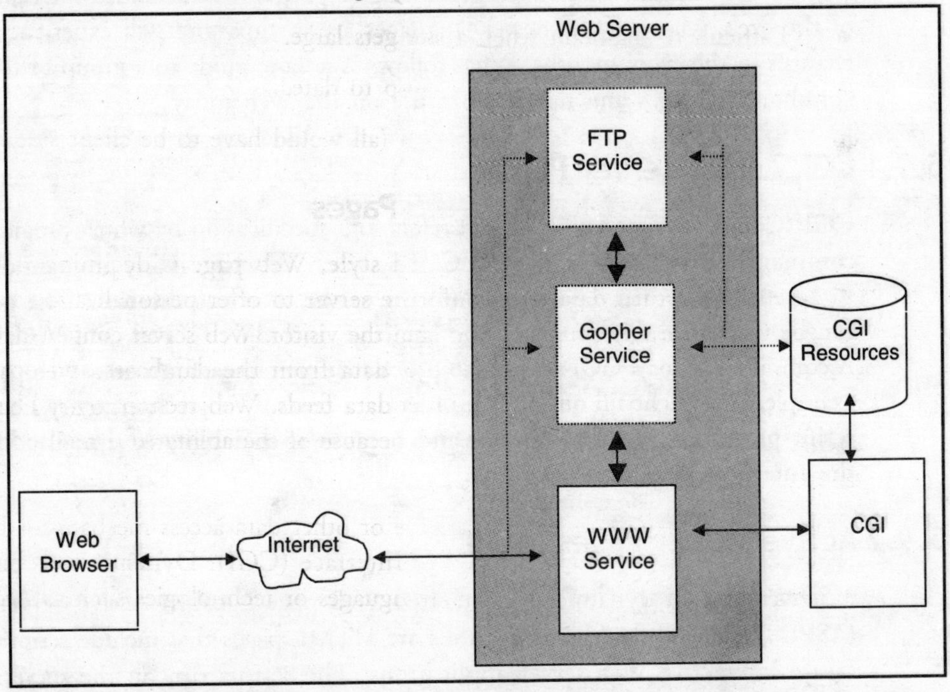

Figure 5.7 ♦ The Web server WWW Service Connects the Web browser to a CGI process over the Internet.

5.8 HOME PAGES ON THE WEB

The World Wide Web consists of files, called pages or home pages, containing links to resources throughout the Internet. Web pages can be created by user activity. For example, if you visit an Internet search engine and enter keywords on the topic of your choice, a page will be created containing the results of your search.

Access to Web pages may be accomplished by:

1. Entering an Internet address and retrieving a page directly.
2. Browsing through pages and selecting links to move from one page to another.
3. Searching through subject directories linked to organized collections of Web pages.
4. Entering a search statement at a search engine to retrieve pages on the topic of your choice.

5.9 PROGRAMMING LANGUAGES AND FUNCTIONS

The uses of existing and new programming languages have extended the capabilities of the Web. Many of the newer languages are in flux, and will experience major changes in the every months. What follows is a basic guide to a group of the more common languages and functions in use on the Web today.

5.9.1 CGI, Active Server Pages

CGI (Common Gateway Interface) refers to a specification by which programs can communicate with a Web server. A CGI program, or script, is any program designed to accept and return data that conforms to the CGI specification. The program can be written in any programming language, including C, Perl, and Visual Basic. A common use for a CGI script is to process an interactive form on a Web page. For example, you might fill out a form ordering a book through Interlibrary Loan. The script processes your information and sends it to a designated e-mail address in the Interlibrary Loan department.

5.9.2 Active Server Pages (ASP)

A newer type of dynamically generated Web page is called Active Server Pages (ASP). Developed by Microsoft, ASPs are HTML pages that include scripting and create interactive Web server applications. The scripts run on the server rather than on the Web browser to generate the HTML pages sent to browsers. Visual Basic and JScript (a subset of JavaScript) are often used for the scripting. ASPs work with only Microsoft's Web servers.

5.9.3 Java/Java Applets

Java is probably the most famous of the new programming languages of the Web. Java is an object-oriented programming language similar to C++. Developed by Sun Microsystems, the aim of Java is to create programs that will be platform independent. A perfect Java program should work equally well on a PC, Macintosh, Unix, and so on, without any additional programming. This goal has yet to be realised. Java can be used to write applications for both Web and non-Web use.

Web-based Java applications are usually in the form of Java applets. These are small Java programs called from an HTML page that can be downloaded from a Web server and run on a Java-compatible Web browser. A few examples include live newsfeeds, moving images with sound, calculators, charts and spreadsheets, and interactive visual displays. Java applets can tend to load slowly, but programming improvements should lead to a shortened loading time.

5.9.4 JavaScript/Jscript

JavaScript is a programming language created by Netscape Communications. Small programs written in this language are embedded within an HTML page, or called externally from the page, to enhance the page's the functionality. Examples of JavaScript include moving tickers, drop-down menus, real-time calendars and clocks, and mouse-over interactions. JScript is a similar language developed by Microsoft and works with the company's Internet Explorer browser.

5.9.5 VRML (Virtual Reality Modelling Language)

VRML (Virtual Reality Modelling Language) allows for the creation of three-dimensional worlds. These may be linked from Web pages and displayed with a VRML viewer. Netscape Communicator comes with the Cosmo viewer for experiencing these three-dimensional worlds. One of the most interesting aspects of VRML is the option to "enter" the world and control your movements within the world.

5.9.6 XML (eXtensible Markup Language)

XML (eXtensible Markup Language) is a Web page creation language that enables designers to create their own customised tags to provide functionality not available with HTML. XML is in the process of being reviewed by the World Wide Web Consortium. At present, this language is little used as Web browsers are only beginning to support it. Some predict that XML may even replace HTML someday.

5.9.7 Real-Time Communication

Text, audio and video communication can occur in real time on the Web. This capability allows people to conference and collaborates in real time. In general, the faster the Internet connection, the more successful is the experience.

At its simplest, chat programs allow multiple users to type to each other in real time. Internet Relay Chat and America Online's Instant Messenger are prime examples of this type of program. The development of a messenging protocols is underway. Such a protocol would allow for the expansion of this capability throughout the Internet.

More enhanced real-time communication offers an audio and/or video component. CU-See Me is one of the most popular software programs of this type. Even more elaborate are programs that allow for true real-time collaboration. Microsoft's NetMeeting and Netscape's Conference (available with Communicator) are good examples of this.

5.10 FEATURED COLLABORATION TOOLS

Audio: conduct a "telephone" conversation on the Web

Video: view your audience

File transfer: send files back and forth among participants

Chat: type in real time

White-board: draw; mark up, and save images on a shared window or board

Document/application sharing: view and use a program on another's desktop machine

Collaborative Web browsing: visit Web pages together

Note: Currently no standard exists that will work among all conferencing programs.

EXERCISE

Objective Type Questions

1. The World Wide Web is
   (A) a network of computer networks
   (B) a domain
   (C) a web of linked documents
   (D) primarily for military use
2. Identify the odd one out from the following list
   (A) JavaScript (B) VBScript
   (C) Java (D) Perl
3. What do you need to put your web pages on the WWW?
   (A) a connection to the internet
   (B) a Web Browser
   (C) a Web Server
   (D) All of the above
4. Script can be inserted in
   (A) head section only
   (B) body section only
   (C) both head and body sections
   (D) only in head and title sections
5. Which one of the following software is used to create and edit JavaScript programs?
   (A) Browsers (B) Text editors
   (C) Compilers (D) All of above
6. Who is making the Web standards?
   (A) World Wide Web Consortium
   (B) Netscape
   (C) Microsoft
   (D) Google
7. Java Script is______ side scripting language.
   (A) Server (B) Client
   (C) Server & Client (D) None of these

8. For handling user interaction______ side scripting is useful.
(A) Server (B) Client
(C) Server & Client (D) None of these

9. ______Scripting is used for data entry validation.
(A) Client side (B) Server side
(C) Client side & Server side (D) None of these

10. Java script is scripting language introduce by
(A) IE (B) Microsoft
(C) Netscape (D) SunJava

11. One of the following web sites does not contain a search engine
(A) www.lycos.com (B) www.yahoo.com
(C) www.excit.com (D) none of the above

12. The following is a synonym for the Internet
(A) cyberspace (B) World Wide Web
(C) Gopherspace (D) Intranet
(E) None of the above

13. Where does the title of a web page appear when it is browsed?
(A) in search engines (B) at top of page
(C) at top of browser window (D) none of the above

14. What is the most commonly used file name for the main page of a WWW site?
(A) default.html (B) index.html
(C) start.html (D) hom
(E) html

15. ______provides the middleware between www server & external databases & information sources.
(A) Perl (B) CGI
(C) Java Script (D) None of these

16. World Wide Web
(A) is another name for internet
(B) world wide connection for computers
(C) a collection of linked information residing on computers connected by the internet
(D) a collection of world wide information

17. Among services available on the World Wide Web are

(i) Encryption (ii) HTTP

(iii) HTML (iv) Firewalls

(A) i and ii (B) ii and iii

(C) iii and iv (D) i and iv

18. What is a Web site?

(A) A computer that stores Web pages

(B) A program that allows surfers to view Web pages

(C) A collection of Web pages that contain related information

(D) A program that runs that runs on a Web server to process forms

(E) None of the above

19. What are CGI scripts?

(A) Browser add-in programs

(B) Programs that extend the capabilities of a server

(C) Both of the above

(D) None of the above

20. What is SSL?

(A) The IP protocol to dynamically assign IP addresses

(B) It allows secure connection

(C) It is a derivative of the scripting language, PHP

(D) It is a Web authoring tool

21. A world wide web contains web pages

(A) residing in many computers

(B) created using HTML

(C) with links to other web pages

(D) residing in many computers linked together using HTML

22. A web page is located using a

(A) Universal Record Linking (B) Uniform Resource Locator

(C) Universal Record Locator (D) Uniformly Reachable Links

23. Which is true?

(A) A Web client and a Web server are both at the TCP/IP network layer

(B) A Web client and a Web server are both at the TCP/IP application layer

(C) A Web client is at the application layer and the server at the network layer

(D) A Web client is at the network layer and the server at the applicatior layer

(E) None of the above - they are both client-server programs

24. HTML and XML are markup languages

(A) Specially development for the web

(B) Are based on SGML

(C) Are versions of SGML

(D) Independent of SGML

25. XML stands for

(A) Extra Markup Language

(B) Excellent Markup Links

(C) Extended Markup Language

(D) Extended Marking Links

26. Which of the following browsers is not free?

(A) Netscape Navigator (B) Internet Explorer

(C) Opera (D) Lynx

27. Which of the following Web sites provides free e-mail service?

(A) www.eudoramail.com (B) www.hotmail.com

(C) www.netaddress.com (D) All of the above

(E) None of the above

28. Which among the following is a Web server application?

(A) Opera (B) Claris

(C) Pegasus (D) Sambar

29. What is a shareware?

(A) Software available for use and distribution free of charge

(B) Software available for trial period after which it must be registered for use

(C) Software which is used in a multi-user/network system

(D) Software which is shared across a network

30. Which of the following is related to Internet security?

(A) CERT (B) MIT

(C) DSL (D) W3C

31. What are emoticons?

(A) Combination of key board characters to express feelings in e-mail

(B) Emotional mail

(C) A multimedia mail attachment with pictures depicting extreme emotions

(D) None of the above

32. What is encryption?

(A) Scrambling of message for security

(B) Invisibly access Internet

(C) Access e-mail without downloading

(D) Messages posted to newsgroups

33. XML uses

(A) User define tags

(B) Pre-defined tags

(C) Both predefined and user-defined tags

(D) Extended tags used in HTML and makes them powerful

34. In order to interpret XML documents one should

(A) Use standardized tags

(B) Have a document type definition which defines the tags

(C) Define the tags separately

(D) Specify tag filename

35. Which of the following is true?

(A) Web server applications extend the functionality and capability of existing Web servers

(B) Web server applications receive HTTP request messages for the Web server and perform actions requested in those messages

(C) They formulate response and pass it back to the server

(D) All of the above

36. What do you call the documents found on the WWW?

(A) A link (B) A page

(C) A node (D) A spider

37. The following is not a reason for using a text based browser such as Lynx
(A) Pages load more quickly
(B) There is no possibility that objectionable images can be viewed
(C) Pages look better formatted with Lynx
(D) It is less taxing on the hardware resources

38. The following is not a field in IP datagram:
(A) Version (B) Header length
(C) Header checksum (D) Source and destination IP address.
(E) None of the above

39. Messages are carried between Internet hosts using ICMP, with a standard IP header. The following is not a typical such message:
(A) Destination unreachable (B) Redirection
(C) Echo request/echo reply (D) Source quench
(E) None of the above

40. The following is not a User authentication method:
(A) SecurID (B) CHAP
(C) PAP (D) None of the above

41. Which browser first popularized the use of plug-in software?
(A) Internet Explorer (B) Netscape Navigator
(C) NCSA Mosaic (D) Chimera

42. What is another term for Web publishing?
(A) Downloading (B) Uploading
(C) Unloading (D) Freeloading

43. What does FTP stand for?
(A) Faster Than Post (B) File Transfer Protocol
(C) Files To Publish (D) Format To Program

44. Which of the following is not an e-mail client?
(A) MS Outlook (B) Eudora Pro
(C) Pegasus (D) Postoffice

45. Which of the following is not a search tool for the Net?
(A) Veronica (B) Archie
(C) Excite (D) Findfast

46. Who created Mosaic, the first graphical Web browser?

(A) Bill Gates (B) Mark Andreesen

(C) Steve Jobs (D) Steve Ballamer

47. The following is not true about NNTP

(i) it stands for Network News Transfer Protocol

(ii) it is a stream-oriented client-server connection

(iii) it is a server-side software package

(iv) news transport is lower than UUCP networks

(A) (i) & (ii) (B) none

(C) (iii) & (iv) (D) (i), (ii) & (iii)

48. The advantages of XML over HTML are

(i) It allows processing of data stored in web-pages

(ii) It uses meaningful tags which aids in understanding the nature of a document

(iii) Is simpler than HTML

(iv) It separates presentation and structure of document

(A) (i),(ii) and (iii) (B) (i),(ii) and(iv)

(C) (ii),(iii) and (iv) (D) (i),(iii) and (iv)

49. A VoIP gateway is

(A) A computer

(B) A network

(C) Neither a computer nor a network

(D) Both a computer and a network

50. Which Internet transfer protocol means you're working through a secure web connection?

(A) https (B) ftp

(C) http (D) stp

51. Which is not a valid web page extension?

(A) htm (B) htl

(C) asp (D) php

52. Which of the following technologies doesn't help in creating dynamic Web pages?

(A) ASP' (B) PHP

(C) Perl (D) Coldfusion

(E) None of the above

53. Which of the following is not a client end scripting language?

(A) HTML (B) XML

(C) XHTML (D) None of the above

54. Which of the following is a special protocol for e-mail?

(A) SMTP (B) POP

(C) IMAP (D) MIME

(E) All

55. Which of the following browsers is different from others in most respects?

(A) Netscape Communicator (B) Internet Explorer

(C) Opera (D) Lynx

56. What type of code is this sample?

Sample: <!--update this page in January-->

(A) Javascript (B) a comment

(C) VBScript (D) a hyperlink

57. Which of the following is not included in a home access point?

(A) A WiFi radio (B) A switch

(C) A Web client (D) A Web server

58. Web pages are uniquely defined using

(A) IP addresses (B) URL

(C) Domain (D) Filename

Review & Discussion Questions

1. What are the main requirements for web hosting?
2. Explain the difference between web server and web client.
3. What protocol is used to communicate between web server and web client?
4. Where do we define the title of the web page? Write a statement to display the title of a web page as "Home Page".
5. What standard file name is generally given to the home page?
6. What is a Local Area Network (LAN)? What are its advantages?
7. Briefly explain a Wide Area Network (WAN).
8. Define the World Wide Web? What are the various features of World Wide Web?
9. What is the difference between Internet and World Wide Web? Explain?
10. What is a Proxy Server? What are the advantages of a Proxy Server?
11. What are the difference between static webpage and dynamic webpage?
12. What are the Web Browsers and Web Serves? How they communicate with each other's? What is World Wide Web (WWW)?
13. What are the Languages used to develop web page?
14. What are the Most commonly use name of default page of website?
15. Which application of Java used with web page?
16. What is CGI?
17. What is Applet?
18. What is Java Script?
19. What is meant by web page and web site?
20. What is computer network and explain its types?
21. What is Web design? List the different types of web pages.
22. What is meant by Script? Write the difference between server side script and client side script?
23. List any two situations when to use server side script and to use client side script.
24. What is mean by entrance page and exit page?
25. Differentiate LAN with MAN.
26. Differentiate LAN and WAN.

27. Describe home page and slash page.
28. What is Web server? Explain the features of WEB Server.
29. Identify the primary deference between relative and absolute Uniform Resource Identifiers (URIs).
30. Describe situations in which it is preferable to use relative URIs rather than absolute URIs for referencing resources.
31. What is good web design?
32. How we design a good web site? List the criterion to define a better web.
33. Which tag is used to embed Java Applet on web page?
34. What is Web browser? Explain Internet Explorer and Netscape Navigator.

CHAPTER 6

HTML Basics

CHAPTER OBJECTIVES

In this chapter, you will take a brief look what HTML is and get a glimpse of the use of the elements. You will able to learn how to use four common tags that are used every HTML document. We are primarily focusing the tag <HEAD> contains general information or meta-information, about the document <TITLE>, <BASE>, <ISINDEX >, <NEXTID>, <LINK>, <META>, <SCRIPT> and <STYLE>.

CHAPTER OUTLINES

6.1 INTRODUCTION

Document tags define the overall structure of an HTML document. An HTML document contains two distinct parts, the head and the body. The head contains information about the document that is not displayed on the screen. The body then contains everything else that is displayed as part of the web page. There are four tags every HTML document should have. These tags define the type of document it is, and the major sections. These tags are <HTML>, <HEAD>, <TITLE>, and <BODY ...>. Under some circumstances you may also wish to use the <!DOCTYPE ...> declaration.

The basic structure then of any HTML page is:

```
<!DOCTYPE HTML PUBLIC "-//W3C//DTD HTML 3.2//EN">
  <html>
  <head>
  <!-- header info used to contain extra information about
       this document, not displayed on the page -->
  </head>
  <body>
  <!-- all the HTML for display -->
       :   :
       :   :
       :   :
  </body>
  </html>
```

Within <HTML> there are two major sections: <HEAD>, and <BODY ...>.

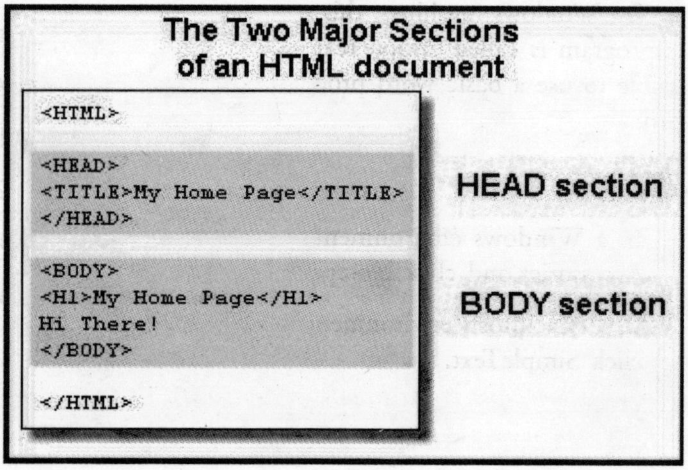

Any Web page you create will contain the following tags at the start of the page:

Tag		Description
<!DOCTYPE ...>	:	Tells the Web browser what version of HTML you are writing in. More specifically, <!DOCTYPE ...> declares that this document conforms to a specific version of HTML, and specifies what version that is. The <!DOCTYPE ...> declaration (technically it's not a "tag") should be the very first thing in your document, if you choose to use it at all.
<HTML>	:	Tells the Web browser that this is the beginning of an HTML document.
<HEAD>	:	Tells that Web browser that this is the header for the page (you'll learn later what goes between "HEAD" tags).
<TITLE>	:	Tells the Web browser that this is the title of the page
<BODY>	:	Tells the Web browser that this is the beginning of the Web page content -- everything you want to say and see on your page will follow this tag.

Creating a Simple Page

There are many ways to create Web pages. Hundreds of companies have created tools to help with the process in one way or another. Some common software are:

For MS Windows	For MacOS X	For Linux
EditPadLite	Taco HTML Edit	Bluefish
CoffeeCup HTML Editor	Arachnophilia	Nvu - Web Editor
1st Page 2000 (Front Page)	HTML Face	Quanta Plus
HTML Kit	Web Minimalist	Screem
Arachnophilia	Plain Old HTML Editor	

Our goal here, however, is to understand how Web pages really work, rather than have a tool hide the process from us. Therefore, we suggest when you are at beginning HTML stage that you use only the most software for Writing HTML, the most basic text editor you can find on your computer (for Windows, use Notepad; for Mac OSX use TextEdit or Plain Old HTML Editor).

On your machine, you have a program, or application, that can create simple text files. On Windows machines, this application is called Notepad. On a Macintosh, this program is called SimpleText. If you cannot find these programs, it is also possible to use a basic word processing program, like WordPerfect or Microsoft Word.

Note

- In a Windows environment, click the Start button, click Programs, click Accessories and click Notepad.
- In a Macintosh environment, click Macintosh HD, click Applications and click SimpleText.

Once you have the proper program open on your screen, type the following HTML text into the window:

```
<html>
<head>
<title>My First Web Page</title>
</head>
<body>
Hello there. This is my first Web Page!
</body>
</html>
```

Whether you put the tags and text side-by-side, row-by-row or indented will not make a difference in how the text is displayed in a browser window. Whether you use uppercase or lowercase letters within your tags also, does not make a difference.

Now you need to save this file somewhere so that you can find it in a moment. Save it to the desktop, or, better yet, to a directory that you set up to hold all of the pages you are going to create. Save it to the filename firstWeb.html or firstWeb.htm.

Next, open the page in your Web browser (e.g., Microsoft Internet Explorer or Netscape Navigator). All Web browsers have a way to open a file stored on the local machine. In Internet Explorer and Netscape, select Open File from the File menu at the top of the window. Open the file first.html. When you open it in your browser, it will look something like this:

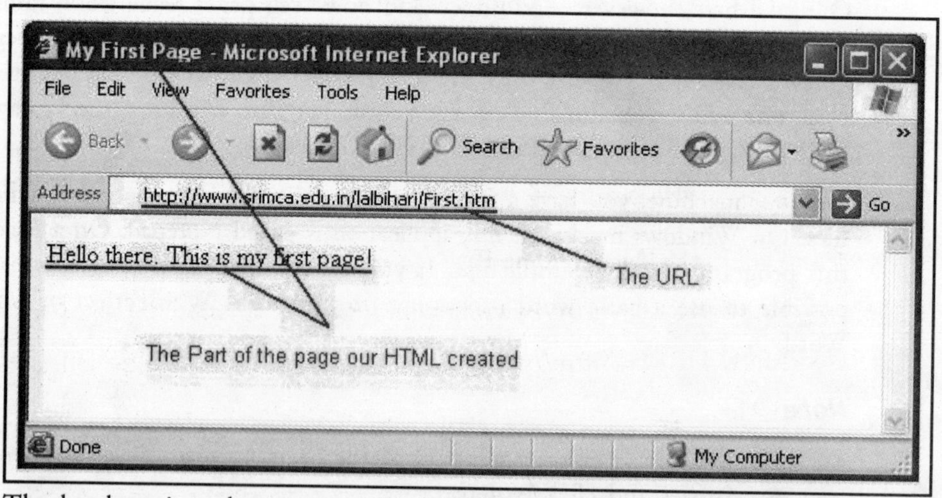

The head section element contains header information (cover page) about the document. Just as the cover page of a book contains information about the book (such as its title, keywords, description, and style sheet). <HEAD> is required in all documents, but its start and end tags are always optional. The <HEAD> element is followed by the <BODY> in HTML 4.0 Strict and Transitional documents. In

HTML 4.0 Frameset documents, the <HEAD> is followed by a <FRAMESET> element.

The contents of the <HEAD> are not displayed as part of the document text, the displayed material is found within the <BODY>. Consequently, only certain mark-up elements can be placed within the <HEAD>. These are:

Tag		Description
<TITLE>	:	The title of the document. This element is mandatory.
<BASE>	:	A record of the original URL of the document.
<ISINDEX>	:	Usually placed in the <HEAD> element by the server or a server script/program to indicate that a document is searchable.
<NEXTID>	:	A parameter used by automated HTML editors to create unique identifiers for the documents. NOTE: This attribute was dropped in HTML 4.0, so you should avoid it in new documents.
<LINK> (Repeatable)	:	Defines the relationship(s) between this document and another or others. A document can have several <LINK> elements.
<META> (Repeatable)	:	A container for document meta-information.
<STYLE> (Repeatable)	:	Stylesheet instructions specify how the document should be formatted for display. Very few browsers currently support stylesheets.
<SCRIPT> (Repeatable)	:	Script program code -- for enclosing, within a document, scripting program code that should be run with -- and that can interact with -- the document. Example lanuages are JavaScript and VBScript.

6.2 <HEAD> ELEMENT

The <HEAD> contains general information, or meta-information, about the document. It is the first thing in any document, lying above the <BODY> and just after the <HTML> tag starting the document.

Example

```
<HTML>
  <HEAD>
    <TITLE> SRIMCA Home Page </TITLE>
    <BASE HREF="http://www.bpkm.org.in/tutorial/headexample.html">
    <LINK HREF="http://www.bpkm.org.in/index.html" REL="index">
  </HEAD>
  <BODY>
    ..... text of the document
  </BODY>
</HTML>
```

6.2.1 <Title> Element

The <TITLE> element is not part of the body text; it is displayed in the window title. The <TITLE> element is required and should contain only text and no markup. Each document can have only one title, which should identify the document content in a general way. Often the title is used to label the window displaying the text, or is used to label a place in a browser's history or bookmark list. Therefore, your title should be descriptive but short, less than 64 characters.

Example

```
<HTML>
<HEAD><TITLE> S Sc...</TITLE> or
<TITLE>Page 5 of report &#174; or <H1>BIG TEXT?</H1></TITLE>
</HEAD> - WRONG
```

```
<HTML>
<HEAD><TITLE>Include only descriptive text here, less than 64 characters</
TITLE>
</HEAD> - RIGHT
```

6.2.2 <BASE> Element

The <BASE> element defines an absolute URL that resolves relative URLs within the document. This is useful if the document is moved away from its original location and the related documents, in which case partial URLs (things like HREF="image.gif"), which are calculated relative to the new URL of the document, become invalid. It is also useful, if your document is downloaded or read out of context. If <BASE> is specified, partial URLs within the document are treated as relative to the <BASE> address.

Example

```
<BASE HREF="http://bpkm.org.in/index.html">
...
<IMG SRC="home/logo.jpg">
```

The image is deferenced to

http://bpkm.org.in/home/logo.jpg

Without the <BASE> element, relative URLs are resolved to the document's URL.

Important <BASE> Extensions

Browsers that support FRAMEs also support a TARGET attribute to the <BASE> elements. This defines the named frame (or window) to which all anchors in the current documents are directed. This can be overriden by TARGET attributes specific to the elements.

Note: <BASE> can cause problems with <ISINDEX> queries, since some browsers will use the BASE URL to determine, where to send the <ISINDEX> query data and some will use the actual URL used to obtain the document.

6.2.3 <ISINDEX> Element

This element tells the browser that the document is an index document. This causes the browser to create a user-input field into which the user can type words to be used in the index search. In a sense, this means that, in addition to being viewed and read, the "document" can in some way be examined or queried.

It is important to realize that this does not mean a simple text search through the document being viewed. When the user types in words and presses ENTER (or whatever key or button is appropriate) the search information is sent back to a server, thus the server machine actually does the searching. In a sense, you can think of an <ISINDEX> document as being a front-end to a kind of indexing or querying program residing on the HTTP server.

- *Construction of ISINDEX Query:* Keywords from <ISINDEX> queries are passed to the server by suffixing, to the URL from which the document originated, a question mark followed by a list of keywords, separated by plus signs. Thus if the URL for a document containing an <ISINDEX> element was

  http://www.bpkm.org.in/classes/search

  Then, typing the word "document" into the <ISINDEX> query window and submitting the query would access the URL http:// www.bpkm.org.in/classes/search? document

- *Appropriate Use of ISINDEX:* The <ISINDEX> element is usually generated automatically by a server-side script, or gateway program. You should not add this element by hand into a regular HTML document.

- *Netscape Enhancements to ISINDEX:* Netscape introduced two new attributes to the <ISINDEX> element, which are commonly supported and with are included in the HTML 4.0 specification.

Example

```
<ISINDEX PROMPT="Enter Strg" ACTION="http://www.bpkm.org.in/
program/prog">
```

Both of these attributes are optional. The PROMPT attribute is not a problem, because if a browser does not understand PROMPT, it will still present the query string.

6.2.4 <NEXTID> Element

This tag has a single attribute, namely 'the number of the next document-wide numeric identifier to be allocated of the form z113'. The <NEXTID> tag is designed for using by automatic hypertext editors, and is not intended for use by mere humans. People writing HTML should generally use mnemonic alphabetical identifiers.

Example

```
<HEAD>
<NEXTID N="z13">
.
.
</HEAD>
```

Note: At present, it is likely that <NEXTID> will be dropped from the HTML specification, since it is not terribly useful. You are therefore advised against wasting your time reading the rest of this page!

6.2.5 <LINK> Element

The <LINK> element defines relationships between the document and other documents. It can be used to create tool bars, link to a style sheet (REV="stylesheet"), a script (REV="script"), or a printable version (like a pdf) of the document (REV="print") and embed authorship details. <LINK> should always be accompanied by an HREF to indicate the resource it refers to, the other attributes are optional. The <LINK> attributes are:

Attributes		Description
REL	:	***"text string"*** describes the relationship to another web page or other internet resource. (Forward link types)
REV	:	***"text string"*** describes the *reverse* relationship, how the other resource views the current document. If the related document is the home page, the current page is probably a child of the home page. (Reverse link types)
TITLE	:	***"suggested title"*** gives a suggested title for the resource be referred to. (Advisory title string)
HREF	:	***"URL"*** URL for linked resource
MEDIA	:	***"SCREEN / PRINT / PROJECTION / AURAL / BRAILLE / ALL / other media"*** indicates which type of media the link applies to. The default is `ALL`, which means that the link applies to any media. (What media type the link applies to)

Contd....

TYPE	:	***"MIME type"*** gives an indication of the MIME type of the resource the tag links to. In practice `TYPE` is most useful when linking to an external CSS style sheet, in which case `TYPE` should have a value of `text/css`. (MIME type of linked resource)

Example

<LINK HREF="summary.html" TITLE="Summary" REV="Home">

<LINK HREF="chapter.html" TITLE="Color Palettes" REL="chapter">

<LINK HREF="mailto:sun@galexy.com" TITLE="Solar King" REV="author">

<LINK REL=STYLESHEET HREF="printonly.css" MEDIA="PRINT">

<LINK REL="stylesheet" TYPE="text/css" HREF="http://www.w3.org/StyleSheets/TR/W3C-REC">

6.2.6 <META> Element

The META element allows for including information about the document not defined by other elements. It is used to supply generic Meta information using name/value pairs. The CONTENT attribute is required, with either the HTTP-EQUIV or NAME attribute to identify the type of action or data identifier to be associated with it.

Attributes		Description
NAME	:	***"GENERATOR / EXPIRE / AUTHOR / KEYWORDS / DESCRIPTION / REFRESH / many others"*** indicates the name of the meta information in the <META ...> tag. The most common values are KEYWORDS and DESCRIPTION (for Search Engines), and REFRESH (for Automatic Refreshing and Forwarding).
HTTP-EQUIV	:	tells the browser to pretend that an additional HTTP header was sent. The name of the header is the value of the HTTP-EQUIV *attribute* and the *value* of the header is the value of the CONTENT attribute. (Name of the pretend HTTP header)
CONTENT	:	**"text string"** specifies the value of the meta information in the <META ...> tag. HTTP-EQUIV and NAME set the name of the content. (Meta information content)

Note: NAME is not necessary if the HTTP-EQUIV attribute is used.

Example

<META Name="description" Content="Home page for bpkm.org.in,

a Web site about creating Web sites. Learn the art of Web site creation.">

<META Name="keywords" Content="bpkm.org.in, HTML,

frames, webmaster reference library, HTML reference, HTML authoring,...>

1. <META NAME="Last-Modified" CONTENT="13-10-00">

Contd....

HTML Ex: (after 10 seconds this page will refresh (move) to the "next" page)

```
<HEAD>
<META HTTP-EQUIV="Refresh" CONTENT="10; URL=next.html">
</HEAD>
<BODY>
<P>...Mr. Tanmoy, this page will self destruct in 10 seconds...</P>
```

6.2.7 <SCRIPT> Element

The <SCRIPT> element is included as a placeholder for future, use with script languages. It is already in use in the newest versions of Netscape and Explorer. Common practice is to surround the script proper with comments so older browsers don't see the script.

- With Navigator 2.0, Netscape introduced a <SCRIPT> element in the document <HEAD> or <BODY>. This element can contain an executable script, written in JavaScript, which can set up program functionality within the document itself. JavaScript is a simple scripting language, loosely based on the Java language. JavaScript can interact with the displayed text, several of the text-display areas on the screen, as well as fill-in FORMS. If you've ever seen a fill-in form that seems to auto-tabulate numbers, or have notices a scrolling marquee appears in the status-line at the bottom of your Netscape window, then you are seeing a JavaScript in action.
- Internet Explorer 3 and greater also supports JavaScript, although they support a slightly different version of the language, which they call Jscript. The result is that some Java/Jscript programs work on IE 3/4 and not on Netscape 3/4, and vice versa. Moreover, scripts that work on IE 4 may not work on IE 3, as the script languages are evolving rapidly, and add many new features from version to version.
- Internet Explorer also supports a second scripting language, known as VBScript, or Visual Basic Scripting. This language is similar to the Visual Basic languages familiar to many Windows developers, and provides essentially the same features as JavaScript.
- As of version 4 of the browsers, Netscape and Microsoft let the script program dynamically interact with the HTML document that is displayed on the page. This is known as dynamic HTML, and makes page design much more interesting. However and unfortunately Microsoft and Netscape have done this in completely different ways, such that dynamic HTML scripts written for Internet Explorer 4 will not work with Netscape Navigator 4, and vice versa.
- This situation will improve with version 5 of the browsers, as they will both support a common way of writing programs that interact with the document.

This common mechanism is known as the Document Object Model or DOM. Both Netscape and Microsoft have promised support for this standard, which will make it much easier to write scripts that work everywhere.

For more information on dynamic HTML and the DOM, please see the following URLS:

Netscape JavaScript and dynamic HTML -- http://developer.netscape.com/tech/javascript/index.html

Microsoft Dynamic HTML -- http://www.microsoft.com/workshop/author/default.asp

The DOM -- http://www.w3.org/DOM/

Example

```
<SCRIPT LANGUAGE="JavaScript">
<!—// hide from other browsers
/* JavaScript Livepopup Navigator
  Generic arrays and select menus
  by Solar King (sun@galexy.com) galexy.com
*/
function createArray() {
this.length = createArray.arguments.length
for (var i = 0; i < this.length; i++)
this[i+1] = createArray.arguments[i]
}
var title = new createArray("Select a page...",
"Developer's Corner",
"Feature Articles",
...
// —>
</SCRIPT>
```

HTML The SRC attribute to the SCRIPT tag allows hiding of scripts.

```
<SCRIPT LANGUAGE="JavaScript" SRC=mySource.js>
```

6.2.8 <STYLE> Element

<STYLE> element is a part of the style sheets. Style sheets are a language, separate from HTML, for specifying formatting and layout properties for a document, such as one marked up in HTML.

HTML does not contain much formatting information. At the same time, authors want the ability to specify, how they want their data displayed. The idea behind style sheets is that this display formatting information can be stored as a separate piece of information, called a style sheet, and that the style sheet can then be applied to a document while it is being formatted for display.

A style sheet is a supplementary document, written in a language different from HTML, which contains style-formatting instructions that can be applied to an HTML document. The <STYLE> element can be used to reference such an external document, or it can contain a set of formatting instructions to be used in the document.

This is done by either:

- referencing an external stylesheet via tags such as <STYLE HREF= "url_to_stylesheet">.

Example

```
<HEAD>
  <STYLE HREF="../styles/style_form.css">
  ...
  </HEAD>
```

Would give the URL of the style sheet to be loaded and used. Here the extension CSS refers to Cascading Stylesheets, one of the methods currently in use. This is discussed in more detail in the <STYLE> element section.

- Enclosing the information between <STYLE> and </STYLE>

Example

```
<STYLE>
BODY
   {
      font-family:      Arial,helvetica,sans-serif;
      color:          black;
       background-color: white;
```

Contd....

```
    }
P  { margin-left: 5%;
       font-family: arial,helvetica,sans-serif
    }
PRE
    { margin-left: 5%;
       font-family: "courier new", courier, monospace;
    }
H2,H3,H4
    { color:  #669999;
       font-family: "arial black", arial, helvetica, sans-serif;
       font-weight: bold;
       margin-left: 0%;
    }
DIV.leftmarg
    {  margin-left: 5%;
       font-family: arial,helvetica,sans-serif
    }
A          {text-decoration: none; }
A:active  {color: #ff0000; text-decoration: underline}
A:visited {color: #999999; }

.note     {color: orange;}
.warning {color: red; font-weight: bold}
</STYLE>
```

Note: The <STYLE> is currently supported by Netscape Navigator 4 and Internet Explorer 4. However, both browsers do not properly support the style sheet language, (known as cascading style sheets), so that the element is not widely used.

EXERCISE

Objective Type Questions

1. A tag is enclosed between

   (A) < > (B) { }

   (C) [ ] (D) " "

2. Every HTML document begins with______ tag.

   (A) </html> (B) <html>

   (C) <Head> (D) <Title>

3. Web pages are created using

   (A) FORTRAN (B) COBOL

   (C) HTML (D) VB

4. HTML is used to______.

   (A) Design a Website (B) Test a Website

   (C) Analyse a Website (D) None of them

5. A file on internet is accessed by______.

   (A) URL (B) HTTP

   (C) FTP (D) HTML

6. The Browser applies the feature of a tag until it encounters _____tag.

   (A) Quit (B) Closing

   (C) Exit (D) Anti

   (E) Deactivate

7. _______are the HTML codes that control the appearance of the document contents.

   (A) Tags (B) Codas

   (C) Slashes (D) Properties

   (E) Code

8. What part of a Web page should the <TITLE> tag be I used in?

   (A) The heading (B) The body

   (C) The footnote (D) Anywhere

9. Extension of HTML document is______.

(A) .doc (B) .exe

(C) .htm (D) .txt

10. ______is a component of Head section.

(A) Title (B) Prologue

(C) Links (D) All of the above

11. The first page of a web is known as______.

(A) Page (B) Web site

(C) Protocol (D) Home page

12. What types of company provides people with access to the Internet?

(A) PSI (B) SPI

(C) ISP (D) IPS

13. Hypertext is

(A) Used to link documents

(B) includes sound and video

(C) a browser

(D) requires plug-in to be viewed by browser

14. An example of browser software is

(A) Gopher (B) ARPAnet

(C) Netscape Navigator (D) Hypertext

15. Hypertext is

(A) used to link document

(B) a search engine

(C) includes sound and video

(D) requires plug-in to be view by a browser

16. Browsers

(A) are software

(B) are needed to find and process the hypertext links

(C) have changed from being only text based to include graphics

(D) all the above

17. When a Web page is displayed in a browser, the title usually appears

(A) in the title bar (B) in the document

(C) in the status bar (D) in blue underline text

18. A closing paired tag must contain a

(A) brace (B) slash

(C) asterisk (D) question mark

19. The <TITLE> tag must be contained in

(A) the body section (B) the style section

(C) the second section (D) the head section

20. Every Web document must begin and end with

(A) <HTML> and </HTML> (B) <BODY> and </BODY>

(C) <HTML> and <HTML> (D) <HEAD> and <HEAD>

21. When a Web page is displayed in a browser, the title usually appears

(A) in the title bar (B) in the document

(C) in the status bar (D) in blue underlined text

(E) all these answers

22. The <BODY> tag must be contained in

(A) the body section (B) the style section

(C) the second section (D) the head section

23. Which one of the following cannot be used as HTML editor?

(A) Paint (B) Word

(C) Photoshop (D) Internet Explorer

24. Which one of the following is used to hide the comments from the old browsers?

(A) // .... (B) /* .... */

(C) <!-- .... -- > (D) * .... *\

25. What does HTML stand for?

(A) Hyperlinks Text Markup Language

(B) Home Tool Markup Language

(C) Hyper Text Markup Language

(D) Hyper Text Machine Language

26. What is HTML?

(A) Hyper Text Marking Language

(B) Hyper Text Machine Language

(C) Hyper Text Middle Language

(D) Hyper Text Markup Language

27. Choose the correct HTML tag for the largest heading

(A) <head> (B) <heading>

(C) <h1> (D) <h6>

28. What is the correct HTML for adding a background color?

(A) <body color="yellow">

(B) <background>yellow</background>

(C) <body bgcolor="yellow">

(D) <body background="yellow">

29. The tag that specifies that style sheet area within an HTML document is

(A) <SHEET> I (B) < STYLE SHEET >

(C) TYPE = "texUcss" (D) < STYLE >

30. The tag that marks the map definition block within the HTML document is

(A) <MAP> (B) <AREA>

(C) <SHAPE> (D) <USEMAP>

31. For largest level of heading which tag is used?

(A) <h1> (B) <h6>

(C) <heading> (D) <head>

32. The language used to develop web page is______.

(A) HTML (B) HTTP

(C) Brower (D) Protocol

33. Java Script is______ side scripting language.

(A) Server (B) Client

(C) Server & Client D) None of these

34. API stands for

(A) Application Programming Interface

(B) Application Programming Index

(C) Applet Programming Interface

(D) None of these

35. Primary aspects of Web design are content, Technology, economics &_______.

(A) visuals (B) site

(C) person (D) graphics

36. Java script is scripting language introduce by

(A) IE (B) Microsoft

(C) Netscape (D) SunJava

37. ______tag is used for document header.

(A) <title> (B) <head>

(C) <html> (D) <body>

38. ______is used to set background image at web page.

(A) <body background> (B) <body bg ground>

(C) <body back> (D) None of these

39. The H in HTML stands for

(A) Hypo (B) High

(C) Higher (D) Hyper

40. A world wide web contains web pages

(A) residing in many computers

(B) created using HTML

(C) with links to other web pages

(D) residing in many computers linked together using HTML

41. HTML is similar to a

(A) word processing language (B) screen editor

(C) scripting language (D) search engine

42. HTML uses

(A) pre-specified tags (B) user defined tags

(C) tags only for linking (D) fixed tags defined by the language

43. HTML tags define

(A) The data types of elements of document

(B) Presentation of specified elements of a document

(C) The contents of the document

(D) The structure of the document

44. What type of code is this sample?

Sample: <!--update this page in January-->

(A) Javascript (B) a comment

(C) VBScript (D) a hyperlink

Review & Discussion Questions

1. Write four tags required in every HTML page.
2. Differentiate between an 'empty tag' and 'container tags'. Give an example each.
3. "An HTML document requires a structure". Justify this statement.
4. Distinguish between empty and container tags. List two tags in each category.
5. Which is the first tag of HTML program?
6. The <TITLE> tag is present inside which tag?
7. What is importance of Web design process models?
8. What is meant by HTML? Why it is used?
9. What is TAG? Explain in Details?
10. Explain pair and unpaired tag in HTML.
11. What are the Advantages & Disadvantages of HTML?
12. Explain the Structure of HTML Program.
13. Explain the Basic Elements of HTML.
14. Explain the procedure to prepare & view HTML document.
15. Write a short note on "web page size and margins".
16. Explain general structure of HTML.
17. Explain <BODY> tag with its all attribute.
18. Explain steps of creating HTML program.
19. What is good web design? List out software html editors for Windows and Linux.
20. Define <HEAD>? List out the elements that are placed in the <HEAD> elements.
21. Explain in brief with example on <LINK> and <META> elements.
22. What is <SCRIPT> element? What is its importance in Web page Design?
23. What is <STYLE> element? How it is different from HTML?

CHAPTER 7

Formatting Basics

CHAPTER OBJECTIVES

In this chapter, you will learn the syntax used for HTML documents. More specifically, HTML documents can contain a variety of text formatting elements that affect the look of the text displayed by the browser. There are elements that deal only with the appearance of the text and those that deal with the meaning of the text as well as heading styles, breaks and horizontal rule. You will able to use these elements anywhere in the body section.

CHAPTER OUTLINES

7.1 INTRODUCTION

In this chapter, you will learn the syntax used for HTML documents. More specifically, HTML documents can contain a variety of text formatting options, similar to the formatting done with a word processor. For an HTML document however, you need to enter codes for the specific formatting you want. The computer then reads these codes and performs the formatting. In most cases, a code must be entered to turn the formatting on and to turn the formatting off.

- Text Formatting
- Heading Styles
- Breaks
- Horizontal Rule

7.2 TEXT FORMATTING

Generally, text is unformatted in your Web documents. However, to emphasize specific letters, words, or phrases which reflects the characteristics about the text. Also, you can use some text formatting options including boldfacing and italicizing. Depending on your browser, you may also be able to add underlining to emphasize characters. There are two major classes of text markup.

a. Character Elements (*Meaning*)

b. Look Elements (*Formatting*)

7.3 CHARACTER ELEMENTS

The character elements describe the type of the text formatting. It is also the treat as *Logical codes* which shows the meaning of the text. For example, if you want to display some programming code, with the help of <CODE> tag can be display. The same font also used with <PRE>; however, <PRE> is for formatted text while the browser will format the text associated with the <CODE>. These elements also called as *Phrase elements*. These elements require start and end tags. There are no required HTML attributes for these elements.

7.3.1 <EM> Element

The <EM> element is an HTML tag that is used to specify emphasized text within an HTML document. The <EM> basic emphasis typically rendered, in an italic font.

Example

```
<BODY>
The witness was <EM>not even there</EM> at the time.
</BODY>
```

.....is rendered similar to.....

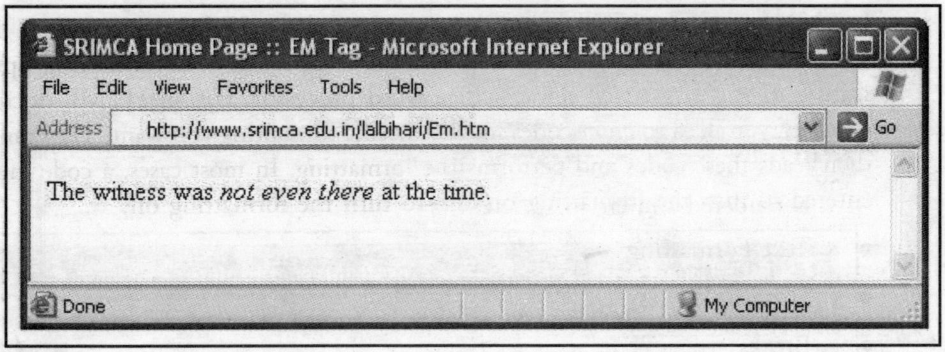

7.3.2 <STRONG> Element

The <STRONG> element indicates text, which should be more forceful than surrounding text. The <STRONG> element emphasizes, usually bold.

Example

```
<BODY>
I will have <STRONG> my bond! </STRONG>/ Speak not against <STRONG> my bond! </STRONG>/ I have sworn an oath that I will have <STRONG> my bond</STRONG>. —The Merchant of Venice
</BODY>
```

.....is rendered similar to.....

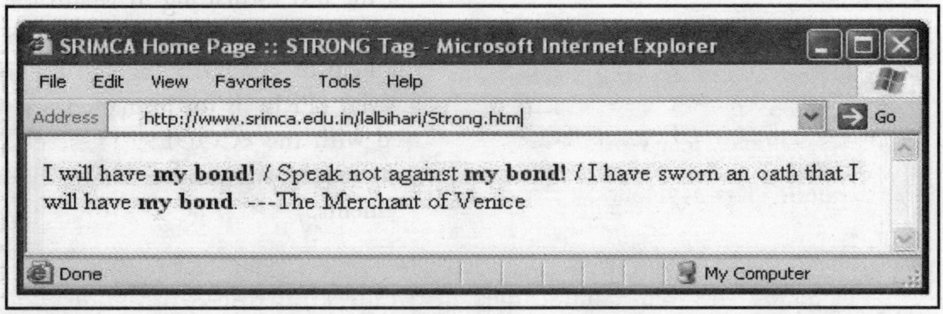

Note: What's the difference between <EM> (emphasis) and <STRONG>? It's a matter of degree: <STRONG> is like <EM> only more so.

7.3.3 <SAMP> Element

The <SAMP> element indicates text, which is an example of something. It is also commonly used to represent some key piece of text that has special meaning.

Example

```
<BODY>
The process of writing Java file names must be the file extension is <SAMP> .java
<SAMP>.
</BODY>
```

.....is rendered similar to.....

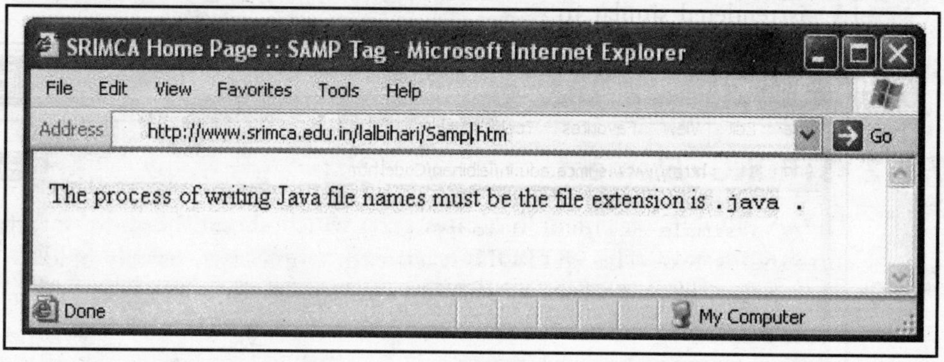

Note: The <SAMP> element is rendered in a fixed width font. The <SAMP> element has a similar purpose to <CODE> element.

7.3.4 <CODE> Element

The <CODE> element indicates text that is the code for a program. <CODE> is rendered in a fixed width font.

Example

```
<BODY>
<code>
// a simple HelloWorld loop
public class MyHello
{
 public static void main(String[] args) throws InterruptedException
 {
   for (int k=1; k <= 5; k++)
   {
     System.out.println("Hello #" + k);
     Thread.sleep (1000 /* millisec */);
```

Contd....

```
    }
  }
}
</code>
</BODY>
```

…..is rendered similar to…..

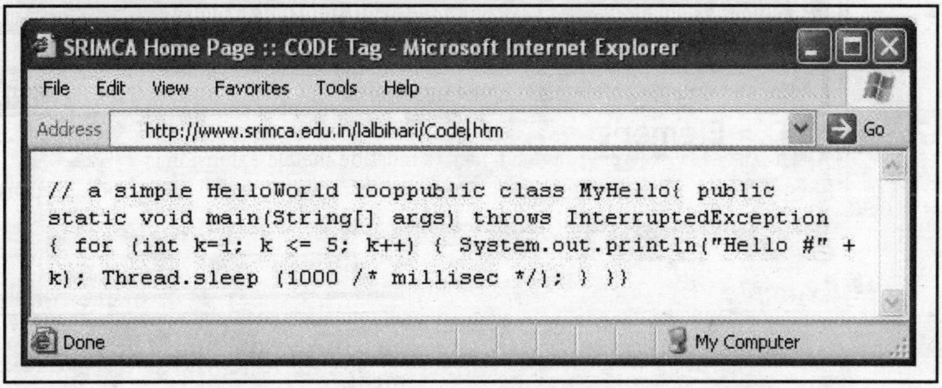

Note: For lengthy code examples, most programmers prefer <PRE ...>, which is much better for showing spacing and indentation.

7.3.5 <ADDRESS> Element

The <ADDRESS> element denotes contact information for the author or an organization of the web site.

Example

```
<BODY>
Site is developed at
<ADDRESS>
Shrimad Rajchandra Institute of Management & Computer Application
Gopal Vidyanagar
Bardoli-Mahuva Road, Tarsadi- 394 350
Surat, Gujarat, INDIA
</ADDRESS>
</BODY>
```

…..is rendered similar to…..

7.3.6 <CITE> Element

The <CITE> element indicates a reference to work, such as a book, report or web site. A citation (typically rendered in italics).

Example

```
<BODY>
Source:
integral - verb controlling "<CITE> ... Hicks and Streeten (1979, p. 568) identify
and review four different approaches... </CITE>"
</BODY>
```

.....is rendered similar to.....

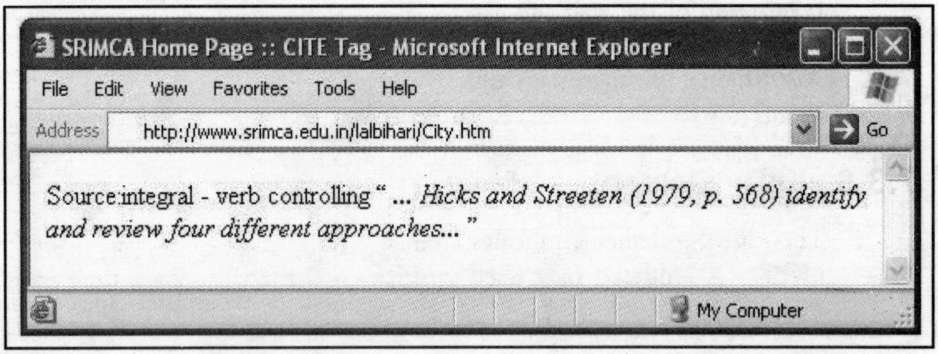

Note: The <CITE> element is also commonly used to indicate ownership and authorship of a web page, usually at the bottom of the page under a <HR ...>

7.3.7 <INS>, <DEL> Element

The <DEL> element indicates that the text has been deleted from the current revision of the document. The <INS> element indicates that the text has been inserted into the document since the last revision. Both of these tags are currently only supported by MSIE. The problem with <DEL> and <INS> elements are that they don't degrade properly. Browsers that don't know these tags will display the contents of both of them as normal, giving an incorrect representation of the intended meaning.

Example

```
<BODY>
Report to Mr.
<DEL>Raj</DEL>
<INS>Suraj</INS>
for further query.
</BODY>
```

.....is rendered similar to.....

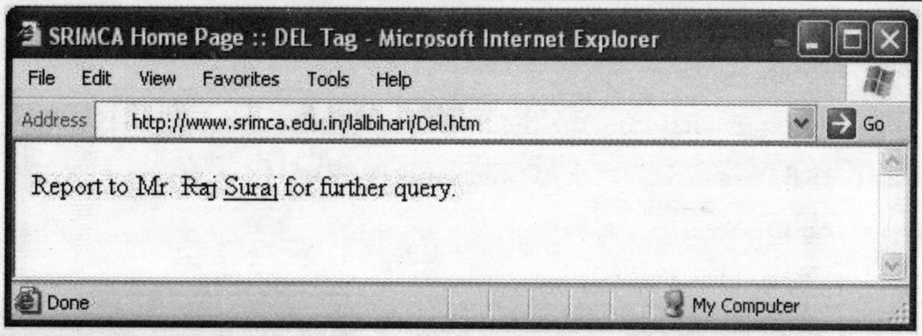

Note: Don't use these tags unless you are sure your audience's browsers support them.

7.3.8 <KBD> Element

The <KBD> element indicates characters that should be typed in at a keyboard. <KBD> is rendered in a fixed width font. Typically this is used in instruction manuals.

Example

```
<BODY>
Finally, type <KBD>logout</KBD> and press the return key.
</BODY>
```

.....is rendered similar to.....

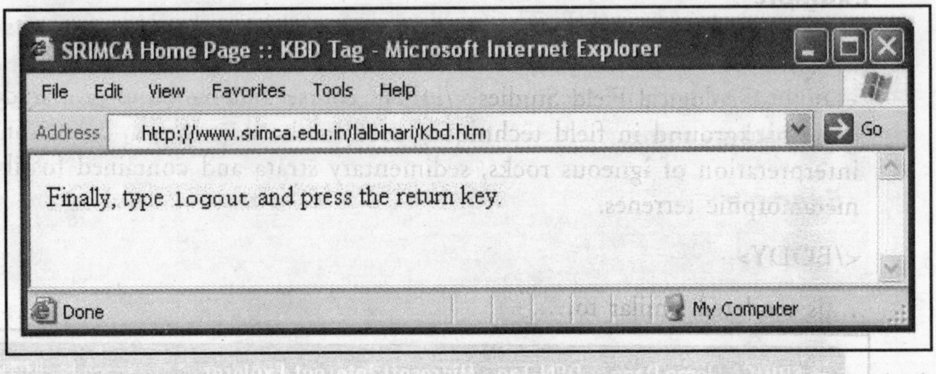

Note: Use the <KBD> element for fixed strings only. To indicate input which varies from one case to another, use the <VAR> element.

7.3.9 <VAR> Element

To indicate that a piece of text (typically, a word) is a variable, a "placeholder", i.e., a generic notation to be replaced by different actual expressions.

Example

```
<BODY>
In the simplest case, the command for deleting a file in Unix is<BR>
<KBD>rm</KBD> <VAR>filename</VAR>
</BODY>
```

.....is rendered similar to.....

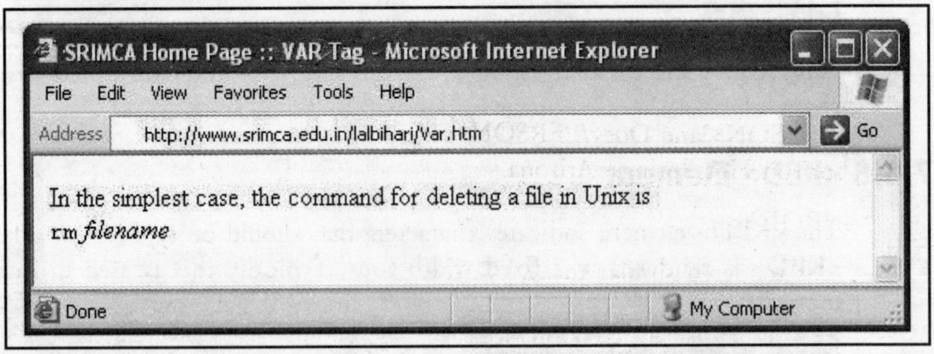

7.3.10 <DFN> Element

The <DFN> element can be regarded as a special kind of emphasis, too, but logically it indicates that a term is used in a context where it is defined.

Example

```
<BODY>
<DFN> Geological Field Studies </DFN> course is designed to give students a basic background in field techniques used in the description, collection, and interpretation of igneous rocks, sedimentary strata and contained fossils, and metamorphic terrenes.
</BODY>
```

.....is rendered similar to.....

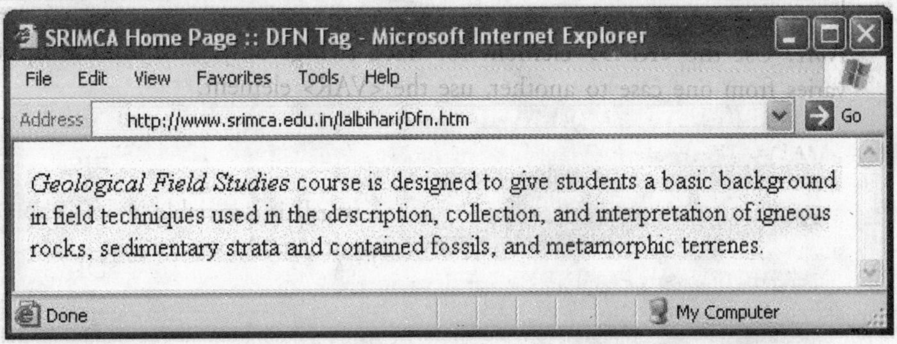

Note: This is a very useful element in principle, but unfortunately, many browsers, including Netscape, do not effectively support it.

7.3.11 <PERSON> Element

The <PERSON> element is used around names of people mentioned in a document. It is typically displayed, just like normal text, but is used by automatic indexers.

Example

```
<BODY>
<PERSON>Jane Doe</PERSON>, former President of United Corporation, was born in Hot Springs, Arizona.
</BODY>
```

.....is rendered similar to.....

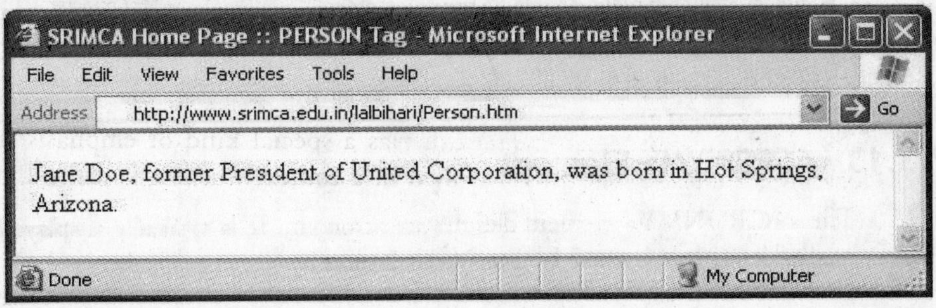

7.3.12 <ABBREV> Element

The <ABBREV> element defines an abbreviation. It is typically displayed just like normal text, but is used by automatic indexers.

Example

```
<BODY>
There are a number of Latin abbreviations, which are sometimes used, in English texts. Here are the commonest ones with their English equivalents:
<ABBREV>e.g.</ABBREV>for example
<ABBREV>cf.</ABBREV>compare
<ABBREV>i.e.</ABBREV>in other words
<ABBREV>v.</ABBREV>consult
<ABBREV>viz.</ABBREV>namely
<ABBREV>etc.</ABBREV>and so forth
<ABBREV>sc.</ABBREV>which means
<ABBREV>et al.</ABBREV>and other people
<ABBREV>ca.</ABBREV>approximately
</BODY>
```

.....is rendered similar to.....

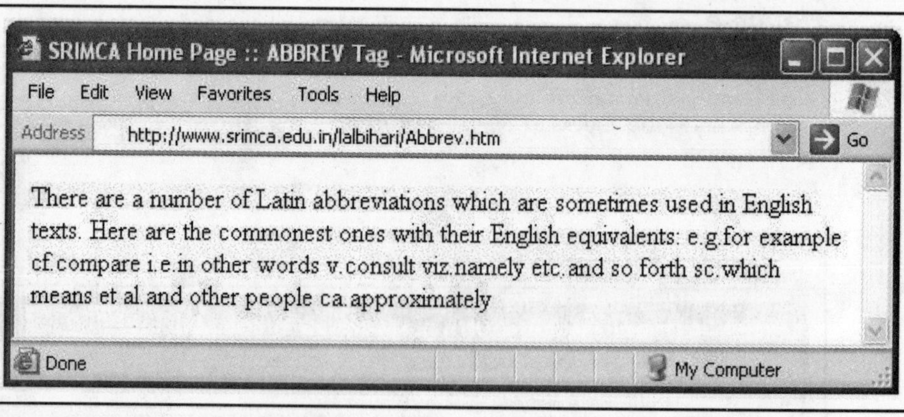

7.3.13 <ACRONYM> Element

The <ACRONMY> element defines an acronym. It is typically displayed just like normal text, but is used by automatic indexers.

Example

```
<BODY>

<ACRONMY>W3C</ACRONMY>'s mission is:<STRONG> "To lead the World Wide Web to its full potential by developing protocols and guidelines that ensure long-term growth for the Web"</STRONG>.

</BODY>
```

.....is rendered similar to.....

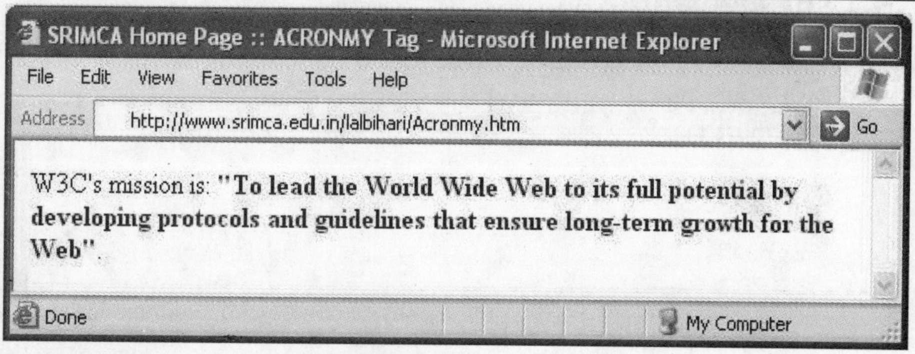

7.3.14 <AUTHOR> | <AU> Element

The <AUTHOR> | <AU> element defines text that names the author of a document. It is typically displayed just like normal text, but is used by automatic indexers.

Example

```
<BODY>

E=MC<SUP>2: A Biography of the World's Famous Education, By <AUTHOR>David Bodanis</AUTHOR>

</BODY>
```

.....is rendered similar to.....

7.4 LOOK ELEMENTS

The look elements deal with the specific text formatting. It is also the treat as Physical codes, which use for how the text is to be displayed and not it's meaning. These tags are useful when bold or idealize a phrase or text.

Note: The logical styles may not be distinct (i.e. different logical styles may be rendered in the same way). Also, some browsers do not support all physical styles. For example, Mosaic does NOT support underlined text.

7.4.1 <B> Element

The <B> element defines text that should be shown in boldface. It can be nested with other logical or physical elements but some browsers will respect only the innermost tag.

Example

```
<BODY>

<P>In mathematics, vectors are usually denoted with boldface letters like <B>x</
B>.

</P>

</BODY>
```

.....is rendered similar to.....

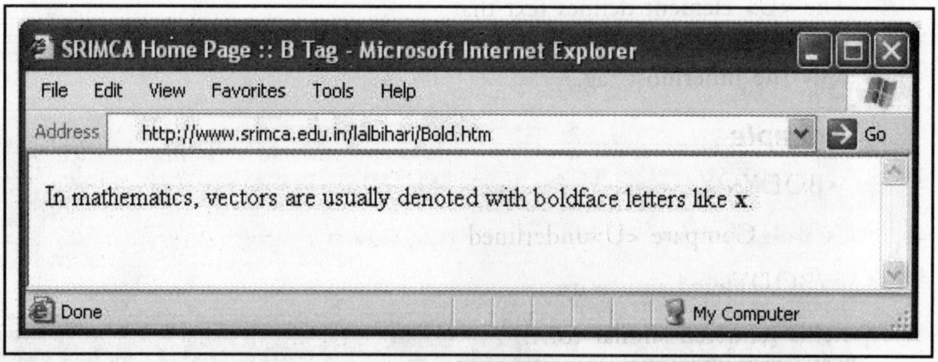

Note: Avoid using <B> element; use logical elements instead. In particular, for emphasis uses <EM> or <STRONG> elements.

7.4.2 <I> Element

The <I> element defines text that should be shown in italics. It can be nested with other logical or physical elements but some browsers will respect only the innermost tag.

Example

```
<BODY>
Usually the dog is said to form the species
<I>Canis familiaris</I>,
but genetically dogs belong to the same species as the wolf,
<I>Canis lupus</I>.
</BODY>
```

.....is rendered similar to.....

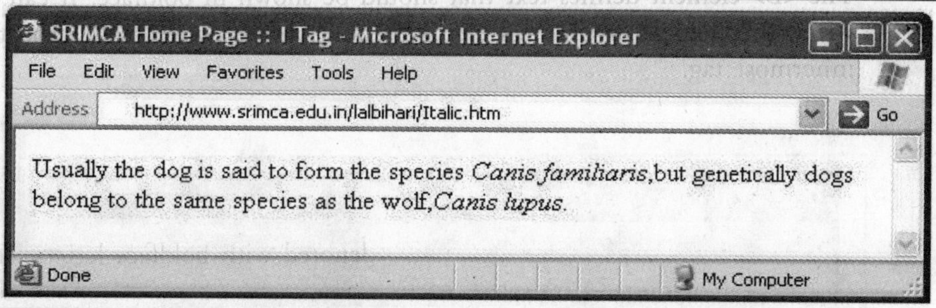

Note: However, don't overuse the <I> element. In particular, for emphasis use <EM> or <STRONG>, and for variables (placeholders) use <VAR>.

7.4.3 <U> Element

The <U> element defines text that should be shown with a line underneath it. It can be nested with other logical or physical elements but some browsers will respect only the innermost tag.

Example

```
<BODY>
        Compare <U>underlined text</U> with normal text.
</BODY>
```

.....is rendered similar to.....

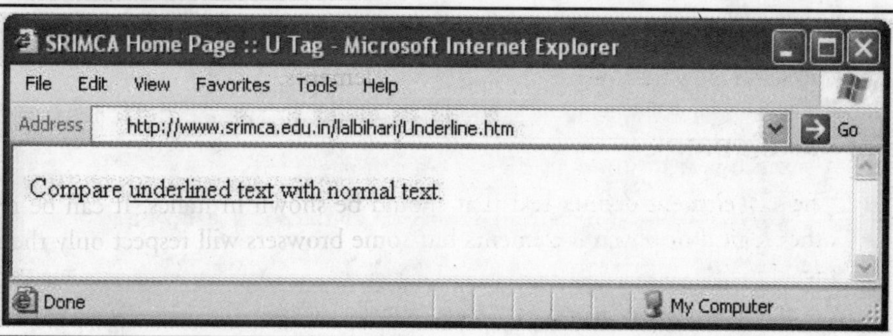

Note: Avoid using <U> element; use logical elements. For example, to emphasize use EM or STRONG. In HTML 4.0, the U element is deprecated .

7.4.4 <TT> Element

The <TT> element defines text that should be shown in a fixed width font. It can be nested with other logical or physical elements, but some browsers will respect only the innermost tag. (Typically rendered in monospaced font)

Example

```
<BODY>
Compare <TT>monospaced font</TT> with normal font.
</BODY>
```

.....is rendered similar to.....

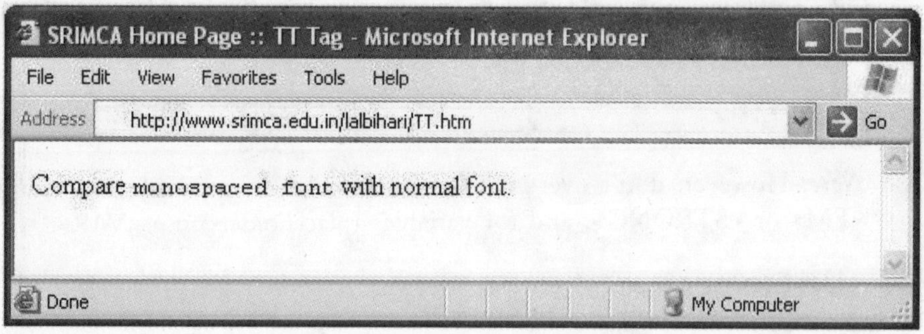

Note: Avoid using <TT> element; use logical elements instead, e.g. <CODE> or <SAMP>.

7.4.5 <STRIKE> Element

The <STRIKE> element defines text that should be shown with a horizontal line through it. It is defined as "font style element". Typically text is striked out to indicate that a text segment belongs to the original version of a text but has been deleted later.

Example

```
<BODY>
"Private agency" means an accredited nonpublic school,
a nonprofit institution of higher education
<STRIKE>eligible for tuition grants</STRIKE>, or a hospital.
</BODY>
```

.....is rendered similar to.....

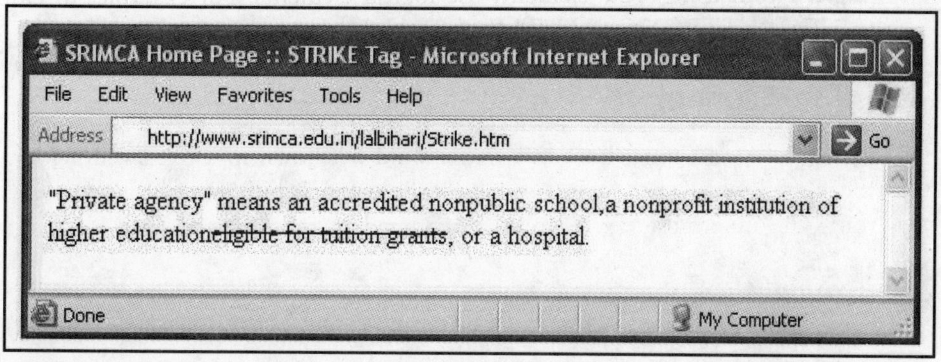

Note: If you use STRIKE in your document, it is advisable to include a note about its meaning.

7.4.6 <BIG> Element

The <BIG> text element defines text that should be displayed in a larger font than usual.

Example

```
<BODY>
That was a <BIG>big</BIG> mistake!
</BODY>
```

.....is rendered similar to.....

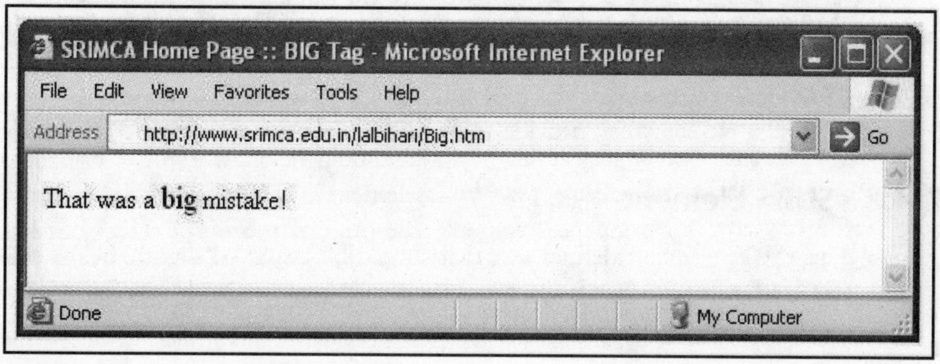

Note: Avoid using <BIG> element; use logical elements instead. In particular, for emphasis use <EM> or <STRONG>.

7.4.7 <SMALL> Element

The <SMALL> text element defines text that should be displayed in a smaller font than usual.

Example

```
<BODY>
<P>
This is normal text.
</P>
<P>
<SMALL>
This text will be presented in a smaller font, if possible.
</SMALL>
</P>
</BODY>
```

.....is rendered similar to.....

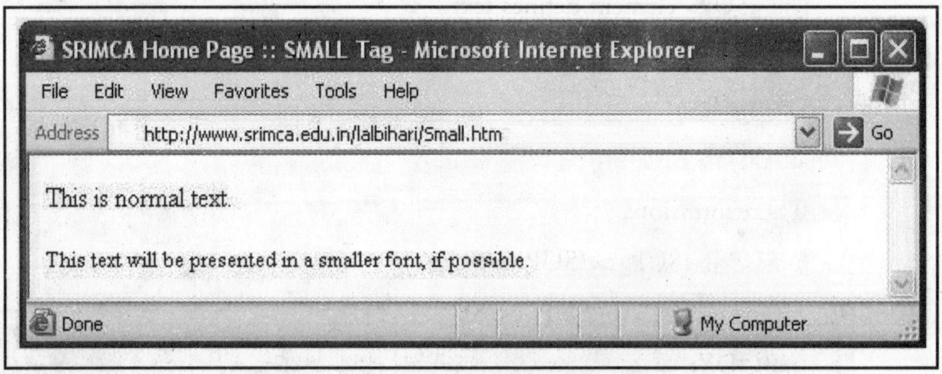

Note: There are no logical elements in current HTML standard; instead, the <FONT> element may provide more alternatives for specifying different font sizes.

7.4.8 <SUB> Element

The <SUB> element defines text that should be displayed slightly below the normal text level, often so that it the text is vertically centered with respect to normal text baseline, and possibly in smaller font.

Example

```
<BODY>
Let us form the sum of all x<SUB>i</SUB>'s, ie
x<SUB>1</SUB> + x<SUB>2</SUB> + ... + x<SUB>n</SUB>.
</BODY>
```

.....is rendered similar to.....

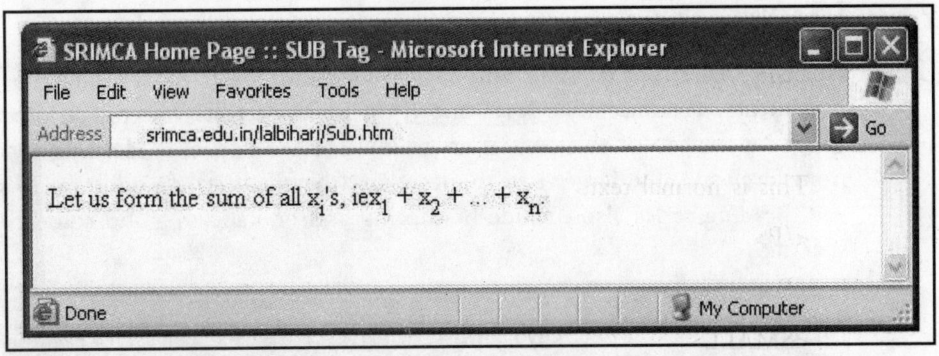

Note: Since this element is new, support for it is not universal. Some browsers simply ignore it, displaying e.g., a₁ as a1. And naturally, text-only browsers cannot truly support <SUB>. Internet Explorer ignores <SUB> elements after nesting level of two.

7.4.9 <SUP> Element

The <SUP> element defines text that should be displayed slightly above the normal text level and possibly in smaller font.

Example

```
<BODY>
The expression:
a<SUP>b<SUP>c</SUP></SUP>
means a<SUP>(b<SUP>c</SUP>)</SUP>
</BODY>
```

.....is rendered similar to.....

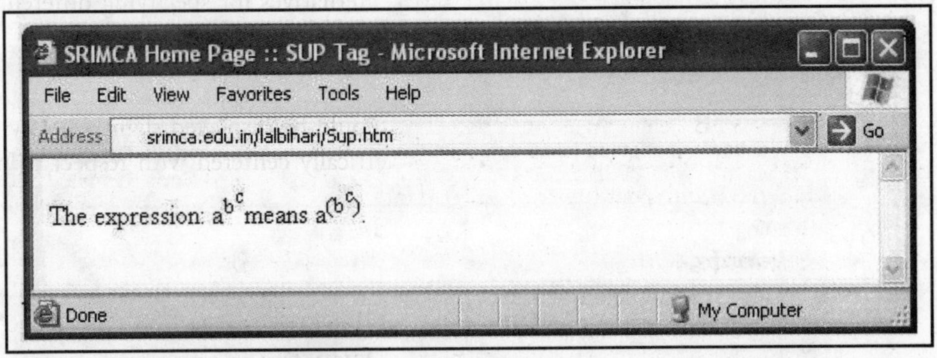

Note: Since this element is new, support for it is not universal. Some browsers simply ignore it, displaying e.g., a^b as ab. And naturally, text-only browsers cannot truly support <SUP>. Internet Explorer ignores <SUP> elements after nesting level of two.

7.5 HEADING STYLE

Heading styles are used to emphasize different levels of information in Web documents. Heading style level one (H1) is the largest. The phrase "formatting basics" at the top of this page is an example of heading one. Heading styles range from level one (the largest) to the level six (the smallest). In addition to the font size, heading styles also include boldfacing and/or italicizing and some paragraph spacing.

Attributes		Description
ALIGN	:	**"LEFT I RIGHT I CENTER I JUSTIFY"** defines the placement of the header on the screen.
SRC	:	**"URL"** identifies a *graphic image* to be embedded before the header text.
DINGBAT	:	identifies an *iconic entity* to be embedded there.
NOWRAP	:	prevents the browser from breaking long header lines; use a element to break those lines yourself.
CLEAR	:	**"LEFT I RIGHT I ALL"** used to position a header after a graphic. It specifies which margin should be clear.
MD	:	"Specifies a message digest or cryptographic checksum for the associated graphic specified by the SRC attribute. It is used when you want to be sure that a linked object is indeed the same one that the author intended, and hasn't been modified in any way. For instance, MD="md5:jV2OfH+nnXHU8bnkPAad/mSQlTDZ", which specifies an MD5 checksum encoded as a base64 character string. The MD attribute is generally allowed for all elements which support URI based links."

Example

```
<BODY>
<H1 ALIGN=CENTER>The Story of Mahatma Gandhi</H1>
<H2>Preface</H2>
<H3>General Remarks</H3>
</BODY>
```

Text Formatted as Heading Level with Code Sample	Text Formatted as Heading Level with Code Sample
Heading 1 <H1>Heading 1</H1>	**Heading 4** <H4>Heading 4</H4>
Heading 2 <H2>Heading 2</H2>	**Heading 5** <H5>Heading 5</H5>
Heading 3 <H3>Heading 3</H3>	**Heading 6** <H6>Heading 6</H6>

7.6 BREAKS

The break codes are used to indicate a new paragraph or the new start of a new line. The paragraph code (<P>) starts a new line of text and leaves a blank line between the paragraphs. The line break (<BR>) code starts a new line but does not leave a blank line.

7.6.1 <P> Element (Paragraph Break)

The <P> element marks a block of text as a paragraph. The <P> element marks the beginning of the paragraph, while the tag </P> marks the end of a paragraph. The end tag, however, is optional, as a paragraph is automatically ended when you start another paragraph, or when you start a heading, blockquote, list, table or form. The <P> element is functionally equivalent to two <BR> elements, and creates a blank line between multiple paragraphs.

Attributes		Description
ALIGN	:	**"LEFT I RIGHT I CENTER I JUSTIFY"** controls the alignment of text within the paragraph. Left and right alignments flush the text with the left and right margins, respectively, while center alignment centers the text. Justify should left and right justify the text.
ID	:	**"name_token"** (not widely supported) mark the paragraph for a possible reference via a URL. Thus, ID should act much like the NAME attribute of a hypertext anchor <A> element. However, this use for ID is currently only supported by the Internet Explorer 4.
NOWRAP	:	causes the browser to not wrap the text to the next line.
CLEAR	:	**"LEFT I RIGHT I ALL I BOTH"** used to position a paragraph after a paragraph. It specifies which margin should be clear.

Example

```
<BODY>

<P ALIGN="LEFT">Harry Potter written by J.K Rawling and 1st published in 1997 in Britain, won immediate and stunning popularity. it is already on Times Best seller list, British best and Adult best seller list. The book is on its way to a movie production and orders are pouring in at Amazon.com for copies by the fans.

<P>With 'Harry' as an orphan child with his uncle and auntie, who are both unfair and cruel, and Dudely as a cousin who leaves no opportunity to hurt humiliate Harry, the story makes a perfect drama to create both sympathy and goodwill for Harry.

</BODY>
```

Note: If you have a collection of closely related small paragraphs, you may wish to consider making them into a list using <UL> and <LI> instead of <P>; this typically results in more presentation that is compact visually.

If you intend to use <P> for alignment purposes, such as centering text, remember that, a <P> element may only contain text elements. The <DIV> element may contain block elements, too.

It is advisable to use explicit </P> tags. The resason behind is that in practice, at least one popular browser (Internet Explorer) fails to infer a closing </P> tag in many occasions. This means that if you do not use an explicit </P> tag, then e.g. a table following a paragraph is rendered immediately after the text, with no space between.

7.6.2
 Element (Line Break)

The line break element indicates that a new line is to start at the given point. There is no extra line inserted between the lines. The <BR> element is used commonly in present poetic text where the division into lines (verses) is essential. To affect the positioning of images <BR> elements with CLEAR attribute is often needed.

Attributes		Description
CLEAR	:	**"LEFT I RIGHT I ALL I NONE"** CLEAR="LEFT" causes the next text line to start down as soon as the left margin is clear, while CLEAR="RIGHT" causes the line to break and start when the right margin is clear. CLEAR="ALL" breaks down until both margins are clear. CLEAR="NONE" means to clear nothing.
ID	:	**"name_token"** (not widely supported) mark the paragraph for a possible reference via a URL. Thus, ID should act much like the NAME attribute of a hypertext anchor <A> element. However, this use for ID is currently only supported by the Internet Explorer 4.

Example

```
<BODY>
<P>
You should always end the terminal session with the command
<BR>
<KBD>logout</KBD>
<BR>
or some other operation with the same effect.
</P>
< BODY>
```

```
<BODY>
```

Contd....

```
<DIV ALIGN=CENTER>
Mieleni minun tekevi<BR>
aivoni ajattelevi<BR>
lähteäni laulamahan<BR>
saa'ani sanelemahan.<BR>
<P ALIGN="RIGHT"><CITE>Kalevala</CITE></P>
</DIV>
</BODY>
```

.....is rendered similar to.....

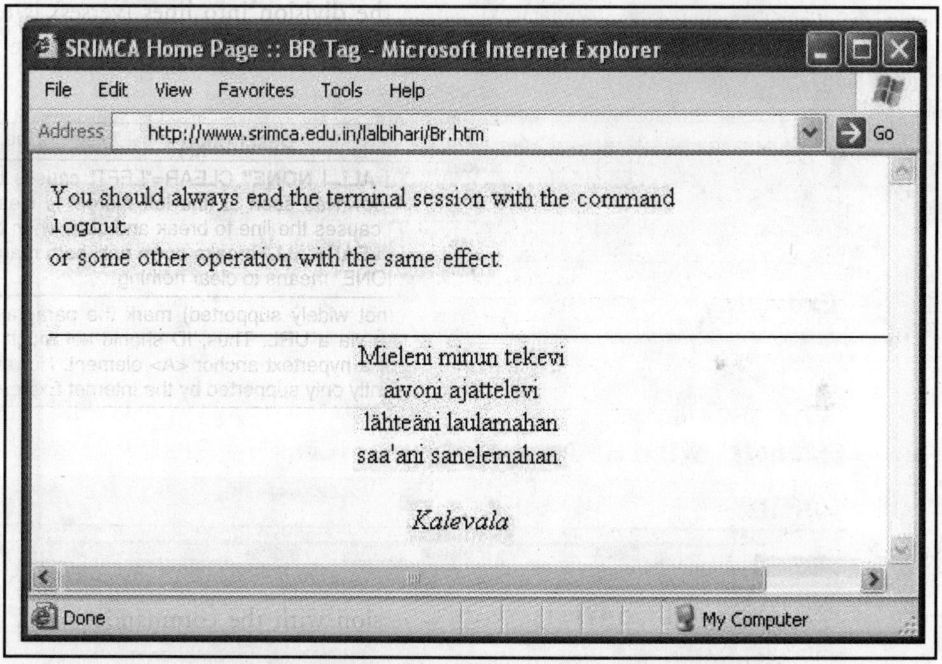

Note: You should not use <BR> elements just in order to force the text to be of some particular width, which you regard as suitable. It is much better to let browsers do such formatting according to each browsing situation.

Some designers use multiple BR elements to force vertical white space. This need not work in all browsers. If you wish to force empty vertical space, consider using a suitable <PRE> element.

7.7 <HR> ELEMENT (HORIZONTAL RULE)

The <HR> element is used to draw a horizontal dividing line completely across the screen. This can be to logically separate blocks of text, or to separate icon lists from the body of the text. The HR is not a container, so the end tag is forbidden.

Attributes		Description
ALIGN	:	**"LEFT I RIGHT I CENTER "** defines the placement of the header on the screen.
SRC	:	**"URL"** identifies a *graphic image* to be embedded before the header text.
NOSHADE	:	draw the dividing line as a solid black bar. The default is a shaded bar. (Ex. <HR NOSHADE SIZE="1">)
SIZE	:	**"n"** specifies the vertical width, in pixels, of the dividing line (n is an integer). (Ex. <HR SIZE="2"> [the default size])
CLEAR	:	**"LEFT I RIGHT I ALL"** CLEAR="LEFT" causes the next text line to start down as soon as the left margin is clear, while CLEAR="RIGHT" causes the line to break and start when the right margin is clear. CLEAR="ALL" breaks down until both margins are clear.
WIDTH	:	**"n", or "n%"** specifies the horizontal width, in pixels or as a percentage of the display width, of the dividing line (n is an integer). (Ex. <HR WIDTH="90%">)
COLOR	:	**"color expression"** allows you to change the color of the text. *RRGGBB* is a six-digit hexadecimal number with the first two digits specifying the red value, the middle two the green value, and the last two the blue value. Color names can also be used in the COLOR attribute. Valid colors are: Aqua, Black, Blue, Fuchsia, Gray, Green, Lime, Maroon, Navy, Olive, Purple, Red, Silver, Teal, Yellow, and White. *Netscape does not support COLOR attribute.*

Example

```
<BODY>

<HR SRC="line.gif" SIZE="5%" WIDTH="100"> - WRONG<HR NOSHADE
SIZE="1" WIDTH="80%" ALIGN="CENTER"> - RIGHT

<BODY>
```

```
BODY>

<HR SIZE="4" WIDTH="80%">

<HR SIZE="10" WIDTH="40">

<HR SIZE="10" WIDTH="40" ALIGN="LEFT">

<HR SIZE="10" WIDTH="40" ALIGN=""LEFT" NOSHADE>

<HR SIZE ="5" WIDTH="20%" ALIGN=""RIGHT">

<HR SIZE ="5" WIDTH="20%" ALIGN="LEFT" COLOR="RED">

</BODY>
```

.....is rendered similar to.....

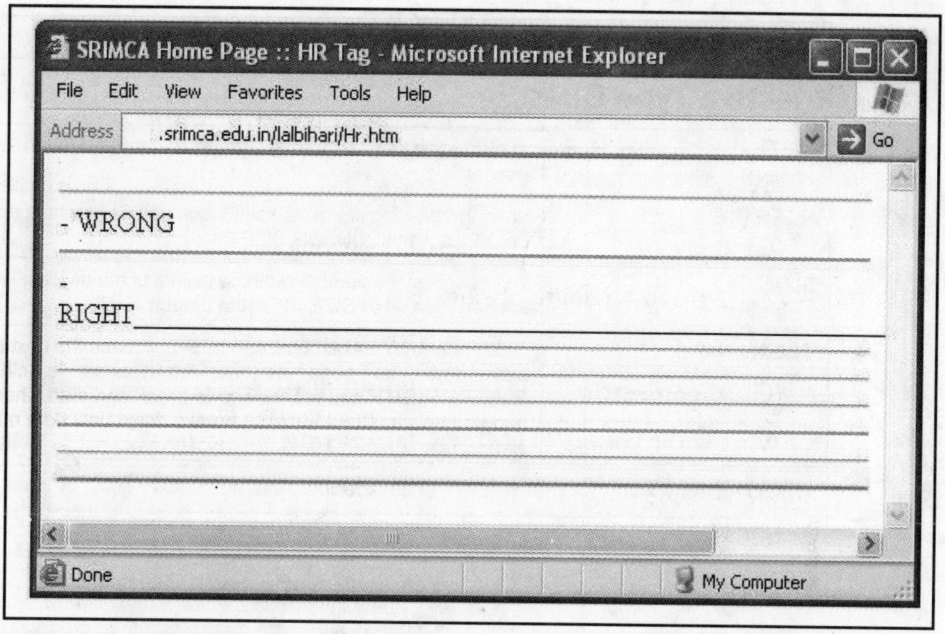

Note: Don't overuse <HR>. The document may not look good if you have lots of rules with just a little text between.

It is usually better to use a percentage specification than absolute number of pixels. The user's window might be very different from yours.

EXERCISE

Objective Type Questions

1. The______tag makes the text bold.

   (A) <b> (B) <i>

   (C) <em> (D) <strong>

2. ______is an attribute of <hr> tag.

   (A) Size (B) Width

   (C) Alignment (D) All of the above

3. What is the correct HTML tag for inserting a line break?

   (A) <break> (B)

   (C) <lb> (D) <nl>

4. Choose the correct HTML tag to make a text bold

   (A) <b> (B) <bb>

   (C) <bld> (D) <bold>

5. Choose the correct HTML tag to make a text italic

   (A) <ii> (B) <italics>

   (C) <i> (D) <italic>

6. Which is correct?

   (A) <b>Click Here<b> (B) <strong>Click Here<strong>

   (C) <b>Click Here</b> (D) </strong>Click Here</strong>

7. The character formatting tag to format the text displayed as bold is

   (A) <BOLD> (B) <STRONG>

   (C) <STRIKE> (D) <SR>

8. ______tag is used to format the text matter.

   (A) <format> (B) <font >

   (C) <form> (D) <frame>

9. In HTML language the tag <U> displays text as

   (A) Boldface (B) Italics

   (C) Underlined (D) Colored

10. ______tag is used to display web pages information such as URL, authors name etc.
    (A) <address> (B) <pre>
    (C) <em> (D) <frame>
11. The tags used for specifying fonts in HTML are
    (i) <B> (ii) <I>
    (iii) <U> (iv) <L>
    (A) (i) and (ii) (B) (i) and (iii)
    (C) (ii) and (iv) (D) (i),(ii) and (iii)
12. Which is the correct code to apply for bold text?
    (A) <b>This is bold text.</b>
    (B) (b)This is bold text.(/b)
    (C) <bold>This is bold text.</bold>
    (D) <b>This is bold text.<b>
13. ______is used to create a new paragraph.
    (A) <form> (B) <img>
    (C) <P> (D) <marque>
14. To group sentences in paragraph which tag is used?
    (A) <para> (B) <p>
    (C) <b> (D)
15. Interpret this statement: <strong>Michelle</strong>
    (A) It makes Michelle strong
    (B) It highlights Michelle as being strong
    (C) It will print out Michelle in bold font
16. What tag produces a divider?
    (A) A <DIVIDER> tag
    (B) A <HR> tag
    (C) A <LINE> tag
17. What do the <P> and <BR> tags have in common?
    (A) They both format text
    (B) They both help create lists
    (C) They have nothing in common

Review & Discussion Questions

1. Write HTML code to generate the following output on browser.

   ENTER STUDENT DETAIL

   NAME

   ROLL NO.

Note:

(i) Heading in bold and underline of Red colour font.

(ii) Text bold and blue colour.

(iii) Page Title is 'CLASS-DATA'.

2. What is the tag for largest level of heading?
3. Which tag is used to insert line brake in HTML code?
4. Which tag is used for smallest heading?
5. Which tag is used to bold the text?
6. Which tag is used to italic the text?
7. Which tag is used to underline the text?
8. Which tag is used to strikethrough the text?
9. Which tag is used to center the text?
10. Which tag is used to subscript the text?
11. Which tag is used to superscript the text?
12. Explain heading tag in html.
13. Explain <BR> and <HR> tag with its attribute.
14. Explain Following HTML tags.

    <P>
 <HR> <PRE>
15. Explain any four Text formatting tags in HTML.
16. What do you mean by text formatting? Explain with suitable examples.
17. What are Character elements? Give examples.
18. What are Looking elements? Give examples.
19. What is the use of <CODE> element? Instead of <CODE> element, which element is preferred in HTML?
20. Explain the <HR> elements and its attributes.

21. List out the break codes used in HTML. In what situation these codes are used.

22. What are the use of <ACRONMY> and <STRONG> tag? Give suitable example.

23. Explain <TT>, <BIG>,<SMALL> and <B> elements. Give the alternative elements for these elements.

CHAPTER 8

Special Characters

CHAPTER OBJECTIVES

This chapter discusses the Code number (character reference) and Phonetic reference (entity reference) which is necessary to include in your HTML document like <,>, or &. These special characters are that cannot be typed in normal keyboard but can be displayed on a graphical display. This chapter explains entity reference which is commonly used for special characters, and it is better use.

CHAPTER OUTLINES

8.1 INTRODUCTION

HTML codes use special characters including the left bracket (<), right bracket (>), ampersand (&), and quote (") to represent certain attributes (starting a tag, ending a tag, etc.). In order for you to be able to visually present these characters, you need to use special referencing. Also, you may occasionally need to use extended characters, which are characters not found on the keyboard, such as those used in foreign languages (like the ñ used in many Spanish words). Two formats can be used to do this.

1. Code number (character reference)
2. Phonetic reference (entity reference)

Although the entity reference is commonly used for special characters, it is better to use character reference with extended characters, because not all browsers recognize entity references.

8.2 CODE NUMBER (CHARACTER REFERENCE)

Character references are composed of three parts:

- A leading ampersand character, (&),
- The decimal number corresponding to the character, preceded by a numbers symbol (#xxx)
- A terminating semicolon (;).

For example the character reference for less than symbol (<) is <

Note: This number depends on the character set being used. For example, in some character sets, the 60th character may not be the less than symbol. Thus, it is more convenient (and universal) to have a symbolic reference for a character, as opposed to an absolute numeric reference. In HTML, (and SGML) such references are called entity references.

8.3 PHONETIC REFERENCE (ENTITY REFERENCE)

Entity references are similar, but use symbolic names to represent the characters. Entity references also have three parts:

- A leading ampersand character, (&),
- The name of the entity (in ascii characters)
- A terminating semicolon (;)

Thus, the entity reference for less than symbol (<) is <

Note: Not all the valid characters have corresponding entity references. In theses cases you need to use the direct numerical character references. Furthermore, some of the newer entity references defined in HTML 4 not understood by all browsers.

8.4 THE MOST POPULAR CHARACTER ENTITIES

This is a quick list of the most popular character entity references.

34	quot	"	Quotation mark = APL quote
38	amp	&	Ampersand
60	lt	<	less-than sign
62	gt	>	greater-than sign
160	nbsp		No-break space = non-breaking space
169	copy	©	copyright sign
174	reg	®	registered sign = registered trade mark sign
8226	bull	•	bullet = black small circle bullet is NOT the same as bullet operator

8.5 COMPLETE LIST OF CHARACTER ENTITIES

This is the complete list of character entity references defined in HTML 4.0. Few browsers (well, none that I know of) support all of these references. If your browser doesn't support the character, it will probably display something like an empty box or a question mark. This list is copied rote from W3C's:

34	Quot	"	quotation mark = APL quote
38	Amp	&	Ampersand
60	Lt	<	less-than sign
62	gt	>	greater-than sign
160	nbsp		no-break space = non-breaking space
161	iexcl	¡	inverted exclamation mark
162	cent	¢	cent sign
163	pound	£	pound sign
164	curren	¤	currency sign
165	yen	¥	yen sign = yuan sign
166	brvbar	¦	broken bar = broken vertical bar
167	sect	§	section sign
168	uml	¨	diaeresis = spacing diaeresis
169	copy	©	copyright sign
170	ordf	ª	feminine ordinal indicator
171	laquo	«	left-pointing double angle quotation mark = left pointing guillemet

Contd....

172	not	¬	not sign
173	shy		soft hyphen = discretionary hyphen
174	reg	®	registered sign = registered trade mark sign
175	macr	¯	macron = spacing macron = overline = APL overbar
176	deg	°	degree sign
177	plusmn	±	plus-minus sign = plus-or-minus sign
178	sup2	²	superscript two = superscript digit two = squared
179	sup3	³	superscript three = superscript digit three = cubed
180	acute	´	acute accent = spacing acute
181	micro	µ	micro sign
182	para	¶	pilcrow sign = paragraph sign
183	middot	·	middle dot = Georgian comma = Greek middle dot
184	cedil	¸	cedilla = spacing cedilla
185	sup1	¹	superscript one = superscript digit one
186	ordm	º	masculine ordinal indicator
187	raquo	»	right-pointing double angle quotation mark = right pointing guillemet
188	frac14	¼	vulgar fraction one quarter = fraction one quarter
189	frac12	½	vulgar fraction one half = fraction one half
190	frac34	¾	vulgar fraction three quarters = fraction three quarters
191	iquest	¿	inverted question mark = turned question mark
192	Agrave	À	latin capital letter A with grave = latin capital letter A grave
193	Aacute	Á	latin capital letter A with acute
194	Acirc	Â	latin capital letter A with circumflex
195	Atilde	Ã	latin capital letter A with tilde
196	Auml	Ä	latin capital letter A with diaeresis
197	Aring	Å	latin capital letter A with ring above = latin capital letter A ring
198	AElig	Æ	latin capital letter AE = latin capital ligature AE
199	Ccedil	Ç	latin capital letter C with cedilla
200	Egrave	È	latin capital letter E with grave
201	Eacute	É	latin capital letter E with acute
202	Ecirc	Ê	latin capital letter E with circumflex

Contd....

203	Euml	Ë	latin capital letter E with diaeresis
204	Igrave	Ì	latin capital letter I with grave
205	Iacute	Í	latin capital letter I with acute
206	Icirc	Î	latin capital letter I with circumflex
207	Iuml	Ï	latin capital letter I with diaeresis
208	ETH	Ð	latin capital letter ETH
209	Ntilde	Ñ	latin capital letter N with tilde
210	Ograve	Ò	latin capital letter O with grave
211	Oacute	Ó	latin capital letter O with acute
212	Ocirc	Ô	latin capital letter O with circumflex
213	Otilde	Õ	latin capital letter O with tilde
214	Ouml	Ö	latin capital letter O with diaeresis
215	times	×	multiplication sign
216	Oslash	Ø	latin capital letter O with stroke = latin capital letter O slash
217	Ugrave	Ù	latin capital letter U with grave
218	Uacute	Ú	latin capital letter U with acute
219	Ucirc	Û	latin capital letter U with circumflex
220	Uuml	Ü	latin capital letter U with diaeresis
221	Yacute	Ý	latin capital letter Y with acute
222	THORN	Þ	latin capital letter THORN
223	szlig	ß	latin small letter sharp s = ess-zed
224	agrave	à	latin small letter a with grave = latin small letter a grave
225	aacute	á	latin small letter a with acute
226	acirc	â	latin small letter a with circumflex
227	atilde	ã	latin small letter a with tilde
228	auml	ä	latin small letter a with diaeresis
229	aring	å	latin small letter a with ring above = latin small letter a ring
230	aelig	æ	latin small letter ae = latin small ligature ae
231	ccedil	ç	latin small letter c with cedilla
232	egrave	è	latin small letter e with grave
233	Eacute	é	latin small letter e with acute

Contd....

234	ecirc	ê	latin small letter e with circumflex
235	euml	ë	latin small letter e with diaeresis
236	igrave	ì	latin small letter i with grave
237	iacute	í	latin small letter i with acute
238	icirc	î	latin small letter i with circumflex
239	iuml	ï	latin small letter i with diaeresis
240	eth	ð	latin small letter eth
241	ntilde	ñ	latin small letter n with tilde
242	ograve	ò	latin small letter o with grave
243	oacute	ó	latin small letter o with acute
244	ocirc	ô	latin small letter o with circumflex
245	otilde	õ	latin small letter o with tilde
246	ouml	ö	latin small letter o with diaeresis
247	divide	÷	division sign
248	oslash	ø	latin small letter o with stroke, = latin small letter o slash
249	ugrave	ù	latin small letter u with grave
250	uacute	ú	latin small letter u with acute
251	ucirc	û	latin small letter u with circumflex
252	uuml	ü	latin small letter u with diaeresis
253	yacute	ý	latin small letter y with acute
254	thorn	þ	latin small letter thorn with
255	yuml	ÿ	latin small letter y with diaeresis
338	OElig	Œ	latin capital ligature OE
339	oelig	œ	latin small ligature oe ligature is a misnomer, this is a separate character in some languages
352	scaron	Š	latin capital letter S with caron
353	scaron	š	latin small letter s with caron
376	Yuml	Ÿ	latin capital letter Y with diaeresis
402	fnof	ƒ	latin small f with hook = function = florin
710	circ	ˆ	modifier letter circumflex accent
732	tilde	˜	small tilde

Contd....

913	Alpha	Α	greek capital letter alpha
914	Beta	Β	greek capital letter beta
915	Gamma	Γ	greek capital letter gamma
916	Delta	Δ	greek capital letter delta
917	Epsilon	Ε	greek capital letter epsilon
918	Zeta	Ζ	greek capital letter zeta
919	Eta	Η	greek capital letter eta
920	Theta	Θ	greek capital letter theta
921	Iota	Ι	greek capital letter iota
922	Kappa	Κ	greek capital letter kappa
923	Lambda	Λ	greek capital letter lambda
924	Mu	Μ	greek capital letter mu
925	Nu	Ν	greek capital letter nu
926	Xi	Ξ	greek capital letter xi
927	Omicron	Ο	greek capital letter omicron
928	Pi	Π	greek capital letter pi
929	Rho	Ρ	greek capital letter rho there is no Sigmaf, and no U+03A2 character either
931	Sigma	Σ	greek capital letter sigma
932	Tau	Τ	greek capital letter tau
933	Upsilon	Υ	greek capital letter upsilon
934	Phi	Φ	greek capital letter phi
935	Chi	Χ	greek capital letter chi
936	Psi	Ψ	greek capital letter psi
937	Omega	Ω	greek capital letter omega
945	alpha	α	greek small letter alpha
946	beta	β	greek small letter beta
947	gamma	γ	greek small letter gamma
948	delta	δ	greek small letter delta
949	epsilon	ε	greek small letter epsilon
950	zeta	ζ	greek small letter zeta

Contd....

951	eta	η	greek small letter eta
952	theta	θ	greek small letter theta
953	iota	ι	greek small letter iota
954	kappa	κ	greek small letter kappa
955	lambda	λ	greek small letter lambda
956	mu	μ	greek small letter mu
957	nu	ν	greek small letter nu
958	xi	ξ	greek small letter xi
959	omicron	ο	greek small letter omicron
960	pi	π	greek small letter pi
961	rho	ρ	greek small letter rho
962	sigmaf	ς	greek small letter final sigma
963	sigma	σ	greek small letter sigma
964	tau	τ	greek small letter tau
965	upsilon	υ	greek small letter upsilon
966	phi	φ	greek small letter phi
967	chi	χ	greek small letter chi
968	psi	ψ	greek small letter psi
969	omega	Ω	greek small letter omega
977	thetasym	Θ	greek small letter theta symbol
978	upsih	□	greek upsilon with hook symbol
982	piv	Π	greek pi symbol
8194	ensp		en space
8195	emsp		em space
8201	thinsp		thin space
8204	zwnj	□	zero width non-joiner
8205	zwj	□	zero width joiner
8206	lrm	‎	left-to-right mark
8207	rlm	‏	right-to-left mark
8211	ndash	–	en dash
8212	mdash	—	em dash

Contd....

8216	lsquo	‘	left single quotation mark
8217	rsquo	’	right single quotation mark
8218	sbquo	‚	single low-9 quotation mark
8220	ldquo	“	left double quotation mark
8221	rdquo	“	right double quotation mark
8222	bdquo	„	double low-9 quotation mark
8224	dagger	†	Dagger
8225	Dagger	‡	double dagger
8226	bull	•	bullet = black small circle bullet is NOT the same as bullet operator
8230	hellip	…	horizontal ellipsis = three dot leader
8240	permil	‰	per mille sign
8242	prime	‘	prime = minutes = feet
8243	Prime	”	double prime = seconds = inches
8249	lsaquo	‹	single left-pointing angle quotation mark lsaquo is proposed but not yet ISO standardized
8250	rsaquo	›	single right-pointing angle quotation mark rsaquo is proposed but not yet ISO standardized
8254	oline	?	overline = spacing overscore
8260	frasl	/	fraction slash
8364	euro	•	euro sign
8465	image		blackletter capital I = imaginary part
8472	weierp		script capital P = power set = Weierstrass p
8476	real		blackletter capital R = real part symbol
8482	trade	™	trade mark sign
8501	alefsym		alef symbol = first transfinite cardinal alef symbol is NOT the same as hebrew letter alef, U+05D0 although the same glyph could be used to depict both characters
8592	larr	←	leftwards arrow
8593	uarr	↑	upwards arrow
8594	rarr	→	rightwards arrow
8595	darr	↓	downwards arrow
8596	harr	↔	left right arrow
8629	crarr		downwards arrow with corner leftwardsc = carriage return

Contd....

8656	lArr	⇐	leftwards double arrow Unicode does not say that lArr is the same as the 'is implied by' arrow but also does not have any other character for that function. So? lArr can be used for 'is implied by'
8657	uArr	⇑	upwards double arrow
8658	rArr	⇒	rightwards double arrow Unicode does not say this is the 'implies' character but does not have another character with this function so ? rArr can be used for 'implies' as ISOtech suggests
8659	dArr	⇓	downwards double arrow
8660	hArr	⇔	left right double arrow
8704	forall	∀	for all
8706	part	∂	partial differential
8707	exist	∃	there exists
8709	empty	•	empty set = null set = diameter
8711	nabla	∇	nabla = backward difference
8712	isin	∈	element of
8713	notin	•	not an element of
8715	ni	∍	contains as member
8719	prod	Π	n-ary product = product sign prod is NOT the same character as U+03A0 'greek capital letter pi' though the same glyph might be used for both
8721	sum	Σ	n-ary summation sum is NOT the same character as U+03A3 'greek capital letter sigma' though the same glyph might be used for both
8722	minus	–	minus sign
8727	lowast		asterisk operator
8730	radic	√	square root = radical sign
8733	prop	∝	proportional to
8734	infin	∞	Infinity
8736	ang	∠	Angle
8743	and	∧	logical and = wedge
8744	or	∨	logical or = vee
8745	cap	∩	intersection = cap
8746	cup	•	union = cup
8747	int	∫	Integral
8756	there4	∴	Therefore

Contd....

8764	sim	~	tilde operator = varies with = similar to tilde operator is NOT the same character as the tilde, U+007E, although the same glyph might be used to represent both
8773	cong	•	approximately equal to
8776	asymp	≈	almost equal to = asymptotic to
8800	ne	≠	not equal to
8801	equiv	≡	identical to
8804	le	≤	less-than or equal to
8805	ge	≥	greater-than or equal to
8834	sub	⊂	subset of
8835	sup	⊃	superset of note that nsup, 'not a superset of, U + 2283' is not covered by the Symbol font encoding and is not included. Should it be, for symmetry? It is in ISOamsn
8836	nsub	•	not a subset of
8838	sube	⊆	subset of or equal to
8839	supe	⊇	superset of or equal to
8853	oplus	⊕	circled plus = direct sum
8855	otimes	•	circled times = vector product
8869	perp	⊥	up tack = orthogonal to = perpendicular
8901	sdot	•	dot operator dot operator is NOT the same character as U+00B7 middle dot
8968	lceil	•	left ceiling = apl upstile
8969	rceil	•	right ceiling
8970	lfloor	•	left floor = apl downstile
8971	rfloor	•	right floor
9001	lang	•	left-pointing angle bracket = bra lang is NOT the same character as U+003C 'less than' or U+2039 'single left-pointing angle quotation mark'
9002	rang	•	right-pointing angle bracket = ket rang is NOT the same character as U+003E 'greater than' or U+203A 'single right-pointing angle quotation mark'
9674	loz	◊	Lozenge
9824	spades	♠	Black spade suit black here seems to mean filled as opposed to hollow
9827	clubs	♣	black club suit = shamrock
9829	hearts	♥	black heart suit = valentine
9830	diams	♦	black diamond suit

EXERCISE

Objective Type Questions

1. How many hex values does a hex triplet consist of?

   (A) Three hex values

   (B) Six hex values

   (C) Twelve hex values

2. How many characters does a hex triplet consist of?

   (A) Three characters

   (B) Six characters

   (C) Twelve characters

3. What color is represented by #AAAAFF?

   (A) Dark blue

   (B) Bright red

   (C) Light blue

4. What are two examples of tags that can incorporate hex triplets?

   (A) The <BODY> and <HEAD> tags

   (B) The <HEAD> and <FONT> tags

   (C) The <FONT> and <BODY> tags

5. Which hex triplet represents the color black?

   (A) The #FFFFFF hex triplet

   (B) The #AAAAAA hex triplet

   (C) The #000000 hex triplet

Review & Discussion Questions

1. How Special characters are represented in HTML?
2. What are the importance of &, # and ;(semi colon) in Character formatting? Explain with suitable example.
3. List out the different special characters that are available in HTML.
4. How will you represent < and > in HTML using special character symbol?
5. How will you represent ©, ®, @, ^, $, % and # symbols in HTML using special character symbol?
6. How can you represent various countries currency symbols using special character symbol?
7. What is the significance of using &copy and &reg in HTML?
8. How will you represent pi, sigma, alpha, beta, delta, gama and epsilon using Phonetic reference?

CHAPTER 9

Target Links

CHAPTER OBJECTIVES

In this chapter, we will introduce you to target links (sometimes referred to as inter/intra document links) that help you determine if they are appropriate for your web documents. This chapter covers the various methods of providing navigation for visitors to a web site. Starting with general navigation tips, the chapter goes on to discuss the two main types of navigation, text-based navigation and graphics-based navigation including tips. When adding links to files other than HTML files, some alternative links and special requirements that may necessary for sites such as FTP, Gopher and newsgroups. It also explains you some alternative links and special requirements to adding links to files other than HTML files.

CHAPTER OUTLINES

9.1 INTRODUCTION

The purposes of this guide are to:

- Introduce you to target links (sometimes referred to as inter/intra document links)
- Help you determine, if they are appropriate for your web documents
- Provide you with the codes necessary for creating links, including tips
- Absolute and Relative Links
- Image Links
- Linking Word Documents, .pdf files
- Mailtos

9.2 ANCHOR ELEMENT

An anchor is a piece of text or some other object (for example an image), which marks the beginning and/or the end of a hypertext link. The <A> element is used to mark that piece of text (or inline image), and to give its hyper textual relationship to other documents. The text between the opening and closing tags, <A attributes> ...text... </A> can be the start or destination (or both) of a link.

Here are some simple examples:

Attributes		Description
NAME	:	**"string"** a name for a link end. It must be unique within the document; case sensitive.
HREF	:	**"URL"** network address for the linked resource. It could be another HTML document, a PDF file, an image, Gopher, Ftp, Telnet, E-mail etc.
REL	:	**"string"** the forward relationship also known as the "link type". In principle, could be used by browsers and other software in several ways, e.g. to determine to how to deal with the linked resource when printing out a collection of linked resources.
REV	:	**"string"** the reverse relationship. A link from document *A* to document *B* with REV="*relation*" expresses the same relationship as a link from *B* to *A* with REL= "*relation*".
TITLE	:	**"string"** a title for the linked resource.

The value of a TITLE attribute might be used e.g.

- For display prior to accessing the destination resource, e.g., as margin note or on a small box, while the mouse is over the anchor or the document is being loaded; thus, the attribute can be used as a hint about the nature of the link.
- As a window title for such resources that do not include a title, such as graphics or plain text.
- As the subject of an e-mail message when the element refers to a mailto: URL.

9.3 ABSOLUTE AND RELATIVE LINKS

There are two types of paths in HTML, known as relative paths and absolute paths. An absolute path contains the full URL of the item being referenced. A relative path contains directions to the item relative to the HTML page.

Absolute paths are essential when linking outside of your site because your browser can't locate a file on the Web unless it knows the site's exact location. When you click on an absolute path to a web page on the Internet, you have to have a live Internet connection to reach that site. This can be a problem if you want to test your own pages on your computer before making them live. For this reason, when you're linking to another page within your own site, it can be helpful to set up your links using relative paths instead of absolute paths.

Example: You are creating a page that will be uploaded to: http://bpkm.org.in/example/ and the page are named index.htm, so that page's URL will be http://bpkm.org.in/example/index.htm. In the example below, you'll see the specifics of that URL:

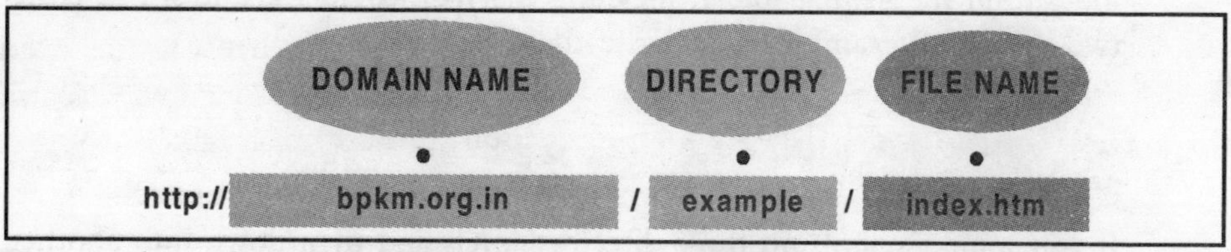

You can have directories within directories as well. In the example shown below, there is a subdirectory of the example directory. The subdirectory is named java.

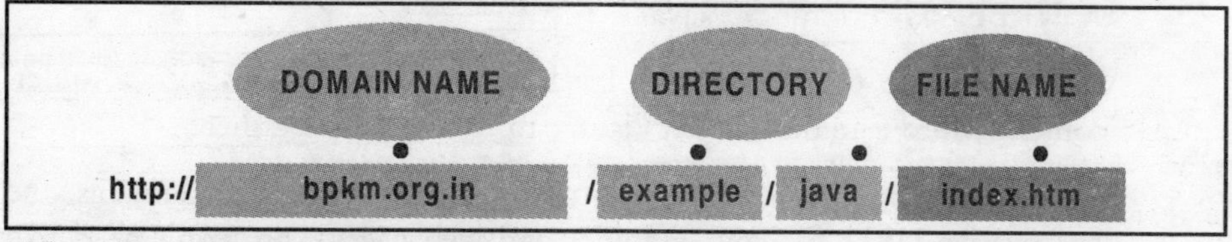

Note: Domain names are not case sensitive, but directories and filenames are!

You'll have an easier time understanding this if you've dealt with DOS or UNIX where files are not kept in icon-assigned folders, but instead you have to navigate the tree structure of your directories.

Relative paths tell your browser the location of other Web pages within your site's folder structure "relative" to the page you happen to be viewing, using a shorthand of "../" to indicate movement one level up in the folder hierarchy. To move two levels up, just double the shorthand by using "../../".

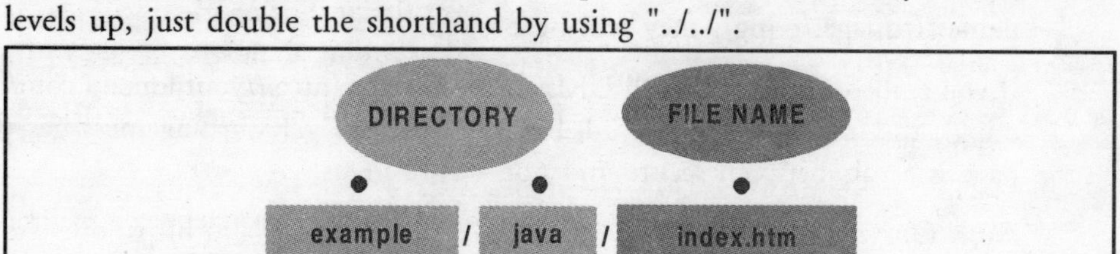

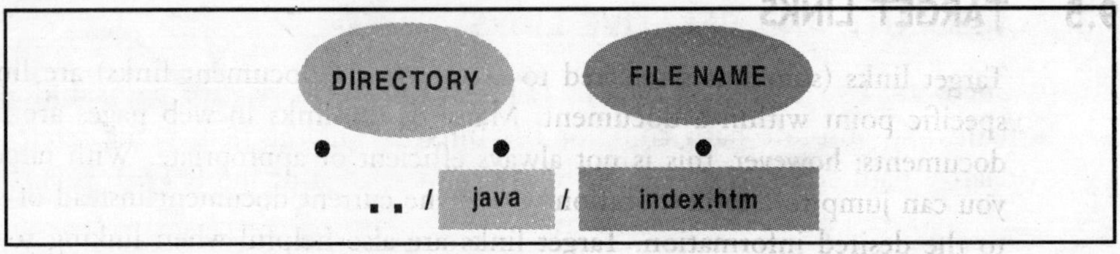

Here are some more examples:

<A HREF="../index.html">

This link would take you to the index page one-folder level above the page, where the link appears.

<A HREF="../../index.html">

This link would take you to the index page two levels above the page, where the link appears.

Note: when you end your URL in a "/" the browser will look for and load the index.html file in that folder, meaning that you could leave it out of either of the two preceding examples, and write them like this:

<A HREF="../">

<A HREF="../../">

If you want to climb up three directory levels and then down into another branch of the filesystem tree, just append the new path like this:

<A HREF="../../../content/java/">

Would take you to a folder two levels up and then downs into a folder named "content", into a folder named "java", to the index page there.

Relative URLs are preferred for your own pages. If you change domains, and you've used relative URLs for your graphics and web pages, you won't need to edit the links if you do change domains. If your web site grows and grows (as ours did!), you might need to change hundreds of links if you ever move your web site.

9.4 PROBLEMS USING ABSOLUTE PATHS WITH SSL

If you are borrowing use of an SSL certificate, such as the one provided free of charge to Internet Connection customers, when a webpage changes from http protocol to https (SSL), if you embed any images by absolute paths without domain names (/images/o.jpg), they will be broken.

If you embed images with full URL absolute paths (http://yourdomain.com/images/o.jpg), the images will show up, but the user will get warning messages that the page is a mix between secure and non-secure items.

Note: On web pages that make transitions between http and https, one should use relative paths to avoid these problems.

9.5 TARGET LINKS

Target links (sometimes referred to as inter/intra document links) are links to a specific point within a document. Many of the links in web pages are to other documents; however, this is not always efficient or appropriate. With target links, you can jump to another location within the current document instead of scrolling to the desired information. Target links are also helpful when linking to specific sections of other documents. Instead of linking just to the page, you can link directly to the relevant section.

<A HREF=" " TARGET="___self">	i.e. same window
<A HREF=" " TARGET="___blank">	i.e. new window
<A HREF=" " TARGET="___parent">	i.e. parent window
<A HREF=" " TARGET="___top">	i.e. whole window

Target links are very appropriate for some documents but not as appropriate for others. The following list covers some considerations for determining if you are going to use targets links or divide the document into separate documents. Your collective answers will help you determine which approach is best for you.

9.5.1 Printing

If the users want to print the document, should they be able to print out just a portion?

Yes: the document should be divided into separate files.
No: the document should be kept in one file with target links to aid navigation.

9.5.2 Number of Subtopics

Does the document contain only one topic with no subtopics?

Yes: the document should remain as one file, probably without target links.
No: if the document has subtopics, target links will help the user identify the subtopics quickly (rather than scrolling) and move to the topics, which are important.

9.5.3 Length

How many screens (or printed pages) does the document contain?

Short (1-2 screens): the document probably does not need target links, should remain as a single document.

Medium (3-6 screens): the document could be kept as one document; target links would be appropriate if there are several subtopics.

Long (more than 6 screens): the document should be divided into separate files or kept in one file with target links to aid navigation.

9.6 TARGET LINK CODE

When writing target links, you first need to identify the section of the document using the <A NAME> command. The links will reference the name by using the pound (#) symbol in the URL.

The following list has the code and examples for naming a section within a document and linking to a specific section.

9.6.1 Naming a Section

The code for the section name is added at the beginning of the section. For example, the code-naming this section (Target Link Codes) is immediately before the section heading.

Code: <A NAME="section_name">

Example

```
<A NAME="intro">
```

9.6.2 Linking to a Section in the Current Document

As with links to other documents, the links to a section surround the "cue" for the reader. This location of the cue is influenced by the content and organization of your document.

Code: <A HREF="#section_name">linking text</A>

Example

```
<A HREF="#Intro">Introduction</A>
```

9.6.3 Linking to a Section in Another Document

When linking to a section in another document you need to include the URL and the name of the section. To avoid confusion, you may want to indicate that the user is going to a section within another document.

Code: <A HREF="URL#section_name">linking text</A>

Example

```
<A HREF="http://bpkm.org.in/resources.html#copyright">Copyright</A>
```

9.6.4 Tips for Working with Target Links

- Provide a link back to the top of the document or to the listing of links (you will need to assign a section name to this area)

- To make maintenance easier, assign meaningful names to your sections.
- If links to other sites are intermingled with target links, you may want to alert the reader.
- Use the comment code to create a summary section of your section names.

9.7 IMPORTANCE OF REL & REV ATTRIBUTES IN CURRENT TREND

At present REL and REV are rarely used. However, they will be of growing importance as HTML documents, and the document development environments, become more sophisticated. The REL attribute is used to give the relationship(s) described by the hypertext link, and describes the relationship of the destination of the link to the document containing the hypertext anchor. Consequently, REL cannot be used unless an HREF is present. The value for REL is a space-separated list of relationship values.

Example

```
<A HREF="http://bpkm.org.in/show.htm" REL="index">show</A>
```

This indicates that the link is to a document that is an index related to the current document (the one you are reading). REV is the converse of REL, thus, an anchor of the form.

Example

```
<A HREF="http://bpkm.org.in/show.htm" REV="index">show</A>
```

This indicates that the document containing this anchor element is an index related to the document show.htm.

9.8 BASICS OF WEB PUBLISHING: LINKING ALTERNATIVES

When you are preparing links for your Web sites (HTML files), be aware that you can link to the Internet sites such as FTP, Gopher, and newsgroups as well as to non-Internet documents that you create, such as PDF and Word documents.

Special Considerations

When adding links to files other than HTML files, it is important to keep in mind the requirements for opening the links. The following table provides a summary of some types of alternative links and special requirements that may exist.

Type of Link		Requirements
Gopher	:	None
UseNet News	:	None
FTP	:	None
Telnet	:	Telnet program and setup
Email	:	Special setup in Netscape
Word	:	Microsoft Word and setup
Adobe Acrobat	:	Adobe Acrobat Reader and setup

9.8.1 Referencing the Link

To help reduce frustration for the user, we recommend that you alert the user of the type of link that you have provided, if it does not open another Web site. The examples below provide two ways that you can alert the user of an alternative link to a telnet site:

- Use the word telnet before the link Telnet to the Library of Gopal Vidyanagar
- Use an icon from SRIMCA Library of Gopal Vidyanagar (the icon for a telnet session)

9.8.2 Gopher

Gopher Link Examples

Shrmad Rajchandra Institute of Management & Computer Application (SRIMCA) Education Gopher

Code for Gopher Links

Sample for the Education Gopher

```
<A HREF="gopher://srimca.edu">Education Gopher</A>
```

9.8.3 UseNet News

UseNet News Link Example

SRIMCA Newsgroup

Code for UseNet News Links

Sample for the UseNet Newsgroup SRIMCA

```
<A HREF="news:srimca.update">SRIMCA Newsgroup</A>
```

9.8.4 FTP (File Transfer Protocol)

When developing FTP links, you want to provide the user with sufficient information about the file that will be downloaded. For example, if you are going to provide a link to download software that has special requirements or installation instructions, you may want to also include a link to the Web page that has that information.

FTP Link Example

SRIMCA FTP Anonymous Login

Code for FTP Links

Sample for the SRIMCA FTP Anonymous Login Site

```
<A HREF="ftp://ftp.srimca.edu">SRIMCA FTP Anonymous Login</A>
```

9.8.5 Telnet

For users to access a Telnet link they must have the software installed on their computer and their browser must be configured to open the software when the link is accessed.

As some telnet sites require a username for connecting or have special instructions for disconnecting, you may want to include some tips for working with the site.

For example, the SRIMCA library catalog requires users to press [Ctrl]+[D] twice to exit. The information is only displayed on one of the login screens.

Telnet Link Examples

Library of Congress

SRIMCA Library Catalog

At the library catalog login prompt, enter library. To exit the library catalog, press [Ctrl]+[D] two times.

Code for Telnet Links

Sample for the Library of Gopal Vidyanagar:

```
<A HREF="telnet://srimca.edu">Library of Gopal Vidyanagar</A>
```

9.8.6 Email Links for Mailto

Web users can contact you more efficiently via email with a mailto link, so you need to make a commitment to respond to the email messages frequently. To access mailto links, users must have email software installed on their computer and have their browser configured to open the software.

Since some users are unable to access mailto links, it is important to include the email address in your Web site (perhaps as the link itself).

Mailto Link Examples

Lal Bihari: lalbihari@bpkm.org.in

Code for Mailto Links

```
Lal Bihari: <A HREF="mailto:lalbihari@bpkm.org.in">lalbihari@bpkm.org.in</A>
```

9.9 WORD DOCUMENTS

For users to access a Word link they must have the right version of Word installed on their computer and their browser must be configured to open the software when the Word link is accessed.

Word Document Link Example

The SRIMCA Online Exam Help is available online as the Word document.

Code for Word Document Links

```
<A HREF="http://bpkm.org.in/document/onlineexam.doc"> Online Exam</A>
```

9.10 ADOBE ACROBAT FILES

For users to access an Adobe Acrobat link they must have the right version of Adobe Acrobat Reader installed on their computer and their browser must be configured to open the software when the Adobe Acrobat link is accessed.

Adobe Acrobat Link Example

This SRIMCA Online Exam was published by the SRIMCA using Adobe Acrobat.

Code for Adobe Acrobat File Links

```
<A HREF="http://bpkm.org.in/document/onlineexam.pdf">Online Exam</A>
```

9.11 AUDIO OR VIDEO FILES

For users to access audio and video links, they must have right version of media files. The most popular these days being the MP3, QuickTime, Real, and Windows Media files. You first place your media file into a subdirectory. As with images, this is a convention, which helps you keep all your various files organized.

```
<A HREF="media/audio-sample.mp3">Link to Audio Sample</A><br /><A
HREF="media/video-sample.avi">Link to Video Sample</A>
```

EXERCISE

Objective Type Questions

1. The tag used in HTML to link it with other URL's is:

   (A) <A> (B) <H>

   (C) <U> (D) <L>

2. Which one of the following is the correct way to code a hyperlink?

   (A) <a hyper:"PageTwo.html">This is a link to page two.</a>

   (B) <a href:"PageTwo.html">This is a link to page two.</a>

   (C) <a ref=PageTwo.html>This is a link to page two.</a>

   (D) <a href="PageTwo.html">This is a link to page two.</a>

3. Digitising audio requires

   (A) Sampling of audio (B) Video input

   (C) Text file (D) None of the above

4. Which of the following can not be compressed?

   (A) text data (B) video data

   (C) image data (D) audio data

   (E) none of the above -- they can all be compressed

5. Which of the link colors you are going to see the least often?

   (A) Visited links (B) Active Links

   (C) Normal Links (D) None of the above

6. What is the term used to describe how background images can display repeatedly on a Web page?

   (A) Cascading (B) Tiling

   (C) Centre (D) None of the above

7. To create a link to an anchor, you use the ______ property in <A> tag.

   (A) Name (B) Tag

   (C) Link (D) Href

8. Relative path make your hypertext links______.

   (A) Portable

   (B) Discrete

   (C) Uniform

9. A____ structure starts with a general topic that includes link to more specific topics.

   (A) Hierarchical

   (B) Linear

   (C) Mixed

10. Which of the following path is supported by HTML?

    (A) Relative

    (B) Defererenced

    (C) Absolute and Relative

11. What is a hot spot?

    (A) A visual representation of a link in a node

    (B) A network of nodes

    (C) A hyperlink that can be multi-directional

    (D) A record of nodes that a user has accessed

12. What is a leaf node?

    (A) No further links (B) A node with multi directional links

    (C) A node full of hot spots (D) None of the above

13. A word that looks underlined on a web page is usually.

    (A) an important word

    (B) the web address

    (C) a "link" to another web page

    (D) a mistake

14. ______is the text on clicking of which other web pages are opened.

    (A) Markup (B) Hypertext

    (C) Link (D) None of these

15. ______tag is used to link a web page.

    (A) <a> (B) <b>

    (C) <td> (D) <tr>

16. If you don't put any links on your page, you have

    (A) forced most visitors to use their browser's Back button to leave the page

    (B) created a dead end

(C) missed the opportunity to lead visitors to other parts of your Web site

(D) All of the above

(E) None of the above

17. Which browser does not support the fonts on page?

(A) Lynx (B) Internet Explorer 3.0

(C) Netscape Navigator 4.0 (D) AOL

18. What are the two main types of links?

(A) Graphical and anchor

(B) Anchor and text

(C) Graphical and text

19. When using a graphical link, what is added to remove the border?

(A) The NOBORDER flag

(B) The IMGBORDER=0 attribute

(C) The BORDER=0 attribute

20. Why is an anchor used?

(A) To link to a specific page

(B) To link to a specific area on a page

(C) To display an image as a link

21. What tag is used to insert a link?

(A) The <ANCHOR> tag

(B) The <LINK> tag

(C) The <A> tag

22. Which piece of code is correct?

(A) <A LINK="Page.html">

(B) <A LINK="Page">

(C) <A HREF="Page.html">

23. How can you open a link in a new browser window?

(A) <a href="url" new>

(B) <a href="url" target="new">

(C) <a href="url" target="_blank">

(D) <a href="url" targer="_new">

Review & Discussion Questions

1. Explain the meaning of anchor tags.
2. What do you mean b hyperlinks? How these are used in HTML? Give an example.
3. How you used a picture as a hyperlink in HTML, give with an example?
4. How to make an email link?
5. How to open a link in new browser window?
6. Which tag is used to create background sound?
7. Which tag is used to play background sound when page is loaded?
8. What is the purpose of creating hyperlink?
9. Explain anchor tag with example.
10. Explain <A> tag in HTML with all its essential attributes.
11. What is Hyperlink? How they are created?
12. Explain the steps to create Image as Hyperlink.
13. Explain different attributes of anchor tag.
14. Write the difference between internal link and external link.
15. What is the use of REL and REV attribute used in <A> tag? Explain the importance of TITLE attribute.
16. What do you mean by link? Explain relative link with example.
17. How link elements help to view current document and other document? Give suitable example.
18. How can you provide link for FTP, TELNET, GOPHER and EMAIL?
19. If you want to play audio and video files in web page, step down code for it.

CHAPTER 10

Working with List and Links

CHAPTER OBJECTIVES

There are times when you want to list items in your document. This chapter provides you several ways to display a list of items. They can be divided into two types: Glossary lists and Regular lists. You will able to know more about glossary lists element <DL> as well as regular lists elements <UL>, <OL>, <MENU> and <DIR> in brief. The appropriate use of active examples illustrates the alignment of the text without using the list option and with the list option.

CHAPTER OUTLINES

10.1 INTRODUCTION

Lists are a great way for displaying information in a clear and organized fashion on the Web. The most common HTML lists are: Glossary lists (definition lists) and Regular lists (ordered lists, unordered lists). There are a few things that you should know before using lists:

1. Lists can be nested. That is, you can have a list inside of a list.
2. Lists can contain many paragraphs, separated by the <P> tag.
3. Lists create their own blank lines before and after their location. Therefore, you do not have put insert you own blank lines.
4. Individual list elements do not need an end tag.

The ordered list displays the information in the list in a numerical fashion. The unordered list follows the same syntax as the ordered list. The only difference in the two is that the unordered list uses bullets instead of numbers to mark each list item. The tag for an unordered lists is <UL> and the end tag is </UL>. Definition lists are a slightly different from the ordered and unordered lists. They have three tags, one to start the list, one to identify the definition term and one to identify the definition (<DL>, <DT>, <DD>).

Similarly, the real power of the internet is found in its ability to link between pages, like a gigantic spider's web. A web page without links doesn't make a whole lot of sense, so we will briefly look at how to insert links in our page. Links can take us to another page or even another section inside of the same page.

10.2 LIST ELEMENTS

Lists are helpful for organizing information to increase the readability and add white space to your page. HTML provides codes for unordered lists with bullets, ordered lists with numbers (1,2,3), and definition lists for multi-line entries, such as a glossary. If you want, you can embed more than one list.

Lists have three components:

1. The code to mark the beginning of the list
2. The code for each item in the list (adding the bullet or the number)
3. The code marking the end of the list

In addition to having bullets or numbers before the list, the list options automatically align the text of multi-line items to help increase readability. The following examples illustrate the alignment of the text without using the list option and with the list option.

HTML supports several elements for making lists. They can be divided into two types:

1. Glossary Lists
2. Regular Lists

10.2.1 Glossary Lists

Glossary Lists are denoted by the element <DL>, while regular lists are denoted by the elements <UL>, <OL>, <MENU> and <DIR>. Lists can be nested. Thus, you can have a regular list within a regular list, a regular list within a glossary list, and so on. Some examples are shown below.

<DL> Element (Glossary Lists)

This list type, also known as a definition list, is used to present a list of items along with descriptive paragraphs. This can be used for glossaries, but is also useful for presenting a named list of items and their meanings. The items within the list are introduced by the two elements

1. <DT> -- The "Term" (a single line)
2. <DD> -- The "Definition" (may be multiple lines)

Attributes		Description
COMPACT		**COMPACT** attribute instructs the browser to reduce the space occupied by the list. Several browsers ignore this attribute.

Note: Although <DL> is basically for definitions, it is often used for descriptions as well. The definition list is like a lookup or glossary.

Example

```
<DL>
<DT>Term one</DT>
<DD>Definition of term one</DD>
<DT>Term two</DT>
<DD>Definition of term two</DD>
<DT>Term three</DT>
<DD>Definition of term three</DD>
</DL>
```

.....is rendered similar to.....

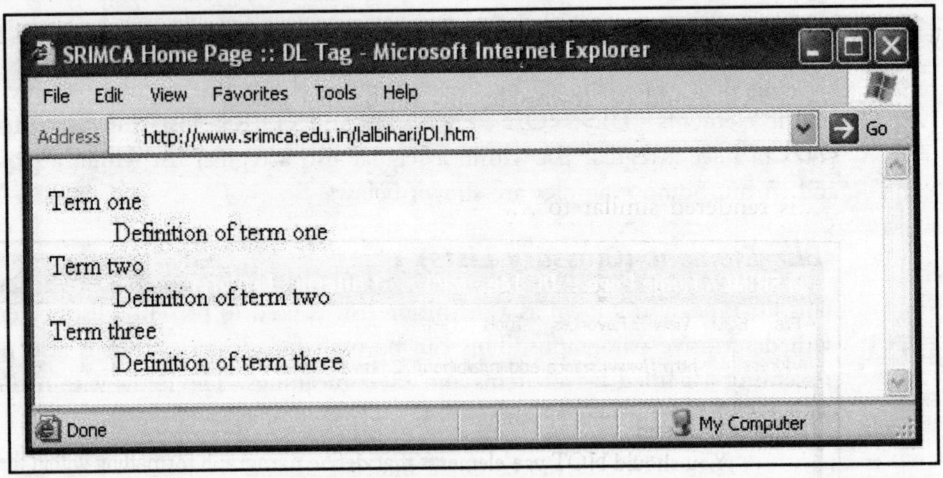

Here is an example from the paragraphs section of this manual (with a small addition to show a nested regular list).

Example

```
<DL>
<DT> Things to Avoid:
    <DD> You should NOT use elements that define paragraph
    formatting within the PRE element. This means you should
    not use <CODE> &lt;P>, &lt;ADDRESS>, &lt;Hn>
    </CODE>and so
    on. You should avoid the use of tab characters — use single
    blank characters to space text apart.
<DT> Things That are OK:
    <DD>You <EM> can </EM> use Anchor.  A typed
    carriage return will cause a new line in the presented text.
    People you should never let format lists include:
    <UL>
    <LI> Bozo the Clown
    <LI> Uncle Fester
    <LI> Knights who go nii
```

Contd....

</UL>

Which would be downright silly in the first place?

</DL>

.....is rendered similar to.....

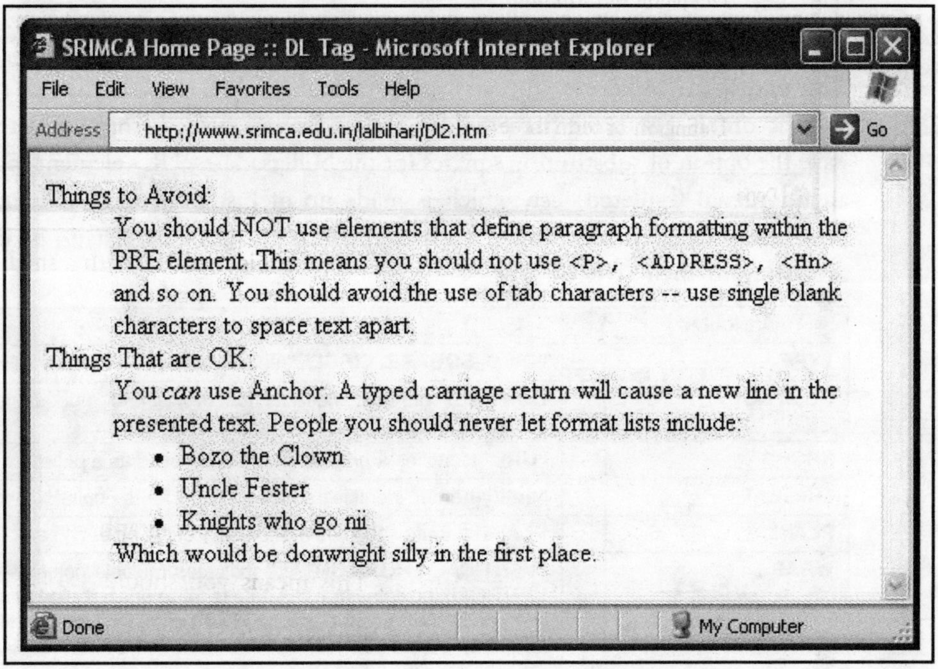

Note: Do not use multiple <DD> elements for the same <DT>, instead use <BR> elements within the <DD>.

10.2.2 Regular Lists

A regular list is a sequence of paragraphs, each of which may be preceded by a special mark, sequence number, or nothing at all. The code is

<UL>

<LI> list element

<LI> another list element...

</UL>

Where the opening element defining the list type can be one of

<UL>: A list of multi-line paragraphs, listed separately and usually marked by a bullet or similar symbol (Unordered List)

<OL>: A list of multi-line paragraphs, listed separately and ordered numerically in some way (Ordered List)

<MENU>: An unordered list of smaller paragraphs, this is similar to UL, but is formatted (if possible) in a more compact manner.

<DIR>: A list of short elements, typically less than 20 characters in length. These may be arranged in columns across the page, as opposed to one above the other. This is browser dependent.

<UL> Element (Unordered List)

The unordered list is helpful for listing related information that doesn't have a specific order. The basic list provides bullets (round dots) before each item. You have the option of substituting squares for the bullets. The <UL> element introduces an unordered (bulleted) list, which is made up of List Item <LI> elements. The presentation is often indented in a manner, which causes nested lists to be indented according to their structure.

Attributes		Description
TYPE		**"DISC, SQUARE, CIRCLE"** specifies the *bullet type.*
COMPACT		**COMPACT** attribute instructs the browser to reduce the space occupied by the list.
SRC		**"URL"** identifies a *graphic image* to be used as a bullet.
DINGBAT		**"entity-name"** identifies an *iconic entity* for the bullet.
PLAIN		**PLAIN** attribute specifies *not to use* a bullet on each item.
WRAP		**"VERTICAL I HORIZONTAL"** indicates multiple columns of data. VERTICAL indicates that the data is to go down the page and then wrap to the next column, and HORIZONTAL indicates that the data is to wrap across each row.

The actual shape of the bullet is dependent on that of the user has selected for his/her browser. For example, Times Roman displays the standard bullets as a circle but Arial displays it as a square. Also, bullets do not always print properly.

Unordered lists are bulleted items.

Example

```
<UL>
<LI>Item 1</LI>
<LI>Item 2</LI>
<LI>Item 3</LI>
</UL>
```

.....is rendered similar to.....

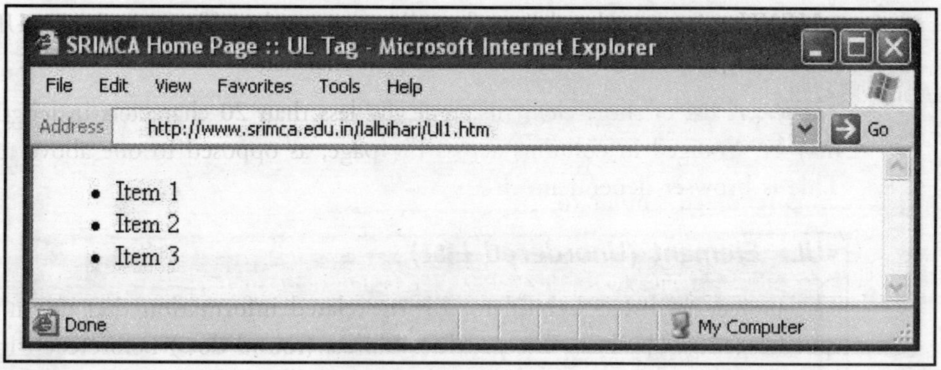

Lists can be nested, one inside another.

Example

```
<UL>
 <LI>Item 1
<UL>
 <LI>Sub-Item 1</LI>
 <LI>Sub-Item 2</LI>
 <LI>Sub-Item 3</LI>
</UL>
 </LI>
 <LI>Item 2
<UL>
 <LI>Sub-Item 4
<UL>
 <LI>Sub-Item 7</LI>
 <LI>Sub-Item 8</LI>
</UL>
 </LI>
 <LI>Sub-Item 5</LI>
 <LI>Sub-Item 6</LI>
```

Contd....

```
</UL>
 </LI>
</UL>
```

.....is rendered similar to.....

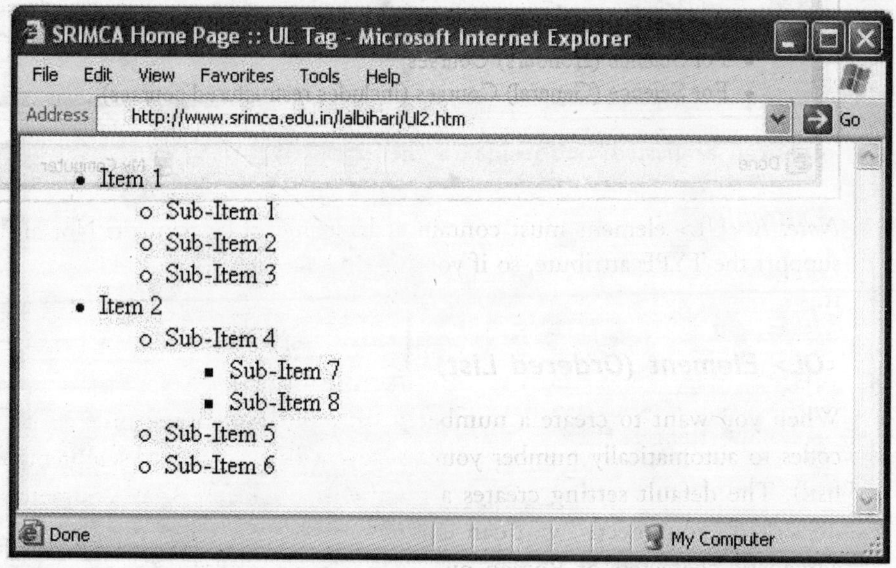

Note: Sub-lists are enclosed in a line item tag set (<LI></LI>) after a line item text section, not directly in the unordered list tag set (<UL></UL>). The unordered list can contain only line item elements, whereas line item elements can contain both inline and general block level elements.

Example

```
   Cut-off marks (Year 2004-2005)
<UL TYPE="DISC">
   <LI> For Arts and Commerce Streams
   <LI> For Science (Honours) Courses
   <LI> For Science (General) Courses (Includes restructured courses)
</UL>
```

.....is rendered similar to.....

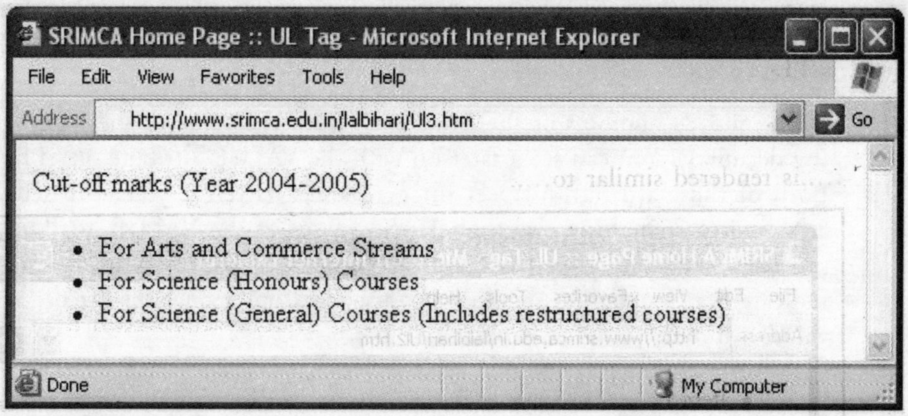

Note: A <UL> element must contain at least one <LI> element. Not all browsers support the TYPE attribute, so if you use it, make sure the list still "works" without it.

<OL> Element (Ordered List)

When you want to create a numbered list, you can use the ordered list HTML codes to automatically number your list (even if you add or delete items from the list!). The default setting creates a numbered list using Arabic numerals. If this doesn't fit your needs, you can explore the options of uppercase or lowercase alphabetic characters or Roman numerals. These codes are entered with the initial code <OL>.

Attributes		Description
TYPE		**"1 I a I A I i I I "** specifies the *numbering style*. The TYPE attribute governs the way items are numbered.
START		**"intger"** allows the first list item to be number instead of the default 1.
COMPACT		**"COMPACT"** attribute instructs the browser to reduce the space occupied by the list.
CONTINUE		**"CONTINUE"** attribute continues the numbering from the previous ordered list.
SEQNUM		**"number"** allows the first list item to be number instead of the default 1.

The meanings of the values of TYPE are the following:

Type	Numbering Style	The First Few Numbers
1	Normal (Arabic) numbers	1, 2, 3, ...
A	Latin letters in lowercase	a, b, c, ...
A	Latin letters in uppercase	A, B, C, ...
I	Roman numbers in lowercase	i, ii, iii, ...
I	Roman numbers in uppercase	I, II, III, ...

It is natural to use an ordered list if the order of the items should be emphasized, e.g., when they are instructions to be followed in that sequence, a description of events in their temporal order, or things in order of importance.

The sequence numbers of the items start from the value of the START attribute (by default 1). You can set it later on with the VALUE attribute on <LI> elements. Both of these attributes expect integer values. (Even if you have set the TYPE attribute to something else than 1, the values of the VALUE attribute must be specified using the normal notation of numbers as sequences of digits.) You can't indicate that numbering should be continued from a previous list or skip missing values without giving an explicit number.

Ordered lists are numbered items:

Example

```
<OL>
 <LI>Item 1</LI>
 <LI>Item 2</LI>
 <LI>Item 3</LI>
</OL>
```

.....is rendered similar to.....

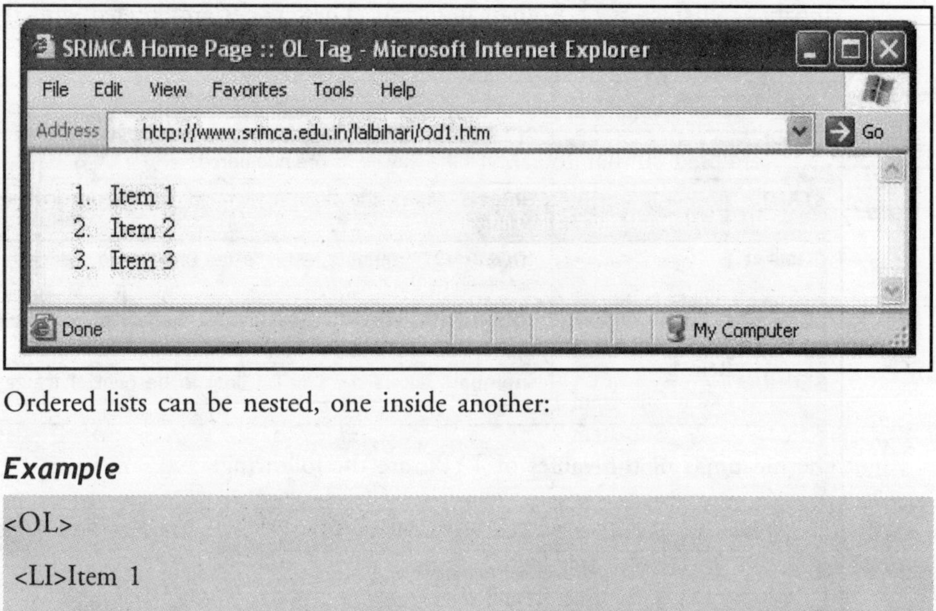

Ordered lists can be nested, one inside another:

Example

```
<OL>
 <LI>Item 1
<OL>
 <LI>Sub-Item 1</LI>
```

Contd....

```
  <LI>Sub-Item 2</LI>
  <LI>Sub-Item 3</LI>
</OL>
  </LI>
  <LI>Item 2
<OL>
  <LI>Sub-Item 4
<OL>
  <LI>Sub-Item 7</LI>
  <LI>Sub-Item 8</LI>
</OL>
  </LI>
  <LI>Sub-Item 5</LI>
  <LI>Sub-Item 6</LI>
</OL>
  </LI>
</OL>
```

.....is rendered similar to.....

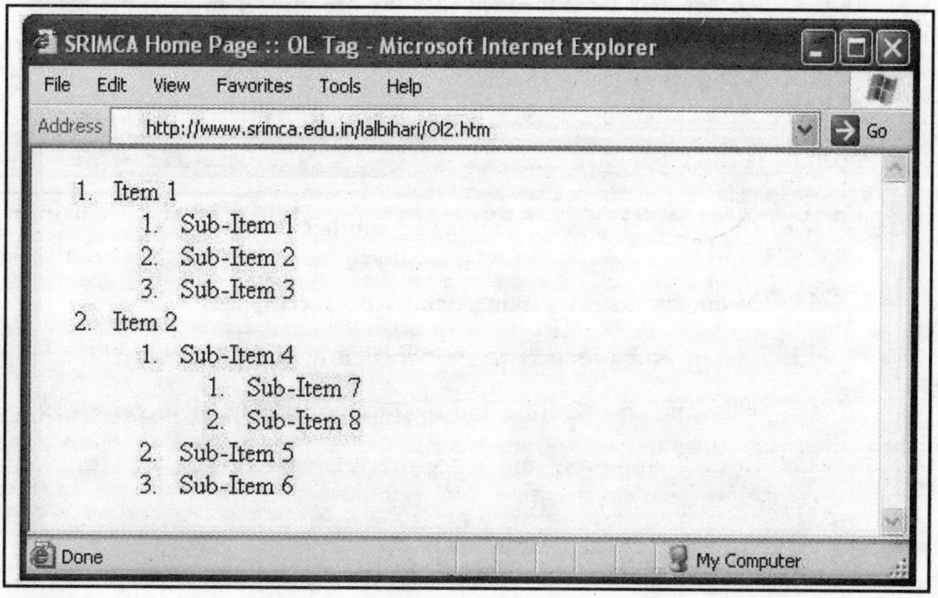

As with unordered lists, ordered sub-lists are enclosed in a line item tagset (<li></li>) after a line item text section.

Example

The <EM>Summer Institute for Linguistics (SIL)</EM> Ethnologue Survey (1999) lists the following as the top languages by population: (number of native speakers in parentheses)

```
<OL TYPE="1">
  <LI>Chinese* (937,132,000)</LI>
  <LI> Spanish (332,000,000)</LI>
  <LI> English (322,000,000)</LI>
  <LI> Bengali (189,000,000)</LI>
  <LI> Hindi/Urdu (182,000,000)</LI>
  <LI> Arabic* (174,950,000)</LI>
  <LI> Portuguese (170,000,000) </LI>
  <LI> Russian (170,000,000)</LI>
</OL>
```

<LH> Element (List Heading)

The list heading tag defines the heading for an ordered, unordered, or definition list. Other tags may be embedded in a list heading. It must come before any List Item <LI> or Definition Term <DT> elements in the list.

Example

```
<OL TYPE="1">
  <LH>This course strips down the operation of a small business to its essentials<LH>
  <LI> Producing quality products and services</LI>
  <LI> Pricing your products and services fairly and profitably</LI>
  <LI> Following an operating and organizational plan to success</LI>
  <LI> Treating employees and subcontractors well</LI>
</OL>
```

.....is rendered similar to.....

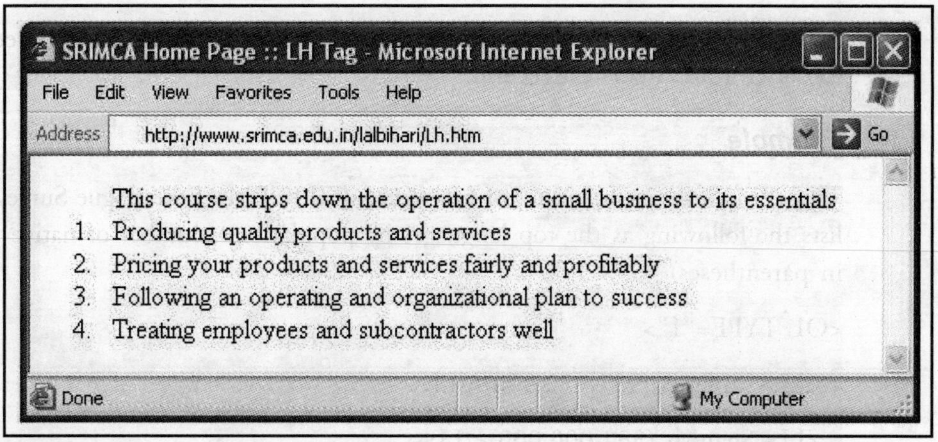

10.3 MENU LIST

The <MENU> element defines a menu list that contains one or more <LI> elements that define the actual items of the list. The <LI> elements must not contain block-level elements or inline elements such as tag like <ADDRESS>, <FORM>, <H1>, <DL> etc. which prevents MENU from being nested.

Example

```
<MENU>
    <LI>HTML</LI>
    <LI>CSS</LI>
</MENU>
...
<MENU>
    <LI>First item in the list.
    <LI>Second item in the list.
    <LI>Third item in the list.
</MENU>
```

Note: MENU is deprecated in HTML 4 in favor of <UL>.

10.4 DIR LIST

The <DIR> element was designed to be used for creating multicolumn directory lists. The <MENU> element was designed to be used for single column menu lists. Both elements have the same structure as <UL>, just different rendering. In practice, a user will render a <DIR> or <MENU> list exactly as a <UL> list.

Example

```
<DIR compact="compact">
Music
Cars
Computers
</DIR>
...
<DIR>
     <LI>A-H<LI>I-M
     <LI>M-R<LI>S-Z
     </DIR>
```

Note: We strongly recommend you to use <UL> instead of these elements.

Common attributes defined in <MENU> and <DIR> list.

Attributes		Description
ID	:	**"name_token"** (not widely supported) mark the paragraph for a possible reference via a URL.
CLASS	:	**"type"** indicates the class that the element belongs too.
LANG	:	**"ENIFR"** language information.
DIR	:	text direction
TITLE	:	element title
STYLE	:	inline style information

10.5 IMAGE MAP

Images can be included within a hypertext anchor. Thus, you can make an image that behaves as a button linked to other documents or resources. The <IMG> element is empty, meaning there is no closing </IMG>.

Attributes		Description
SRC	:	**"URL"** SRC give the URL of the image document. This attribute **must** be present. The naming scheme is the same as for hypertext links, thus relative URLs such as SRC="shrimad.gif" or SRC="../shrimad.gif" are commonly used. At present, you can only inline GIF images and X-bitmaps (standard extensions are .gif, .xbm, .xpm), although many (but not all) browsers also support inline JPEG (standard extensions .jpeg or .jpg) images as well.
ALT	:	**"alternative text"** Some browsers cannot display images, while users connecting via phone lines often turn off image loading. The ALT attribute lets you specify a text alternative to the image, for use in these circumstances. You should **always** include an ALT alternative, particularly if the image is a button linked to some other resource. If the image is unimportant, you can always put ALT="".

Contd....

ALIGN	:	**"TOP I MIDDLE I BOTTOM I LEFT I RIGHT"** tells the browser how to align the image with the neighboring text. "Bottom" aligns the bottom of the image with the baseline of the text, and is the default. "Middle" aligns the middle of the image with the baseline of text, and "top" aligns the top of the image with the top of the tallest item in the line. This attribute is **optional**.
HEIGHT / WIDTH	:	**"integer"** HEIGHT & WIDTH specify the display height and width (in pixels) for the image. If the picture does not fit, the browser should rescale the image to fit in the specified box. An example is HEIGHT="30" WIDTH="50". This is supported by most of the current browsers. Some also support percent values (a percentage of page size, or sometimes a percentage of available size inside a table cell), but you had better test percentage values, to make sure things work as expected.
ISMAP	:	**"ISMAP"** indicates that the image is a server-side image map. It marks the image as an active *image map*. This allows the user to click the mouse over the image and have different regions of the image cause different actions. Most browsers also support the ISMAP attribute.
BORDER	:	**"integer"** specifies line border width, in pixels. If ISMAP is used, then the image is a hypertext link, and will be surrounded by a border to indicate this. In particular, BORDER=0 specifies no border.
HSPACE / VSPACE	:	**"integer"** specifies the horizontal gutter (width of white space to the immediate left and right of the image) and vertical gutter (height of white space above and below the image) in pixels, to leave between the image and the surrounding elements.
LOWSRC	:	**"integer"** *(Netscape only)* specifies a low-resolution image file. Netscape browsers will first load the smaller, low-resolution file specified by LOWSRC and will then load the larger SRC-specified image file.
USEMAP	:	**"URL"** Specifies a URL pointing to a client side image map that is, a MAP element. For example, if the map element starts with <MAP NAME="sri">, then the map would be referenced as <IMG USEMAP="#sri"... >. Smaller, low-resolution file specified by LOWSRC and will then load the larger SRC-specified image file.

There are two ways of implementing clickable image maps in HTML documents.

10.5.1 Server Side Image Map

Requires specific support in a Web server, but such support exists in most servers. The client (browser) essentially just sends the coordinates of the clicked location to the server, which then must take care of the rest. To use a server side image map, you use an <A> element containing an <IMG> element with ISMAP attribute. The HREF attribute of the <A> element specifies the address of the server (typically a script named imagemap or htimage; consult the documentation of the server).

10.5.2 Client Side Image Map

Requires a client (browser), which supports <MAP> and <AREA> elements. (Newest versions of most popular browsers support them.) The HTML document uses these elements to specify the correspondence of areas of an image and associated documents (URLs). Usually some special program (image map editor) is used for the purpose.

Since client side image maps are faster and have other benefits as well but are not supported by all browsers, you may wish to combine server side and client side image maps in the following way.

Example

```
<A HREF="/cgi-bin/htimage/your.map">
<IMG SRC="image/your.gif" ... ISMAP USEMAP="#yourmap"></A>
```

That way new browsers will use the client side image map, whereas old browsers will ignore the USE MAP attribute and pass the request to the server.

Image maps can be very useful in association with geographical maps. (See, e.g. the "Virtual Tourist" map at http://www.vtourist.com/travel/.) They might conceivably be used in other contexts as well, for instance to allow the user select an item in a display of purchasable objects or a detail in a plan of a house or to request information about a part of a device described by a drawing. In general, an imagemap can be very useful for things, which are inherently visual in two or more dimensions. However, in actual practice most use of image maps is abuse.

10.5.3 Adding Width and Height Values

Specifying the height and width of your image is a good idea, since doing so can help increase the speed at which the image loads on the page. You should always include the correct width and height. If the width and height values are larger than the actual image, the browser will stretch the image to make it fit. If you note smaller values, the browser will squeeze the image into the smaller size, scrunching it up.

Example

```
<IMG SRC="photo.jpg" WIDTH="250" HEIGHT="188" />
```

10.5.4 Providing Alternative Text

Some people still don't have high-speed access, so images can slow down their access to your page's content, and they will disable the images. Another important concern is that many people visiting the Web are visually impaired or blind. In all these cases, it's helpful to provide some clues to your visitor as to what the image represents. (Image Source Code) To inserts an image from the designated URL. The ALT text gives an alternate description of the image, which is used by browsers who cannot display images, or when the displaying images has been disabled.

Example

```
<IMG SRC="photo.jpg" WIDTH="250" HEIGHT="188" ALT="photograph of
a delicious Vietnamese noodle dish from restaurant Pho 88" />
```

10.6 LINKING THE IMAGE

Many times, you will want to link an image to either another HTML document or a detailed version of the image. In either case, linking an image works the same way as linking text. You surround the image code with the anchor element and the reference to where the image is linking, just as if it were the text content.

Example

```
<A href="detail.html">
<IMG SRC="images/photo.jpg" WIDTH="250" HEIGHT="188" ALT=
"photograph of a delicious Vietnamese noodle dish from restaurant Pho 88" />
</A>
```

If the image link is followed, the browser will use the default visited link color around the image. Of course, many people find the link border unsightly. If you'd like to get rid of your border immediately, you can do so by turning it off directly in the HTML.

Example

```
<a href="detail.html">
<img src="images/photo.jpg" width="250" height="188" alt="photograph of a
delicious Vietnamese noodle dish from restaurant Pho 88" border="0" />
</a>
```

10.7 LINKING TO AN AUDIO OR VIDEO FILE

Embedding Files Using the object Element

Another means of providing audio, video, and other multimedia such as Flash animations and Java applets is to embed them directly into the page. This means that the software plug-in automatically loads with the page. All external files are considered objects. This includes images as well as multimedia files. In contemporary HTML and XHTML specifications, the proper way to include all multimedia is to use the object element to embed a file directly.

```
<OBJECT DATA="media/video-sample.avi" TYPE="video/avi" />
```

Of course, you can do a lot more in terms of providing advanced settings. In instances with Flash files, you use the object element to achieve inline results.

```
<OBJECT CLASSID="clsid:d27cdb6e-ae6d-11cf-96b8-444553540000" WIDTH="100" HEIGHT="100" CODEBASE="http://active.macromedia.com/flash6/cabs/ swflash.cab#version=6,0,0,0">
<PARAM NAME="movie" VALUE="media/ava.swf" />
<PARAM NAME="play" VALUE="true" />
<PARAM NAME="loop" VALUE="true" />
<PARAM NAME="quality" VALUE="high" />
</OBJECT>
```

More Relative URL Tips

Let's say that the page you are writing will be uploaded as:

```
http://bpkm.org.in/example/index.htm
```

and a graphic, in another folder, at the URL

```
http://bpkm.org.in/images/kishor.gif
```

The path from the HTML page to the graphic:

Absolute Path:

```
<IMG SRC="http://bpkm.org.in/images/kishor.gif">
```

Relative Path:

```
<IMG SRC="images/kishor.gif">
```

The relative path tells the browser to look in a directory named images for a file named kishor.gif. If the image was located at the URL:

```
http://bpkm.org.in/images/music/kishor.gif
```

The relative path would appear as:

```
<IMG SRC="images/music/kishor.gif">
```

Let's say that the page you are writing will be uploaded as:

```
http://bpkm.org.in/example/index.htm
```

And the graphic you want to link to is located at:

```
http://bpkm.org.in/amitab.gif
```

The path from the HTML page to the graphic would look like this:

Absolute Path:

```
<IMG SRC="http://bpkm.org.in/amitab.gif">
```

Relative Path:

```
<IMG SRC="../amitab.gif">
```

The ../ in the HTML, tag tells the browser to go up one directory level. If the graphic was up two directory levels, the relative path would look like this:

<IMG SRC="../../amitab.gif">

At this point, we have created relative paths to images that are in the same directory, in a directory on the same level, and in a directory that is up one level, and a directory that is up two levels. Most HTML editors will create links for you. However, some HTML editors will create an absolute link to a graphic...on your hard drive! This will of course, be useless once you upload your web page. A bad link to a graphic created by an HTML editor will look like this:

<IMG SRC="c:\\pagemill\images\filename.gif">

If you see anything like that in a problem web page, edit the HTML to create a correct link. The give away that this link won't work is that it contains slashes going the wrong direction, and a reference to c:, or the c drive on a computer.

Also, remember that you will need to mirror your directory structure on your computer and on your web site. This way, links will work both, when you test the page on your computer and once you upload both the HTML file and the graphic.

EXERCISE

Objective Type Questions

1 <OL> tag is used for creating

(A) List (B) Ordered List

(C) Unordered List (D) Open List

2. ______attribute is used for setting a start value = 5 for an individual list item.

(A) <ul start = 5> (B) <start ul = 5>

(C) <ol start = 5> (D) <start ol = 5>

3. The list tag which specifies that the information appear as an ordered list is

(A) <IL> (B) <LI>

(C) <OL> (D) <LO>

4. Which tag is used to create a list that displays items with bullets?

(A) <OL> (B) <UL>

(C) <list> (D) <DL>

5. Font tag has following attribute

(A) type (B) face

(C) value (D) caption

6. The following is not a type of list in HTML

(A) Bulleted (B) Glossary

(C) Menu (D) None of the above

7. How can you make a list that lists the items with bullets?

(A) <ol> (B) <dl>

(C) <ul> (D) <list>

8. Which one is the proper opening/closing code tags for a numbered list?

(A) <nl></nl> (B) <ol></ol>

(C) <ul></ul> (D) <li></li>

9. ______represent lower case Roman Numerals in List.

(A) 1 (B) A

(C) i (D) I

10. How can you make a list that lists the items with numbers?

(A) <list> (B) <dl>

(C) <ul> (D) <ol>

11. A picture can be inserted using______tag.

(A) <Image> (B) <Picture>

(C) <pic> (D) <img>

12. What is the correct HTML for inserting an image?

(A) <img>image.gif</img> (B) <img href="image.gif>

(C) <image src="image.gif"> (D) <img src="image.gif">

13. What is the correct HTML for inserting a background image?

(A) <background img="background.gif">

(B) <img src="background.gif" background>

(C) <body background="background.gif">

(D) <body src="background.gif">

14. The tag that marks an image within an HTML document is

(A) <IMAGE> (B) <ALIGN>

(C) <SRC> (D) <IMG>

15. The tag that marks the map definition block within the HTML document is

(A) <MAP> (B) <AREA>

(C) <SHAPE> (D) <USEMAP>

16. For inline images______ tag is used in an HTML document.

(A) <input> (B) <map>

(C) <img> (D) None of these

17. ______is used to set background image at web page.

(A) <body background> (B) <body bg ground>

(C) <body back> (D) None of these

18. ______tag is used to link a web page.

(A) <a> (B) <b>

(C) <td> (D) <tr>

19. What is another term for a bulleted list?

(A) Unnumbered list (B) Numbered list

(C) Hit list (D) Sequenced list

20. What text is the placeholder for a bulleted list?

(A) No. (B) #

(C) > (D) !

21. ______tag defines client-side image map.

(A) <map> (B) <img>

(C) <align> (D) <iframe>

22. ______tag defines an active area in the associated image map.

(A) <img src> (B) <area>

(C) <map> (D) <align>

23. The tag used in HTML to link it with other URL's is:

(A) <A> (B) <H>

(C) <U> (D) <L>

24. It is possible to display pictures (i.e, images) in HTML specification by using the tag.

(A) <GR src = Picture file> (B) <PIC src =Picture file>

(C) <IMG src =Picture file> (D) <GIF src=Picture file >

25. To make an image map one uses the

(A) map tag and the area attribute

(B) map attribute and the area tag

(C) map tag and the area tag

(D) map attribute and the area attribute

26. Which one of the following is the correct way to code a hyperlink?

(A) <a hyper:"PageTwo.html">This is a link to page two.</a>

(B) <a href:"PageTwo.html">This is a link to page two.</a>

(C) <a ref=PageTwo.html>This is a link to page two.</a>

(D) <a href="PageTwo.html">This is a link to page two.</a>

27. How can you open a link in a new browser window?

(A) <a href="url" new>

(B) <a href="url" target="new">

(C) <a href="url" target="_blank">

(D) <a href="url" targer="_new">

28. Anchor tag is used for

(A) Line (B) Subscript

(C) Linking (D) Paragraph

29. What is the correct HTML for making a hyperlink?

(A) <a name="http://www.srimca.com">srimca.com</a>

(B) <a href="http://www.srimca.com">srimca</a>

(C) <a>http://www.srimca.com</a>

(D) <a url="http://www.srimca.com">srimca.com</a>

30. How can you make an e-mail link?

(A) <a href="xxx@yyy"> (B) <mail href="xxx@yyy">

(C) <a href="mailto:xxx@yyy"> (D) <mail>xxx@yyy</mail>

Review & Discussion Questions

1. Explain any two types of lists in HTML.
2. What types of Lists used in HTML? Describe each with suitable examples.
3. Which tag is used to create a list that displays items with bullets?
4. What is the item of unordered list are preceded with?
5. Which tag is used to make numbered list?
6. Which tag is used to define area of image map?
7. What are the lists? How they are created?
8. Define list. What are the components of list elements?
9. Explain different attributes of list tag.
10. Define <UL>. Discuss its various attribute with suitable example.
11. Define <OL>. Discuss its various attribute with suitable example.
12. Explain image map.
13. Explain client side and server side image map with example.
14. How you used a picture as a hyperlink in HTML, give with an example?
15. Give output of the following:

(i)
```
< HTML >
< TITLE > MULTIMEDIA < /TITLE >
< UL>
< L1 > VIDEO
< L2 > AUDIO
< /UL>
</HTML>
```

(ii)
```
< HTML >
< TITLE > PRINTER < /TITLE >
< BODY >
< MARQUEE >< U >< I > LASERPRINTER < /I >< /U >< /
MARQUEE >
< /BODY >
< /HTML >
```

16. Which tag is used to list the items in the form of 1,2,3...?
17. Which tag is used to play background sound when page is loaded?
18. Explain <MAP> tag & different shapes used in image map with suitable example.
19. Explain different attributes of image tag.
20. Write the difference between internal link and external link.
21. Which tag is used to create background image?
22. Explain the steps to create Image as Hyperlink.
23. What is <IMG> tag? What are the attributes that can be used with <IMG> tag?
24. What is Navigation? Explain the advantage of Top/Bottom/Left/Right Navigation.
25. Explain the advantage of Center Navigation, and when to use center navigation.
26. "Placement of Navigation should be consistent within a page layout" Comment.
27. Which is the best place to place navigation element as your opinion why?

CHAPTER 11

Table Elements

CHAPTER OBJECTIVES

This chapter discusses the use of tables to structure data and how to create page templates from tables. Tables can be used for more than just displaying a table of data that can also be used as a formatting tool. You will able to learn the major purpose and uses of several elements that are used to build a table as well as how to adjust various properties and attributes of <CAPTION>, <TBODY>, <TH>, <TR>, <TD>, <TFOOT> and <THEAD>. This chapter helps you better illustration of web page design using this heart of HTML element.

CHAPTER OUTLINES

11.1 INTRODUCTION

HTML tables are awesome; with them, you can create pages that look so good they look professional. You can use HTML tables to display data in rows and columns that helpful to divide the page into different sections. Tables are also used to line up text and images in some ways that are not possible using the attributes for the tags. Almost all major sites on the web are using invisible tables to layout the pages. One thing you have to remember while making HTML tables, keep the table neat, otherwise you will never be able to catch mistakes or update it very well.

Tables are used on websites for two major purposes:

- The obvious purpose of arranging information in a table.
- The less obvious - but more widely used - purpose of creating a page layout with the use of hidden/invisible tables.

The major aspects that can be done with tables are:

- ***Creating Layout:*** Helps to divide the page into separate sections. An invisible table is excellent for this purpose.
- ***Creating Menus:*** Typically with one color for the header and another for the links following in the next lines.
- ***Adding Interactive Form Fields:*** Typically a gray area containing a search option.
- ***Creating Fast Loading Headers for the Page:*** A colored table with a text on it loads, like a bullet compared to even a small banner.
- ***Image Slices:*** Easy alignment of images that have been cut into smaller pieces.

Most important is that the content of a table is not shown until the entire table is loaded. If you have extremely long pages, you should divide it into two or more tables - allowing the user to start reading the upper content while the rest of the page is loading.

As we know table is made up of rows of cells, it takes three basic tags to create a table:

<TABLE> </TABLE> for the table itself

<TR> </TR> for each table row

<TD> </TD> for each table cell

The cell tags are nested between the row tags and all rows are nested between the table tags.

Example

```
<table border="1">
  <tr>
      <td>row 1 cell 1</td>
      <td>row 1 cell 2</td>
      <td>row 1 cell 3</td>
  </tr>
  <tr>
      <td>row 2 cell 1</td>
      <td>row 2 cell 2</td>
      <td>row 2 cell 3</td>
  </tr>
</table>
```

Tables are made up of many parts, all inside one another, which is where much of the complications come from. The <TABLE> element's sub elements are as follows.

Element		Description
<CAPTION>	:	Contains the caption of the table, the title of sorts. It will appear across the top unless specified otherwise. This tag should not be contained in a <TR> or <TD>.
<TR>		Starts a new table row. Cells go inside this. Attributes are the same as <TD>'s.
<TD>		Encloses a table cell. Content goes in these.
<TH>		Same as table cells, but with all contents bold and aligned to the center.
<THEAD>		Defines the header part of a large table. Wrap the tags around the rows/cells you wish to define as the header.
<TBODY>		Defines the main body of a complex table.
<TFOOT>		Wrap this around the footer part of your table.
<COLGROUP>		Allows you to set attributes for the entire column. Each column has to be defined sequentially.

The TABLE may contain a number of optional elements to provide a rich structure to the table. The optional CAPTION element gives a caption for the table and is followed by optional COL, COLGROUP elements that specify column widths and groupings. The THEAD, TFOOT, and TBODY elements then follow with groups of rows. The optional THEAD and TFOOT elements contain header and footer rows, respectively, while TBODY, elements supply the table's main row groups. A row group contains TR elements for individual rows, and each TR contains TH or TD elements for header cells or data cells, respectively.

11.2 <TABLE> ELEMENT

The <TABLE> element defines a table for multi-dimensional data arranged in rows and columns. This is the top level-containing element for HTML table structures. All formatting information are lies between the <TABLE>...</TABLE> elements. By default, tables have no borders. All attributes of the TABLE element apply globally to each cell in the table unless overridden at a sub-element level (row, cell, etc.) by other attributes.

Some attributes to the <TABLE> element are only applicable when the table is constructed using the Complex Table Model, which allows a finer level of control than the Simple Table Model while maintaining backward compatibility with the simpler model.

Attribute		Description
ALIGN	:	**"LEFT I CENTER I RIGHT I BLEEDRIGHTI JUSTIFY"** causes the table to be aligned in one of a variety of ways on the page. Here LEFT: To the left text margin, CENTER: In the center of the page (Turns on NOFLOW.), RIGHT: To the right text margin, BLEEDRIGHT: To the rightmost edge of the window, BLEEDLEFT: To the leftmost edge of the window, JUSTIFY: To both text margins (The table size is adjusted. Turns on NOFLOW.)
WIDTH/HEIGHT		**"n", or "n%"** specifies the width/height of the table, not the columns, in pixels or as a percentage of the display width/height (n is an integer). (Ex. <TABLE WIDTH="90%">)
BORDER		**"integer"** specifies the width in pixels of the border around a table.
CELLPADDING		**"n", or "n%"** defines the amount of space within table cells (i.e., between the border and cell contents). The value may be given as a number of pixels or as a percentage (n is an integer), though most browsers do not support percentages, treating CELLPADDING= "20%" as if it were CELLPADDING="20".
CELLSPACING		**"n", or "n%"** defines the amount of space between table cells. The value may be given as a number of pixels or as a percentage (n is an integer), though most browsers do not support percentages, treating CELLSPACING="20%" as if it were CELLSPACING="20".
BGCOLOR		**"color expression"** sets the background color for the entire table. *RRGGBB* is a six-digit hexadecimal number with the first two digits specifying the red value, the middle two the green value and the last two the blue value. Color names can also be used in the COLOR attribute. Valid colors are: Aqua, Black, Blue, Fuchsia, Gray, Green, Lime, Maroon, Navy, Olive, Purple, Red, Silver, Teal, Yellow, and White.
BORDERCOLOR		**"color expression"** sets the border color for the entire table.
BORDERCOLORLIGHT		**"color expression"** sets the border highlight color for the entire table.
BORDERCOLORDARK		**"color expression"** sets the border shadow color for the entire table.
VALIGN		**"TOPIBOTTOM"** sets the vertical alignment for the entire table.
CLEAR		**"LEFTIRIGHTIALL"** specifies which margin should be clear.

Contd....

NOFLOW		Prevents text flow around the table and is equivalent to setting the CLEAR attribute on the element after the table.
COLSPEC		**"colspec"** is a list of column alignments and widths, separated by spaces. There should be one entry for each column in the table, and each should be an optional capital letter for alignment (one of L (left,) R (right,) C (centre,) J (justify,) or D (decimal)) followed immediately by a number describing the width.
UNITS		**"units"** makes sense only, if the COLSPEC or WIDTH attributes are being used and specifies the units to be used for the column or table widths. units should be one of **en**: widths are in en spaces, proportional to font size, **relative**: column widths are percentage of entire table width, table width is percentage of entire window width and **pixels**: widths are in pixels
DP		**"character"** is the character (the default is ".") to be used in aligning for decimal point alignment.
NOWRAP		Prevents word wrap within table entries.
SUMMARY		**"text"** describe the purpose and/or structure of the table. The overview provided by the SUMMARY attribute is particularly helpful to users of non-visual browsers. With simple tables, a good <CAPTION> is usually a sufficient summary, but complex tables may benefit from a more detailed overview via the SUMMARY attribute.

11.3 <CAPTION> ELEMENT

The caption tag defines the caption of a figure or table. It is valid only within <FIG> or <TABLE> tags.

Attribute		Description
ALIGN	:	**"alignment"** arranges for the caption to be at the TOP or BOTTOM of the table or figure (in NE). For IE the ALIGN attribute sets the alignment of the caption within the table or figure border. It can be LEFT, RIGHT, or CENTER.
VALIGN	:	**"vertical-alignment"** arranges for the caption to be at the TOP or BOTTOM of the table or figure.

11.4 <TBODY> ELEMENT

The <TBODY> element is used to group together a number of rows within a table, for assigning ID or STYLE values.

Attribute		Description
CLASS	:	**"type"** indicates the class that the element belongs too.
ID	:	**"value"** specifies a unique value for the element over the document.
STYLE	:	**"css1"** specifies the style information.

11.5 <TH> ELEMENT

The table header <TH> element is valid only in a <TR> element. The <TH> element defines a header cell. The attributes are:

Attribute		Description
COLSPAN	:	**"number"** specifies the number of columns this header occupies.
ROWSPAN	:	**"number"** specifies the number of rows this header occupies.
NOWRAP	:	This attribute prevents word wrap within the cell.
ALIGN		**"align"** governs the alignment of the text within the table cell. The "align" can be LEFT, RIGHT or CENTER. Table Header cells default to centered.
VALIGN		**"TOP I MIDDLE I BOTTOM I BASELINE"** governs the alignment of the text within the table cell.
BGCOLOR		**"#rrggbb"** sets the background color for the header cell.
BORDERCOLOR		**"#rrggbb"** sets the border color for the header cell.
BORDERCOLORLIGHT		**"#rrggbb"** sets the border highlight color for the header cell.
BORDERCOLORDARK		**"#rrggbb"** sets the border shadow color for the header cell.

11.6 <TR> ELEMENT

The table row <TR> element is valid only in a <TABLE> element. The <TR> element defines a row of cells that are defined with <TH> and <TD> elements. The attributes are:

Attribute		Description
ALIGN		**"align"** governs the alignment of the text within the table cell. "align" can be LEFT, RIGHT or CENTER. Table Header cells default to centered.
VALIGN		**"TOP I MIDDLE I BOTTOM I BASELINE"** governs the alignment of the text within the table cell.
NOWRAP	:	This attribute prevents word wrap within the cell.
BGCOLOR		**"#rrggbb"** sets the background color for the table row.
BORDERCOLOR		**"#rrggbb"** sets the border color for the table row.
BORDERCOLORLIGHT		**"#rrggbb"** sets the border highlight color for the table row.
BORDERCOLORDARK		**"#rrggbb"** sets the border shadow color for the table row.
CLASS		**"class"** is one of <Header>, <Body>, or <Footer> and allows the browser to arrange for header or footer rows to be displayed as the user scrolls through the document.

Note: If ALIGN is specified for any cell in the row, the cell alignment overrides the row alignment.

11.7 <TD> ELEMENT

The table data <TD> element is valid only in a <TR> element; the <TABLE> element defines a table cell. The attributes are:

Attribute		Description
COLSPAN	:	**"number"** specifies the number of columns this cell occupies.
ROWSPAN	:	**"number"** specifies the number of rows this cell occupies.
NOWRAP	:	This attribute prevents word wrap within the cell.
ALIGN	:	**"align"** governs the alignment of the text within the table cell. "align" can be LEFT, RIGHT or CENTER.
VALIGN	:	**"TOP I MIDDLE I BOTTOM I BASELINE"** governs the alignment of the text within the table cell.
BGCOLOR	:	**"#rrggbb"** sets the background color for the table cell.
BORDERCOLOR	:	**"#rrggbb"** sets the border color for the table cell.
BORDERCOLORLIGHT	:	**"#rrggbb"** sets the border highlight color for the table cell.
BORDERCOLORDARK	:	**"#rrggbb"** sets the border shadow color for the table cell.

11.8 <TFOOT> ELEMENT

The <TFOOT> element defines the table footer. The footer tag is used to group all footers.

Attribute		Description
CLASS	:	**"type"** indicates the class that the element belongs too.
ID	:	**"value"** specifies a unique value for the element over the document.
STYLE	:	**"css1"** specifies the style information.

11.9 <THEAD> ELEMENT

The <THEAD> element defines the table heading. The <THEAD> element is used to group all headers together.

Attribute		Description
ALIGN	:	**"LEFT I CENTER I RIGHT I JUSTIFY"** specifies the alignment of text in the heading, the default is center.
CLASS	:	**"type"** indicates the class that the element belongs too.
ID	:	"value" specifies a unique value for the element over the document.
STYLE	:	**"css1"** specifies the style information.
VALIGN	:	**"MIDDLE I TOP I BOTTOM"** specifies the vertical alignment of text in the heading. The default is MIDDLE.

11.10 EXAMPLES OF <TABLE> ELEMENTS

11.10.1 <Table Border> </Table>

Defining a Table Border without a border size.

Foo Bar and Waffle

Using the Border attribute without parameters will display a default border with a width of "1", i.e, <table border>. (The <TABLE> ... </TABLE> tag pair without attributes will not show any border at all. The following attributes and characteristics will not default either)

11.10.2 <Table Border=??> </Table> (Pixels)

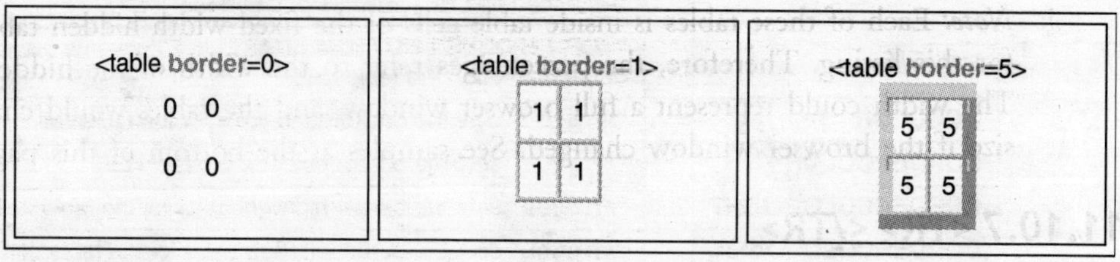

11.10.3 <Table Cellspacing=?> </Table> (Pixels)

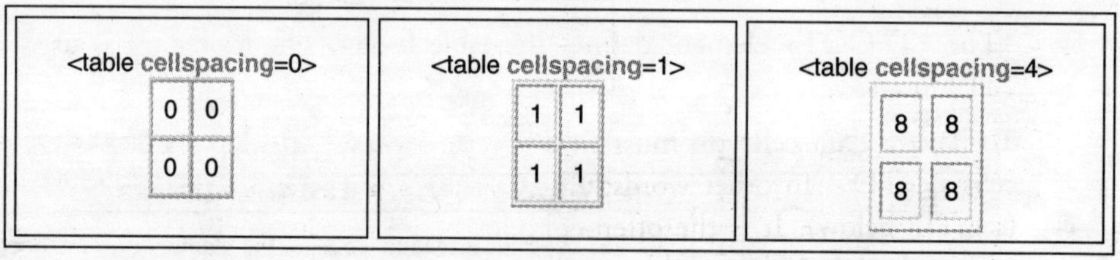

Note: Cellspacing refers to the width between borderlines. It can be used to put space between cells/objects in invisible tables - i.e., border=0.

11.10.4 <Table Cellpadding=?> </Table> (pixels)

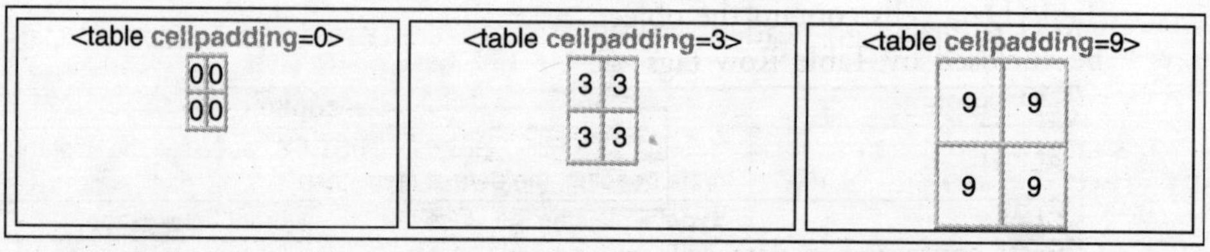

Note: Cellpadding refers to the minimum space between objects and the inner table border. It can be used to put space between cells/objects in invisible tables - i.e., border=0.

11.10.5 <Table Width=?> </Table> (in pixels)

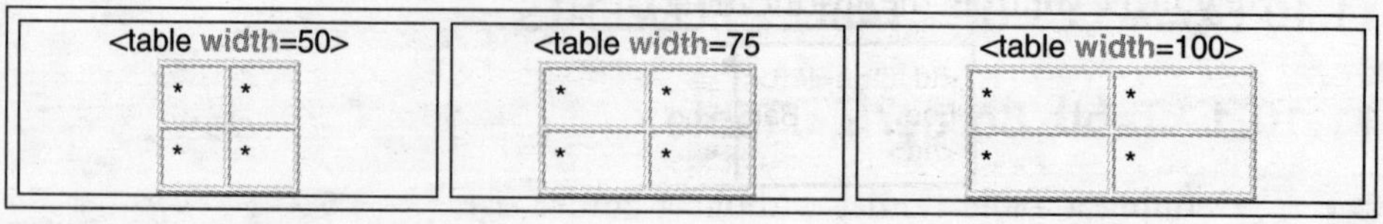

Note: The widths of these tables have been set to a fixed number of screen pixels.

11.10.6 <Table Width=%> </Table> (percentage of ??)

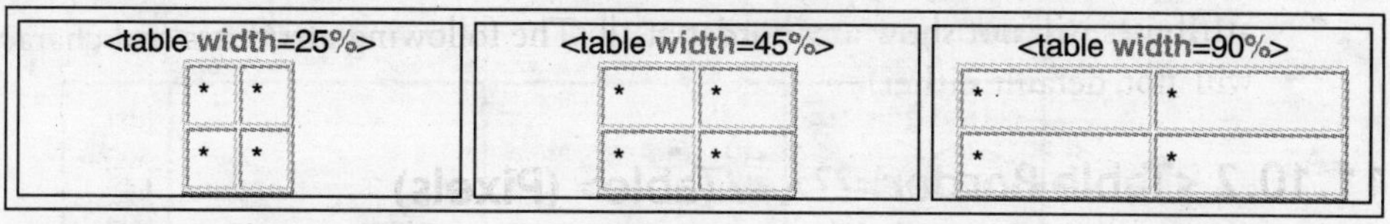

Note: Each of these tables is inside table cells of the fixed width hidden table used for this listing. Therefore, the percentages refer to the width of the hidden cells. The width could represent a full browser window, and the tables would change in size if the browser window changed. See samples at the bottom of this page.

11.10.7 <TR> </TR>

Table Rows <TR> enclose the Table Data Cells <TD>. TR tags must be a pair. <TR>...</TR>

<table><tr><td>......</td>
<td>......</td></tr></table>

To have a data cell you must first have a Table, a Row <TR> and then the data cells(s) <TD>. In other words, all data cells must be contained within Table Rows (see TD below). It is the often-complex combination of table rows and data cells within the rows, that enables specific placement of objects other than by the very basic left, right and center object attributes.

11.10.8 <TD> </TD> (must appear within table rows)

Table Data cells contain the objects placed in a table. Table Data cells <TD> must be enclosed by Table Row tags <TR>. TD tags must be a pair. <TD>...</TD>

<table><tr><td>......</td>
<td>......</td></tr></table>

Objects contained in data cells can be text, bitmap images or any other object that can be placed into a Web page (i.e, Java Applets, Forms, Embedded Sound Devices/ Objects, etc).

11.10.9 <TD ALIGN=left | right | center> </TD>

Alignment controls the justification of objects in a data cell.

<td align=left> Foo Bar </td>	<td align=center> Foo Bar </td>	<td align=right> Foo Bar </td>

The alignment attributes listed in the heading should be self-explanatory.

11.10.10 <TD VALIGN=top | middle | bottom> </TD>

Vertical Alignment controls the position of objects in a data cell.

<td valign=top> ...</td>	<td valign=center> ...</td>	<td valign=bottom> ...</td>	just some fill text

The vertical alignment attributes listed in the heading should be self explanatory.

11.10.11 <TD NOWRAP> </TD>

Nowrap means no line breaks in text objects.

Foo Bar and waffle!	Foo Bar and waffle etc! <td nowrap>...</td>

Here the table has been forced to a minimum size of 100 pixels, although it can not reduce to this size, because the right hand cell is set with the <TD NOWRAP>...</TD> attribute. The text in the left hand cell has wrapped because its width is minimised by the force of the text in the "nowrap" cell.

No wrap simply means don't wrap the text to multi lines even if the width (cell, table, page, etc.) happens to be smaller. Consider the ramifications of using this attribute if you design at high resolution when many surfers will view your page with low-resolution video monitors. They may have to scroll sideways to read each line and will probably go elsewhere very quickly.

11.10.12 <TD COLSPAN=?> </TD>

Make one data cell wider than others above and/or below. (Spans multiple columns)

Table Data 1	Table Data 2
<tr> <td>Table Data 1</td> <td>Table Data 2</td> </tr><tr> <td colspan=2>This cell</td> </tr>	

The top row contains two data cells. To force the bottom single data cell to the width of the top two (and the width of the table in this case), the COLSPAN = attribute is used. Note this order of <TR>s and <TD>s. Each data cell in a table (horizontally) represents a column.

Make one column cell higher than others next to it. (Spans multiple rows)

Table Data 1	<tr> <td>Table Data 1</td> <td rowspan=2>This cell</td> </tr><tr> <td>Table Data 2</td> </tr>
Table Data 2	

The left hand column contains two data cells compared to the single data cell in the right hand column. Note this order of <TR>s and <TD>s. The higher data cell is described in the first row, similar to the "colspan" sample above. But, the rowspan attribute creates a very different result.

11.10.13 <TD WIDTH=?> </TD> (in pixels)

Set the width of individual Table Cells in pixels.

75	15	40
"	"	"

Each data cell <TD> tag includes a width=??? attribute. (A minimum width in the screen pixels) <TD>.

11.10.14 <TD WIDTH="??%"> </TD> (percentage of table)

Equal Table Data cells.

33	33	33
%		

Uneven cells

15	35	50
%		%

Each of these tables are inside table cells of the fixed width hidden table used for this listing, and each table has been set to 70% of the hidden cell width. The percentages displayed in each cell refer to the width of the table the cell is in. Therefore, if each table was on a page and not in hidden cells as they are here, these table cells would change in width if the browser window and the table changed in width.

11.10.15 <TD BGCOLOR="#rrggbb"> </TD>

Setting the background colour of individual Table Data cells

#999900	#FF9900	#996699

This attribute is a recent NS & IE extension, not standard HTML 3.2. Use it cautiously. i.e., a dark color with light text will hide your text in many browsers.

<TH> </TH> (same as TD, except text is bold)

Table Header cell.

<table>
<tr><th>Table Header cell</th><th>Table Data cell</th></tr>
<tr><td colspan="2"><tr>
<th align="center" width="50%">Table Header cell</th>
<td align="center" width="50%">Table Data cell</td>
</tr>
<tr>
<td colspan="2" align="center">This is this cell</td>
</tr></td></tr>
</table>

The TH tag can be used in place of the TD tag. All attributes are the same as for <TD>, except all text, objects are forced to bold. Not used very often.

11.10.16 <CAPTION> </CAPTION> (above or below table)

A Table Caption appears without table borders.

<table>
<tr><td colspan="2"><table><caption>Foo Bar</caption>...</td></tr>
<tr><td>Table Data cell</td><td>Table Data cell</td></tr>
<tr><td colspan="2">Table Data cell - colspan=2</td></tr>
</table>

This table tag and its attributes are used to place captions at the top or bottom of tables.

<CAPTION ALIGN = top|bottom> </CAPTION>

Table Captions can be placed at the top or bottom of a table.

<table>
<tr><td colspan="2"><table><caption align=top>Foo Bar</caption>....</td></tr>
<tr><td>Table Data cell</td><td>Table Data cell</td></tr>
<tr><td colspan="2">Table Data cell - colspan=2</td></tr>
</table>

<table>
<tr><td colspan="2">....<caption align=bottom>Foo Bar</caption></table></td></tr>
<tr><td>Table Data cell</td><td>Table Data cell</td></tr>
<tr><td colspan="2">Table Data cell - colspan=2</td></tr>
</table>

11.10.17 A Complex Table

<table>
<tr><td rowspan="4">1</td><td colspan="3">2</td><td rowspan="4">3</td><td rowspan="2">4</td></tr>
<tr><td rowspan="2">5</td><td colspan="2">6</td></tr>
<tr><td>7</td><td>8</td><td rowspan="2">9</td></tr>
<tr><td colspan="3">10</td></tr>
</table>

The CODE for the Complex Table:

```
<center>
<table border="2" cellpadding="2" cellspacing="3" width="565">

Row 1 <TR>
    <td valign="middle" align="center" width="94" rowspan="4">1</td>
    <td valign="middle" align="center" width="282" colspan="3">2</td>
    <td valign="middle" align="center" width="94" rowspan="4">3</td>
    <td valign="middle" align="center" width="95" rowspan="2">4</td>
</tr>
Row 2 <TR>
    <td valign="middle" align="center" width="94" rowspan="2">5</td>
    <td valign="middle" align="center" width="188" colspan="2">6</td>
</tr>
Row 3 <TR>
    <td valign="middle" align="center" width="94">7</td>
    <td valign="middle" align="center" width="94">8</td>
    <td valign="middle" align="center" width="95" rowspan="2">9</td>
</tr>
Row 4 <TR>
    <td valign="middle" align="center" width="282" colspan="3">10</td>
</tr>
 </table>
</center>
```

Note: Cells 1, 2, 3 and 4 all start at the top of Row 1. Cells 5 and 6 start at the top of the Row 2 etc. Follow these steps between the table and code above to understand the order that must be followed. You will see that the order is set by rows, top to bottom. Table data cells are ordered left to right, within each row, only if they start in that row (the cell top). Their height is irrelevant as to which row they are listed in, but is relevant to the rows they are not listed in if they span multiple rows.

EXERCISE

Objective Type Questions

1. <Caption> tag is used for______
   (A) Name of the table (B) Name of web page
   (C) Name of the list (D) None of them
2. ______tag specifies the table item
   (A) <th> (B) <ti>
   (C) <tr> (D) <caption>
3. Which of these tags are all <table> tags?
   (A) <thead><body><tr> (B) <table><tr><tt>
   (C) <table><tr><td> (D) <table><head><tfoot>
4. Choose the correct HTML to left-align the content inside a tablecell
   (A) <td align="left"> (B) <td leftalign>
   (C) <tdleft> (D) <td valign="left">
5. Which of the following is a two sided tag?
   (A) DT (B) LI
   (C) DD (D) DL
6. <CAPTION> tag is used
   (A) within a table to identify the text of the table caption
   (B) place the caption at the top
   (C) place the caption at the bottom
   (D) None of the above
7. In BORDER="n" to specify a table border-width, "n" is measured in
   (A) Points (B) Picas
   (C) Pixels (D) Millimeters
8. The attribute which specifies outside edges of the table that will have a border is
   (A) RULES (B) cols
   (C) ROWS (D) FRAME

9. In table row is created by

(A) <tr> (B) <th>

(C) <ta> (D) None of these

10. ______tag is used to create a caption on top or below the table.

(A) <table> (B) <caption>

(C) <align> (D) <border>

11. To change the table border size______ attribute is used.

(A) cell padding (B) cell spacing

(C) Border (D) colspan

12. What is the limit of tables you can nest within another table?

(A) four (B) unlimited

(C) ten (D) two

13. Which code will display two cells on top of each other in one column?

(And yes, notice how much harder code is to read when it's not properly aligned!)

(A) <table><tr><td></td></tr><tr><td></td></tr></table>

(B) <table><tr><td></td><td></td></tr></table>

(C) <table><th><tr><td></td></tr></th></table>

(D) <tr><td></td></tr><tr><td></td></tr>

14. In HTML, in order to mark a row within a table, the tag is

(A) <TD> (B) <TR>

(C) <TH> (D) <TA>

15. Which of the following is not a feature of tables on web pages?

(A) every cell in a row has the same size

(B) rows are only a little bigger than the widest item in any of their cells

(C) every row has the same size

(D) none of the above

16. What tag is used to define a table?

(A) The <TABLESET> tag

(B) The <TABLE> tag

(C) The <DEFINE> tag

17. Is a table cell or a table row defined first?

(A) A table row

(B) A table cell

(C) Neither one

18. What two attributes define the height and width of a table?

(A) The HEIGHT and WIDTH attributes

(B) The SIZE and SHAPE attributes

(C) The DEPTH and LENGTH attributes

19. What attribute defines a table's border size?

(A) The SIZE attribute

(B) The BORDERSIZE attribute

(C) The BORDER attribute

20. What tag defines a table caption?

(A) The <CAPTION> tag

(B) The <TABLE> tag

(C) The <TEXT> tag

Review & Discussion Questions

1. Write HTML code to generate the following table:

Serial No.	Name	Date of Birth

2. Sketch the table which will be generated by the following HTML code:

```
<HTML>
<HEAD><TITLE>TABLE</TITLE></HEAD>
<BODY>
<TABLE BORDER=1px>
<TR>
<TH colspan = 2>GENDER</TH>
</TR>
<TR>
    <TD>Male</TD>
    <TD>Female</TD>
</TR>
</TABLE>
</BODY>
</HTML>
```

3. Differentiate between 'cell spacing' and 'cell padding'.
4. The resolution of a computer screen is 1024 pixels across and 768 pixels down. You are asked to create a table in HTML with the width of 75% of the screen resolution and a height of 400 pixels.
   (i) How wide is your table in pixels?
   (ii) Write down the HTML code for the above table with the border of 1 pixel.
5. Kumar wants to change the background color of a table in his web page. Which attribute of <TABLE> tag is used for this purpose?
6. Distinguish between cell spacing and cell padding attributes of <TABLE> tag.
7. How table is used in HTML, describe with an example?
8. Draw the output for the following code:

```
<HTML>
<HEAD>
```

```
<TITLE>New Page 1</TITLE>
</HEAD>
<BODY>
<TABLE BORDER="1" CELLPADDING="0" CELLSPACING="0"
   BORDERCOLOR="red" WIDTH="100%">
<TR>
<TD WIDTH="25%" ROWSPAN="3">  ;</TD>
<TD WIDTH="25 %">   ;</TD>
<TD WIDTH="25%" ROWSPAN="2">  ;</TD>
<TD WIDTH="25 %">   ;</TD>
</TR>
<TR>
<TD WIDTH="25%" ROWSPAN="2">  ;</TD>
<TD WIDTH="25 %">   ;</TD>
</TR>
<TR>
<TD WIDTH="25 %">   ;</TD>
<TD WIDTH="25 %">   ;</TD>
</TR>
</TABLE>
</BODY>
</HTML>
```

9. Which tag is used to left align the content is table cell?
10. Which attribute is used to change the table border?
11. The table caption is set by using which tag?
12. What is <TABLE> tag? What are the attributes that can be used with table tag?
13. Explain the Use of Following Tags in HTML.

    a. CAPTION b. TR c. TD d. TH
14. Explain <TABLE> tag.
15. Explain different attributes of <TABLE> tag.

CHAPTER 12

Form Elements

CHAPTER OBJECTIVES

Form elements are probably one of the most important aspects of HTML that we come across when browsing the web. This chapter describes the characteristics of form elements, including some of the basic elements and their attributes. The list of attributes is not necessarily complete, but rather includes a subset that is used in this book. This chapter explains how to organize documents for user input by combining forms and tables; and how to send the contents of a form back to its creator.

CHAPTER OUTLINES

12.1 INTRODUCTION

Forms are the most popular way to make web pages interactive. Like forms on paper, a form on a web page allows the user to enter requested information and submit it for processing. (Fortunately, forms on a web page are processed much faster.) The <form> tag tells the browser where the form starts and ends. You can add all kinds of HTML tags between the <form> and </form> tags.

The purpose of a form element is to present a fill-out form to be used for user actions such as registration, ordering, or queries. Forms can contain a wide range of HTML markup including several kinds of form fields such as single and multi-line text fields, password fields, radio button groups, check boxes, submit and reset buttons, hidden fields, file upload, image buttons and menus. More generally, forms are processed by CGI scripts.

12.2 <FORM> ELEMENT (FORM ELEMENTS)

Attributes		Description
ACTION	:	**URL** attribute values are Uniform Resource Identifiers (URIs), as defined in RFC 2396. The value of the action attribute specifies what is to be done when the form filling is complete. Its value will be simply a URL, if this is the name of an executable file then the file will be executed, however it may simply refer to a WWW page, however this is unusual. URI attribute values may include full URIs such as http://www.bpkm.org.in/ as well as relative URIs such as index.htm and../aboutus/. While parts of a URI may be case-insensitive, in general URI values are case-sensitive.
METHOD	:	**"GETIPOST"** HTTP method to be used to send the contents of the form to the server. Default is GET, but POST is more common.
ENCTYPE	:	**"multipart/form-data I application/x-www-form-urlencoded I text/plain I text/html I image/jpeg I model/vrml I video/quicktime I application/java I text/css I text/javascript"** determines how the form data is encoded. Whenever data is transmitted from one place to another, there needs to be an agreed upon means of representing that data. Music is translated into written music notation, English is written using letters and punctuation. Default is *application/x-www-form-urlencoded.*
NAME	:	The name attribute can be used with client functions. However, client functions are not recommended for content developers.
TARGET	:	**"_blank I _parent I _self I _top"** The area tag forces the load of that link into the targeted window. **_blank** makes the link to load into a new blank window. This window is not named. **_parent** makes the link load in the immediate FRAMESET parent of this document. This defaults to acting like "_self" if the document has no parent. **_self** causes the link to always load in the same window the anchor was clicked in. This is useful for overriding a globally assigned BASE target. **_top** makes the link load in the full body of the window. this defaults to acting like "_self" if the document is already at the top. It is useful for breaking out of an arbitrarily deep FRAME nesting.

Note: The value of the METHOD attribute specifies the HTTP method (as defined in the HTTP specification) to be used to send the contents of the form to the server (when the ACTION attribute specifies an HTTP server). In principle, the GET method is to be used when the processing of the form is "idempotent", i.e., has no lasting observable effect on the state of the world; this applies typically by query forms, the processing of which may involve extracting information from a database but no changes to the content of the database. If the processing of the form has side effects (such as modification of a database or subscription to a service), the method should be POST. In practice, the POST method is often used even if the form submission has no side effects. As regards to technicalities.

For the GET method, a browser starts with the action URL (the value of the ACTION attribute or, by default, the base URL of the document), then appends a? character and the form data set, in the format specified by ENCTYPE or in the application/x-www-form-urlencoded format by default. Finally, the browser processes the resulting URL as if it were a link anchor.

For the POST method, the browser conducts an HTTP POST transaction using the action URL and a message body in the in the format specified by ENCTYPE, or in the application/x-www-form-urlencoded format by default.

A web page (i.e., an HTML document) may include multiple forms; however, forms may not be nested (you cannot create a form within a form). You must end the current form with < /FORM > before you can start a new form.

Example

```
<form METHOD="GET" ACTION="http://bpkm.org.in/testfile">
</form>
```

12.2.1 <INPUT> Elements (Input Elements)

</input> tag is used to obtain user input in a variety of ways. The particular type of input is indicated by the value of the type attribute.

Attributes		Description
TYPE	:	**"TEXT I CHECKBOX I RADIO I PASSWORD I HIDDEN I SUBMIT I RESET I BUTTON I FILE I IMAGE"** type of the input field. Default is TEXT.
NAME	:	**"string"** name to be used to identify the field when submitting the contents to the server.
VALUE	:	**"string"** initial value of the input field. VALUE sets the default values for text and password fields, sets the button text in submit, reset and plain buttons, sets the values of the choices in radio buttons, sets the permanent values of hidden fields, and has no effect on file, and image fields. When TYPE is SUBMIT or RESET, provides a textual label. VALUE is obligatory, if TYPE is RADIO or CHECKBOX.

Contd....

CHECKED	:	**"CHECKED"** when TYPE is RADIO or CHECKBOX, initializes the field to checked state.
SIZE	:	**"integer"** visible size of the field, as number of average character widths.
MAXLENGTH	:	**"integer"** maximum number of characters permitted in a text field.
SRC	:	**"URL"** address of an image. It is used for fields with background images.
ALIGN	:	**"TOP I MIDDLE I BOTTOM I LEFT I RIGHT"** image alignment for graphical submit buttons.

The different values of the TYPE attribute correspond to different kinds of input fields as follows.

<INPUT TYPE= "TEXT"> (the default)

type="text" attribute is used to create a single line text input field. The size of the text input area and the maximum number of characters that may be typed into the input area may be specified using the size="" and maxlength="" attributes. To add default text to the field use the value="" attribute.

Example

Default text field:

```
<form><input type="text"></form>
<form>
<input type="text" size="17" maxlength="60" name="url" value="http://">
</form>
```

<INPUT TYPE= "PASSWORD">

type="password" a modified TEXT field, displays typed characters as bullets/ asterisks instead of the character actually typed. Possible attributes to include within the type PASSWORD include NAME (required), SIZE, MAXLENGTH, and VALUE.

Example

```
<form><input type="password"></form>
<form>
```

<INPUT TYPE= "CHECKBOX">

type="checkbox" check boxes allow for multiple choices and multiple selections that can be checked or left empty. Possible attributes to include with the TYPE text include NAME (required), VALUE, and CHECKED (which defaults the check box as checked). A check box can be pre-checked by including the "checked" attribute.

Example

```
<FORM METHOD="POST" ACTION="someplace/foo.cgi"
        ENCTYPE="application/x-www-form-urlencoded">
Computer Experience:<BR>
<INPUT TYPE="checkbox" NAME="choice"
        VALUE="Less than 1">Less than 1 year.<BR>
<INPUT TYPE="checkbox" NAME="choice"
        VALUE="1 to 5">1-5 years.<BR>
<INPUT TYPE="checkbox" NAME="choice"
        VALUE="More than 5">More than 5 years.
<BR><INPUT TYPE="reset" VALUE="Clear Form">
<INPUT TYPE="submit" VALUE="Submit">
</FORM>
```

Note: You want to be especially careful when using check boxes and radio buttons in HTML documents with custom backgrounds or background colors. Depending on the Web browser used, check boxes and radio buttons sometimes do not show up with dark backgrounds.

<INPUT TYPE= "RADIO">

type="radio" radio button is a more complex version of check box, allowing only one of the related set to be chosen. Possible attributes to include with the TYPE text include NAME (required), VALUE, and CHECKED. Only one button can be selected and this will be the only information sent with the form. To pre-check a radio button use the "checked" attribute.

Example

```
<FORM METHOD="POST" ACTION="someplace/foo.cgi">
<TR>
<CAPTION="TOP"><B><B>T-Shirt Order</B></CAPTION>
<TD></TD><TD>White</TD><TD>Blue</TD>
</TR>
<TR>
<TD ALIGN="LEFT">Small</TD>
```

Contd....

```
<TD><INPUT NAME="torder" TYPE="radio" VALUE="smwhite"></TD>
<TD><INPUT NAME="torder" TYPE="radio" VALUE="smblue"></TD>
</TR>
<TR>
<TD ALIGN="LEFT">Medium</TD>
<TD><INPUT NAME="torder" TYPE="radio" VALUE="medwhite"></TD>
<TD><INPUT NAME="torder" TYPE="radio" VALUE="medblue"></TD>
</TR>
<TR>
<TD ALIGN="LEFT">Large</TD>
<TD><INPUT NAME="torder" TYPE="radio" VALUE="lgwhite"></TD>
<TD><INPUT NAME="torder" TYPE="radio" VALUE="lgblue"></TD>
</TR>
<TR>
<TD></TD>
<TD><INPUT TYPE="reset></TD>
<TD><INPUT TYPE="submit" VALUE="Order"></TD>
</TR>
</TABLE>
</FORM>
```

Note: If you don't specify a set of radio buttons or check boxes with one of the values as CHECKED, then you could receive an empty field for that <INPUT> name.

<INPUT TYPE= "SUBMIT">

type="submit" to change the text on the button use the value="Button Text" attribute. A form may have more than one "Submit" button. When this is done each button should contain a different name="" and value="" attribute, so you know which button was used.

Example

```
<FORM><INPUT TYPE="Submit"></FORM>
<FORM><INPUT TYPE=" Submit " VALUE="Button Text"></FORM>
```

Note: A button with text like "Submit" or "Send" is fine. Try to avoid more oblique values like "Tell Us!" or "Done!".

<INPUT TYPE= "RESET">

type="reset" this button will reset the form to the original state before any information was entered. Use the value="" attribute to change the text on the button.

Example

```
<FORM><INPUT TYPE="Reset"></FORM> <FORM>
<INPUT TYPE="Reset" VALUE="Clear Form"></FORM>
```

<INPUT TYPE= "FILE">

type="file" attribute is used to upload a file from the user's computer to the server. To use this function the form tag will require the enctype attribute, enctype=multipart/form-data". The types of files to be uploaded can be restricted by using the accept="" attribute, which specifies a MIME content type.

Below are some examples:

- accept="text/*" (will upload text only files)
- accept="text/html" (will upload html only files)
- accept="image/*" (will upload images only files)
- accept="image/gif" (will upload only .gif files)
- accept="image/gif,jpg,jpeg" (will upload only .gif & .jpg files)

Example

```
<form action="/cgi-bin/myscript.cgi" method="POST" enctype="multipart/form-data">
<input type="file" name="upload" accept="text/html"></form>
```

<INPUT TYPE= "HIDDEN">

type="hidden" fields are used to "save state" within an HTML form. Used in forms having multiple pages where certain information needs to be passed from one page to the next. Neither the form nor the information appears on the web page, the user can alter or see the info, but the information is sent along with other form input fields.

<INPUT TYPE= "BUTTON">

type="button" generates a "clickable" button (similar to the "Submit" button) normally used with the javascript "onClick" attribute. The button text is specified using the value="" attribute.

<INPUT TYPE= "IMAGE">

type="image" allows for the use of an image in place of the "Submit" button. This attribute requires using the image src="" attribute. The width="", height="", border="", alt="" align="", hspace="". and vspace="" attributes may be used just as in a normal image tag.

Note: Image fields cause problems to people using text-only or speech-based user agents or graphical browsers with automatic loading of images disabled.

12.2.2 <SELECT> Element

The <SELECT> element shows a list of choices in either a menu or a scrolling list. To specify, within a form, a select menu box from which the user can select one or more alternatives. Effectively, a <SELECT> element defined a form field where user's input is restricted to an enumerated list of values. SELECTED attribute may be used to pre-select an item(s).

Attributes		Description
NAME	:	**"string"** attribute is required. It defines the name for the data.
Size	:	**"integer"** This attribute determines how many choices to show. If you omit SIZE or set it to 1, the choices are shown as a drop-down list. If you set it to 2 or higher, it shows the choices in a scroll box. If you set SIZE large than the number of choices you have within <SELECT>, a nothing is added. When the end user chooses this, it's returned as an empty field. It is applicable when MULTIPLE is set.
MULTIPLE	:	"MULTIPLE" signifies multiple selections. If you specify multiple, a scrolling window displays—regardless of the number of choices or the setting of SIZE.
DISABLED	:	READONLY locks the field: the user cannot change the value. DISABLED locks the field where user can't change the value. This means that the user cannot use the field in any way, not to highlight the text for copying, not to select the checkbox, not to submit the form. In fact, a disabled field is not even sent if the form is submitted.

Note: As an alternative to <SELECT>, you may wish to consider using a set of <INPUT> elements with TYPE="CHECKBOX" or TYPE="RADIO", typically resulting in a rendering which allows the user see all alternatives at a glance.

You should always provide a default choice (an OPTION element with attribute SELECTED set) within a SELECT element. For reasons to this, see my document choices in HTML forms.

<SELECT ...> does not have a READONLY attribute. The reason is that technically <SELECT ...> lists don't have values. They have selected options, which themselves have values. You may wish to see <SELECT DISABLED>, which disables the <SELECT ...> list.

Some WWW browsers don't properly display a scrolling window if the SIZE is 2 or 3. In that case, leave it as a drop-down list or think about using the <INPUT> field's radio buttons.

12.2.3 <OPTION> Element

<OPTION ...> is used along with <SELECT ...> to create select lists. <OPTION ...> indicates the start of a new option in the list. <OPTION ...> can be used without any attributes, but you usually need the VALUE attribute, which indicates what is sent to the server. The text which follows <OPTION ...> is what is displayed in the browser. Each item in the list is placed within a set of <option></option> tags.

Attributes		Description
SELECTED	:	**SELECTED** indicates that the option should be selected by default.
VALUE	:	**"string"** indicates the value that is sent to the server if that option is chosen. The value of VALUE is not seen by the user. It is defaults to the contents of the element; however, several browsers ignore leading and/or trailing spaces in the content.

Note: In a SELECT element without the MULTIPLE attributes, at most one OPTION element may have SELECTED attribute.

The VALUE attribute is optional, but most CGI programs require it to process the information.

Example

```
Drop-Down Menu
<form>
<label for="favcity">Which is your favorite city?</label>
<select id="favcity" name="favcity">
<option value="1">Amsterdam</option>
<option value="3">Interlaken</option>
<option value="4">Moscow</option>
<option value="5">Dresden</option>
<option value="2">New York</option>
```

Contd....

```
<option value="6">Salt Lake City</option>
<option value="7">Logan</option>
<option value="8">Buenos Aires</option>
<option value="9">Asuncion</option>
<option value="10">Hong Kong</option>
<option value="11">Tokyo</option>
<option value="12">New Dehli</option>
</select>
</form>
```

To improve the accessibility of this list even further, we could add OPTGROUP tags, to group the information. Note that the optgroup tag is not widely supported by a browser. Window Eyes, for example, does not yet support this tag. JAWS supports it, but only in virtual PC mode, not in forms mode.

Example

```
Drop-Down Menu
<form>
<label for="favcity2">Which is your favorite city?</label>
<select id="favcity2" name="favcity2">
<optgroup label="Europe">
<option value="1">Amsterdam</option>
<option value="3">Interlaken</option>
<option value="4">Moscow</option>
<option value="5">Dresden</option>
</optgroup>
<optgroup label="North America">
<option value="2">New York</option>
<option value="6">Salt Lake City</option>
<option value="7">Montreal</option>
</optgroup>
<optgroup label="South America">
```

Contd....

```
<option value="8">Buenos Aires</option>
<option value="9">Asuncion</option>
</optgroup>
<optgroup label="Asia">
<option value="10">Hong Kong</option>
<option value="11">Tokyo</option>
<option value="12">New Dehli</option>
</optgroup>
</select>
</form>
```

Example

```
Scrolling Menu
<form>
<select name="SelectBox" size="2">
<option value="1">Option 1</option>
<option value="2">Option 2</option>
<option value="3">Option 3</option>
<option value="4">Option 4</option>
</select>
</form>
```

Example

```
Scrolling Menu
<form>
<select name="SelectBox" size="4" multiple>
<option value="1">Option 1</option>
<option value="2">Option 2</option>
<option value="3">Option 3</option>
<option value="4" SELECTED>Option 4</option>
<option value="5">Option 5</option>
```

Contd....

```
</select>
</form>
```

12.2.4 <TEXTAREA> Element

An input area which appears as a separate box, where you can enter multiple lines of information, possibly having a distinct background color, and usually with some kind of scroll bars for both vertical and horizontal direction.

The area is initialized with the contents of the TEXTAREA element, using monospaced font. The content is displayed as it is written, similarly to PRE elements.

Any text, including spaces or breaks, placed between the <textarea> and </textarea> tags will appear in the text area field when the form loads. To eliminate any text or spaces keep the tags together, <textarea></textarea>.

Attributes		Description
NAME	:	**"string"** a property name that is used to identify the <textarea> field when the form is submitted to the server.
ROWS	:	**"integer"** COLS indicates how many characters (not pixels) wide the text area should be.
COLS	:	**"integer"** ROWS indicates how many rows should be in the text area. ROWS & COLS attributes do not set any limit on how much can be typed in, just how much of the <textarea> is visible.
WRAP	:	**"SOFT I HARD I OFF"** determines how the lines of text entered into the <textarea> will be displayed. *wrap="off"*, the text is displayed exactly as typed, no lines will wrap. This is the default wrap attribute. *wrap="physical"*, any line of text longer than the text area input field will wrap to the next line. The text is sent with the physical (hard) wraps in place. *wrap="virtual"*, same as wrap="physical" except the wrap applies only to the visual text area input field. The virtual (soft) wraps are removed before the form is sent.
READONLY	:	**READONLY** locks the field where the user cannot change the value.
DISABLED	:	**DISABLED** does the same thing but takes it further where the user cannot use the field in any way, not to highlight the text for copying, not to select the checkbox, not to submit the form. In fact, a disabled field is not even sent if the form is submitted.

Note: The contents are interpreted as text only; HTML markup is ignored. Theoretically, the user can type unlimited amounts of text into the <textarea> field. In reality, the browser sets the limit, usually no more than 32 K. If you want users to send in their latest novel, consider using file upload.

Browsers do not always honor the ROWS and COLS attributes exactly. Rather often, the visible input area is somewhat larger than specified by them.

Example

```
<form>
<textarea name="example" cols="50" rows="6" wrap="hard">
</textarea>
</form>
```

12.2.5 <FIELDSET> Element

<FIELDSET> defines a group of form elements as being logically related. The browser draws a box around the set of fields to indicate that they are related. For example, a form might contain a few fields about name and email, some fields asking for opinions, and a field for "other comments".

<FIELDSET> could be used to group those fields like this:

```
<form>
<FIELDSET>
name: <INPUT NAME="realname"><BR>
email: <INPUT NAME="email">
</FIELDSET><P>
<FIELDSET>
favorite color: <INPUT NAME="favecolor"><BR>
<INPUT TYPE=CHECKBOX NAME="onions"> like green onions<BR>
<INPUT TYPE=CHECKBOX NAME="cookies"> like cookies<BR>
<INPUT TYPE=CHECKBOX NAME="kimchee"> like kim chee<BR>
</FIELDSET><P>
<FIELDSET>
other comments:<BR>
<TEXTAREA NAME="comments" ROWS=5 COLS=25></TEXTAREA>
</FIELDSET>
</form>
```

Note: <FIELDSET> is a block level element, so theoretically we didn't need the <P ...> tags between the fieldsets. However, because <FIELDSET> is not yet supported by major browsers such as Netscape, we put in the <P ...>s to keep the groups separated.

12.2.6 <LEGEND> Element

<LEGEND ...> is used with <FIELDSET> to give a title to each set of fields.

Example

```
Scrolling Menu
<form>
<FIELDSET>
<LEGEND>Personal Stuff</LEGEND><P>
name: <INPUT NAME="realname"><BR>
email: <INPUT NAME="email">
</FIELDSET>
</form>
```

12.2.7 <LABEL> Element

Labeling a form control means more than just making sure the text that appears on the Web page is clear. It also means that you've used the LABEL element to clearly mark and describe what type of information you want the visitor to enter into each form control.

A little background information: A "form control" is a fancy term for a text box, checkbox, radio button, or any element in a form that allows the user to enter information or submit the form.

The LABEL element is an "explicit label" for the form control. By explicit, we mean that you're specifically providing information about each form element. Each form control should have its own LABEL. Add the FOR attribute to tie the LABEL to the form control's ID attribute.

```
<form method="post" action="../cgi-bin/FormMail.pl" name="emailForm">
<label for="em_add">Email Address</label>
<input type="text" name="email" id="em_add">
<br>
<label for="comment_here">Send us your Comments!</label> <br>
<textarea name="comments" id="comment_here" cols="20" rows="5">
</textarea>
<br>
<input type="submit" value="Submit">
</form>
```

Note: Do not add a LABEL attribute for the SUBMIT button. That's because browser read the text that's on the button. That's a handy feature, but does mean that you need to clearly define the button's use.

The FOR attribute is required. The value of FOR should be the same as the value of ID in the form field that the label applies to.

You can also add the ACCESSKEY attribute to your LABEL element and make keyboard navigation easier for visitors.

12.2.8 Other Considerations with LABEL

Always place the <LABEL> element immediately before or after the form control related to it. Although it's not a good idea, you could create a LABEL like this for a table inside a form:

```
<form ... form attributes here>
<table>
<tr>
<td><label for="em_add">Enter Your Email Address</td>
<td>Need an email address? The University offers them free to all students!</td>
</tr>
<tr>
<td><input type="text" name="email" id="em_add"></td>
<td> </td>
</label>
</tr>
</table>
</form>
```

First, you have nesting problems and HTML Toolbox would probably alert you that your tags aren't closed properly. But, even more important, you've created an "implicit" LABEL instead of an explicit one.

12.2.9 Other Attributes of <INPUT> element

The other attributes associated with the INPUT element are the disabled, alt and usemap. When an element is disabled, its contents are not only unalterable but also unusable. The alt attribute is used for those web browsers that can't accept Forms. It only allows the users to see what elements the Form is composed of, but does not interact with those elements in any way. The usemap attribute can be used to include a client-side image map in the INPUT element.

Example

```
<INPUT alt = "this is a submit button"
        type = "submit">
<INPUT usemap= "#mapx">
<ISINDEX ...>
```

12.3 TIPS FOR FORM TAG & ATTRIBUTES

Put Cursor Into Form Field When Page Loads

Image here

Notice that when this page loaded the cursor was already activated in the form text field above.

This can be accomplished with the following steps:

Give the form a name using the name=name" attribute. For the example we are using name="myform".

Give the form input tag element a name. For the example we are using name="email".

Place the javascript onLoad event handler in the opening <body... tag.

<body onLoad="document.myform.email.focus()">

Note: The form name "myform" is placed in the object position of the onLoad event handler. The input tag name "email" is placed in the element position of the onLoad event handler. Just replace these with your form name and input tag name where you want the cursor to appear when the page loads.

Here is the code for the above form:

```
<form name="myform" method="POST" action="myscript.cgi">
Email <input type="text" name="email">
</form>
```

Remove Default Content From A Form Field

This onClick removal script will remove default text from a form field when the cursor is activated. Thus saving the user having to highlight and remove the text before entering their information.

Name the form using the name="name" attribute. (name="FormName")

The form name is used as the document object in the onClick command.

Name the form element input tag. (name="userinfo")

The form element name is used as the onClick reference in the command.

Example

```
<form name="myform" method="POST" action="myscript.cgi">
Email <input type="text" name="email">
</form>
```

EXERCISE

Objective Type Questions

1. ______is not an element of form.
   (A) Selection List Box (B) Input Box
   (C) Text Area (D) Output Box
2. ______is not an attribute of <frame> tag.
   (A) Src (B) Name
   (C) Scrolling (D) Color
3. ______button is used to select one option from a form.
   (A) Check Box (B) Radio
   (C) Select (D) Submit
4. What is the correct HTML for making a checkbox?
   (A) <input type="check"> (B) <check>
   (C) <checkbox> (D) <input type="checkbox">
5. What is the correct HTML for making a text input field?
   (A) <textinput type="text"> (B) <textfield>
   (C) <input type="textfield"> (D) <input type="text">
6. What is the correct HTML for making a drop-down list?
   (A) <list> (B) <input type="list">
   (C) <select> (D) <input type="dropdown">
7. What is the correct HTML for making a text area?
   (A) <input type="textbox"> (B) <input type="textarea">
   (C) <textarea> (D) <textbox>
8. Write a code for making text area?
   (A) <textarea> (B) <input ="textarea">
   (C) <input type ="textbox"> (D) <input type="text area">
9. Form tag has 2 attributes
   (A) action & method (B) form & action
   (C) method & form (D) all of these

10. ______button send the current information held in each field of the form to the web server for further processing.

(A) submit (B) reset

(C) normal (D) all of these

11. ______value of method attribute send information to the server.

(A) POST (B) GET

(C) form (D) none of these

12. ______tag is used with <option> tag to give list of items.

(A) <input> (B) <frame>

(C) <select> (D) a and b

13. ______element is used to check one element at a time.

(A) Radio (B) Menu

(C) List (D) Checkbox

14. The______ element replicates asterisk for any keystroke.

(A) password (B) radio

(C) text (D) checkbox

15. What are the general syntax for inline image?

(A) src=img (B) src=image

(C) img=file (D) img src=file

(E) image src=file

16. What values can the METHOD attribute have?

(A) The GET and POST values

(B) The PUT and PLACE values

(C) The POST and REQUEST values

17. What tag is used for pull down and scrolling menus?

(A) The <SELECT> tag

(B) The <TEXT> tag

(C) The <FORM> tag

18. What attribute does every <INPUT> tag contain?

(A) The TYPE attribute

(B) The SIZE attribute

(C) The COLS attribute

19. What shape is a radio button?

    (A) A diamond

    (B) A circle

    (C) A square

20. What tag is used to define a text area?

    (A) The <AREA> tag

    (B) The <TEXTAREA> tag

    (C) The <TEXT> tag

Review & Discussion Questions

1. Arrange the following objects according to object hierarchy: Form, Window, Document, and Checkbox.

2. You are asked to design an HTML form for a survey where name, age group and gender information of the person will be entered.

   What input type will you use for collecting information in each of the following cases? Give reason for your choice.

   (i) Age group: ______ (ii) Gender: ______

3. Specify the tag and attributes used to create a textbox which can accept maximum of 20 characters with a default value "Enter Name".

4. How to create Forms in HTML, give an example?

5. Design a feedback form for any of the University/s websites. Use HTML. Your form should have basic formatting features. Make necessary assumptions and indicate them.

6. Draw the output for the following code:

```
<HTML>
<BODY>
<FORM NAME="input" ACTION="html_form_action.asp"
METHOD="get">
Type your first name:
<INPUT TYPE="text" NAME="First Name" VALUE="Mickey" SIZE="20">
<BR>Type your last name:
<INPUT TYPE="text" NAME="Last Name" VALUE="Mouse" SIZE="20">
<BR>
<INPUT TYPE="submit" VALUE="Submit">
</FORM>
<P>
If you click the "Submit" button, you will send your input to a new page
called html_form_action.asp.
</P>
</BODY>
</HTML>
```

7. Which tag is used to create checkbox?

8. Which tag is used to create drop-down list?

9. Which attribute of <OPTION> element is used to select the default option from list?

10. Which tag is used to create multi-line textbox?

11. Explain form tag.

12. Explain different attributes of FORM tag.

13. Differentiate between get and post method of form tag.

14. What is meant by FORM? What are essential steps while designing the idle form?

15. Explain following tags used to construct web form:

    (a) FORM

    (b) INPUT

    (c) SELECT

16. What is FORM? Give different object of form with tags.

CHAPTER 13

Frames

CHAPTER OBJECTIVES

This chapter discusses the major advantages and disadvantages of using frames in a Web site. The proper syntax for building frames is covered as well as some very useful frame designing tips. Frames can either be a designer's best friend that enhances a site by consistently displaying navigation and content at the same time, or a designer's worst enemy if the frames have been poorly designed, leading to user confusion and detracting from his/her overall experience.

CHAPTER OUTLINES

13.1 Introduction

13.2 Getting Started with Frames

13.3 <FRAMESET> Element

13.4 <FRAME> Element

13.5 < NOFRAMES> Element

13.6 Targeted Frames

13.7 Creating Borderless Frames

13.8 Guide to Frames Usage

Exercise

13.1 INTRODUCTION

Frames allow you to divide the page into several rectangular areas and to display a separate document in each rectangle. Each of those rectangles is called a "frame". Frames are very popular because they are one of the few ways to keep part of the page stationary while other parts change. Frames are also one of the most controversial uses of HTML, because of the way the frames concept was designed, and because many web framed web sites are poorly implemented. A frames master page uses the <FRAMESET> element pair instead of <BODY>. Each frameset must be defined before frame objects.

13.2 GETTING STARTED WITH FRAMES

With frames, which divide Web pages into multiple, scrollable regions - you can present information in a more flexible and useful fashion. Each region, or frame, has several features:

- It can be given an individual URL, so it can load information independent of the other frames on the page.
- It can be given a NAME, allowing it to be targeted by other URLs.
- It can resize dynamically, if the user changes the window's size. (Resizing can also be disabled, ensuring a constant frame size.)

These properties offer new possibilities:

- Elements that the user should always see, such as control bars, copyright notices, and title graphics can be placed in a static, individual frame. As the user navigates the site in "live" frames, the static frame's contents remain fixed, even though adjoining frames redraw.
- Tables of contents are more functional. One frame can contain TOC links that, when clicked, display results in an adjoining frame.
- Frames side-by-side design allows queries to be posed and answered on the same page, with one frame holding the query form, and the other presenting the results.

13.3 <FRAMESET> ELEMENT

The <FRAMESET> element is a frame container for dividing a window into rectangular subspaces called frames. In a Frameset document, the outermost <FRAMESET> element takes the place of <BODY> and immediately follows the <HEAD>. The <FRAMESET> element contains one or more <FRAMESET> or <FRAME> elements, along with an optional <NOFRAMES> element to provide alternate content for browsers that do not support frames or have frames disabled. A meaningful <NOFRAMES> element should always be provided and should at the very least contain links to the mainframe or frames.

Attributes		Description
ROWS	:	**"pixels I percents"** define the row height of each row (vertical) within the frameset. The value for each row height is a comma separated list of sizes (in pixels or percents).
COLS	:	**"pixels I percents"** define the column width of each column (horizontal) within the frameset. The value for each column width is a comma separated list of sizes (in pixels or percents).
ONLOAD		**"script"** to specify client-side scripting actions to perform when the frames have all been loaded.
ONUNLOAD		"script" to specify client-side scripting actions to perform when the frames have all been removed.
FRAMEBORDER		**" YES I 1 I NO I 0"** controls the visibility of the borders around all frames. The FRAMEBORDER attribute enables you to turn off the border around frames in the frameset. FRAMEBORDER can also be used with the <frame> tag for single frames. Use the values "yes" or "1" to enable borders and "no" or "0" to disable borders. This attribute is handled differently in IE and Netscape, so if you want to use it, you should define the borders in all frames in your frameset so that you get a consistent view.
BORDER		**"integer"** controls the width of all borders. This attribute allows you to set the width of the borders in a NE. frameset; defined in pixels.
BORDERCOLOR		**"color expression"** allows you to change the color of the frame borders. *RRGGBB* is a six-digit hexadecimal number with the first two digits specifying the red value, the middle two the green value, and the last two the blue value. Color names can also be used in the COLOR attribute. Valid colors are: Aqua, Black, Blue, Fuchsia, Gray, Green, Lime, Maroon, Navy, Olive, Purple, Red, Silver, Teal, Yellow, and White. *With Netscape, you can change the color of the frame's border using this tag. Keep in mind that if two adjacent frames have different bordercolor's the border color will end up undefined.* Bordercolor can be used with the <FRAME> tag for single frames.

Note: The ROWS and COLS attributes define the dimensions of each frame in the set. Each attribute takes a comma-separated list of lengths, specified in pixels, as a percentage, or as a relative length. A relative length is expressed as i* where i is an integer. For example, a frameset defined with ROWS="3*,*" (* is equivalent to 1*) will have its first row allotted three times the height of the second row.

The values specified for the ROWS attribute give the height of each row, from top to bottom. The COLS attribute gives the width of each column from left to right. If ROWS or COLS is omitted, the implied value for the attribute is 100%. If both attributes are specified, a grid is defined and filled left-to-right then top-to-bottom.

13.4 <FRAME> ELEMENT

The <FRAME> element defines a frame i.e., a rectangular subspace within a Frameset document. Each FRAME must be contained within a FRAMESET that defines the dimensions of the frame. The FRAME element also accepts a number of attributes to specify the presentation on visual browsers. Style sheets provide a more flexible method of defining the presentation of frames, but the element's presentational attributes are more widely supported.

Attributes		Description
SRC	:	***"text string"*** describes the relationship to another web page or other internet resource. (Forward link types) This is the only required attribute for the frame tag. The value of this attribute is the URL of the document you would like to be displayed in the frame. **"URLIPATH"** defines the path or full URL to the HTML page you want to appear in a named frame. Path refers to a local document, and URL refers to a page on another server. You can reference any HTML object, image, or multimedia element that could normally be displayed by a Web browser. (Keep in mind, if you use an image, it will not be tiled like a background image, but rather just displayed once.)
NAME	:	The NAME attribute gives a name to the frame for use with the TARGET attribute of the <A>, <AREA>, <BASE>, <FORM>, and <LINK> elements. The NAME attribute value must begin with a character in the range A-Z or a-z. "_selfl_parentl_topl_blank" use for Frame or Window targeting. This allows you to label your frames so that you can open new pages in specific frames. If you do not name your frames, all links will open in the frame that they are in.
NORESIZE	:	Prevent visitors from resizing frames created with this non-value attribute. By default, the browser allows frames to be resized by dragging the frame border.
SCROLLING	:	**"YESINOIAUTO"** enables you to control when scrollbars are to appear on each frame window. The browser default is always 'auto', allowing the browser to decide if the frame needs scrollbars when objects appear outside the frame window boundaries. You can often use the "no" value if you design your objects to appear within the boundaries of fixed size frames.
MARGINHEIGHT	:	This attribute defines how tall the margin between frames will be. It cannot be less than 1 pixel. Also, if the browser cannot display the desired values, then this attribute will be ignored.
MARGINWIDTH	:	This attribute defines how wide the margin between frames will be. It cannot be less than 1 pixel. Also, if the browser cannot display the desired values, then this attribute will be ignored.
FRAMEBORDER	:	**"YESINO"** controls the visibility of the borders around individual frames. The frame FRAMEBORDER attribute enables you to turn off the border around individual frames. Frames connected to the preferred borderless frame should also include this attribute/value. Use the values "yes" or "1" to enable borders and "no" or "0" to disable borders. This attribute is handled differently in IE and Netscape, so if you want to use it, you should define the borders in all frames in your frameset so that you get a consistent view.
LONGDESC	:	**"URI"** provide the URI of a full HTML description of the object.
BORDERCOLOR (Netscape only)	:	**"color expression"** allows you to change the color of the individual frame. *RRGGBB* is a six-digit hexadecimal number with the first two digits specifying the red value, the middle two the green value and the last two the blue value. Color names can also be used in the COLOR attribute. Valid colors are: Aqua, Black, Blue, Fuchsia, Gray, Green, Lime, Maroon, Navy, Olive, Purple, Red, Silver, Teal, Yellow, and White. *With Netscape, you can change the color of the frame's border using this tag. Keep in mind that if two adjacent frames have different bordercolor's the border color will end up undefined.*

13.5 < NOFRAMES> ELEMENT

The <NOFRAMES> element contains content that should only be rendered when frames are not displayed. <NOFRAMES> is typically used in a Frameset document to provide alternate content for browsers that do not support frames or have frame disabled.

The <NOFRAMES> element pair is a very simple method of doing this. All you have to do is create a page that you want these visitors to see instead of your frames view, and paste everything from the <BODY> element to the closing </BODY> element, between the <NOFRAMES> element pair. If you do not use <NOFRAME> element, then the visitor will see nothing and quickly leave your site.

Note: A meaningful <NOFRAMES> element should always be provided in a Frameset document and should at the very least contain links to the mainframe or frames. <NOFRAMES> should not contain a message telling the user to upgrade his or her browser. Some browsers support frames but allow the user to disable them.

Example

```
<html>
<head>
<title>Frames Set with Header</title>
</head>
<frameset rows="45,*">
<frame name="top" scrolling="no" noresize target="main" src="frmhead1.htm">
<frame name="main" src="frmmain1.htm" scrolling="auto">
<noframes>
<body>
<p>This page uses frames, but your browser doesn't support them.<br>
Please <a href="home.htm">click here</a> to view a non-frames home page. Thank you.</p>
</body>
</noframes>
</frameset>
</html>
```

Note: This tag pair and content should appear before the last closing </FRAMESET> tag.

Frame Examples

```
<FRAMESET ROWS="10%, 80%, 10%">
    <FRAME NAME="window1" SRC="document.html">
    <FRAMESET COLS="50%, 50%">
      <FRAME NAME="window2" SRC="doc.html">
      <FRAME NAME="window3" SRC="doggy.html">
    </FRAMESET>
    <FRAME NAME="window4" SRC="doc444.html">
    <NOFRAMES>
     <BODY BACKGROUND ......>
     .... stuff to display if the browser does not understand FRAMESET...
    </NOFRAMES>
  </FRAMESET>
```

This first divides the display into three slices, the top and bottom being thing (10% of the display height), the remainder going to the middle frame. The first slice is named window1, and is initially loaded with the document document1.html. The <FRAME> element defines the initial content of the cell (frames may be empty, in which case you leave out the SRC). The second slice is divided by columns into two frames i.e. window2 and window3 and so on.

```
<frameset                                   cols="20%,*">
        <frame        name="left"           src="col1.html">
        <frame        name="right"          src="col2.html">
</frameset>
```

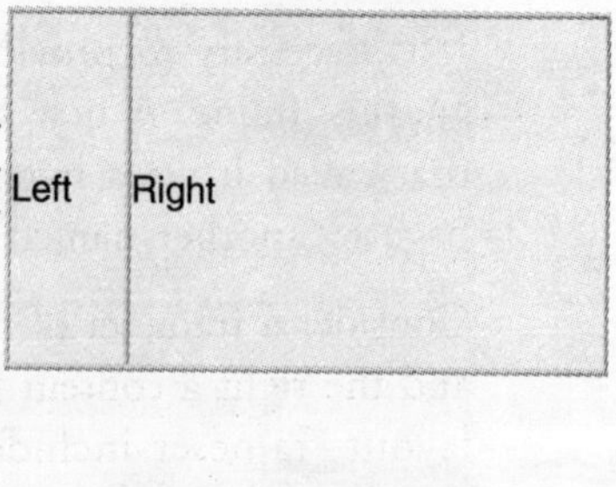


```
<frameset                                   cols="20%,*">
        <frame        name="left"           src="col1.html">
             <frameset                      rows="33%,33%,*">
         <frame       name="top"            src="row1.html">
        <frame        name="middle"         src="row2.html">
        <frame        name="bottom"         src="row3.html">
   </frameset>
</frameset>
```

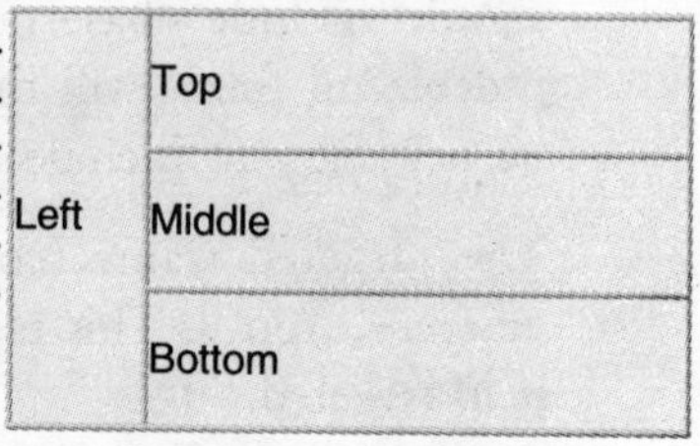

```
<frameset                                        cols="80%,*">
        <frameset                           rows="33%,33%,*">
        <frame        name="top"             src="row1.html">
        <frame        name="middle"          src="row2.html">
        <frame        name="bottom"          src="row3.html">
    </frameset>
    <frame           name="right"            src="col2.html">
</frameset>
```

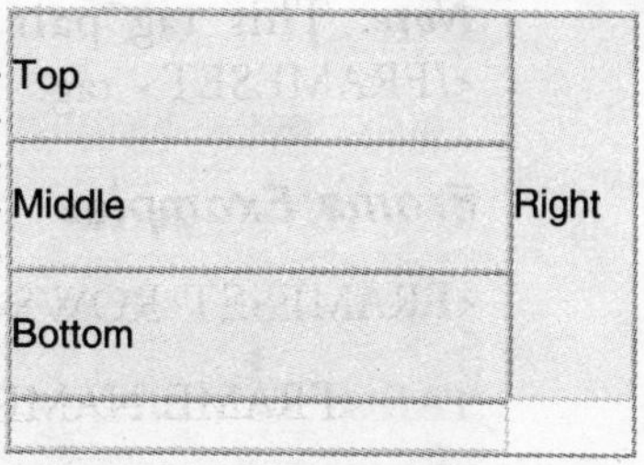


```
<frameset                                        rows="15%,*">
        <frame        name="upper"           src="row1.html">
        <frame        name="lower"           src="row2.html">
</frameset>
```

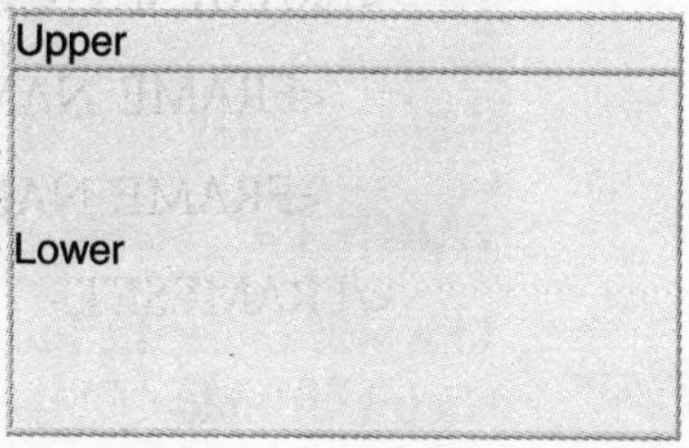


```
<frameset                                        rows="20%,*">
        <frame        name="header"          src="row1.html">
           <frameset                             cols="20%,*">
        <frame        name="left"            src="col1.html">
        <frame        name="right"           src="col2.html">
    </frameset>
</frameset>
```

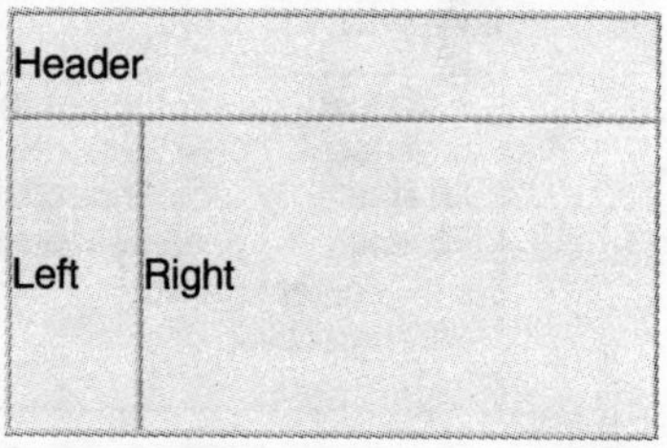

Note: All of these examples can be adjusted in size to meet the needs of your task. Comparing the code to its illustration should aid in the further understanding of frameset layouts and how you might develop others. Remember, frame sizes may be specified in pixels as well as percentage.

13.6 TARGETED FRAMES

It is necessary to provide "control" within the frame that changes information in another frame. A new page will appear by default in the same frame as the page that called it via a hyperlink, unless the target attribute is used to direct the new page to another named frame (see _top and _blank exceptions).

Consider a frameset of two columns, the left an index frame for making a selection and the right a content frame for displaying the selection. If the <frame> tag in the layout frameset included name="content", the controlling frame (index.html) should include <base target="content"> within the <head> tag. All links in the index.html frame will then target the "content" frame. Without this entry, it will be necessary to include target="content" within each of the links.

The targeted frame (content.html) name="content" needs to include the tag, <target="_top">. This tag will make the "content" frame load over itself each time it is targeted.

TARGET="_self"

This causes a document to load into the same frame as the link.

TARGET="_parent"

This forces a document to load into the same frameset window as the link.

TARGET="_top"

This makes the document load into the full area of the browser window, removing all frames. ie linking from a frameset to another site, or offering the visitor the ability to "not use" or "get out of" frames view.

TARGET="_blank"

This will cause the linked page to load into a new and completely separate window. Useful for links to other reference sites while keeping your site loaded in its original window. These show a few uses of the target attribute for framesets and general hyperlinks etc.

Example Layout:	*Frame, index.html:*	*Frame, content.html:*
<frameset cols="20%, 80%"> .<frame src="index.html"> .<frame name="content" src="content.html"> </frameset>	<head> <base target="content"> </head> <body> . </body>	<target="_top"> <body> . </body>

<FRAME TARGET="|_self|_parent|_top|_blank> </FRAME>

<a href="your.html" target="framename">Load the Page</a>

<a href="your.html" target="_blank">View the Page</a>

<form method="POST" action="http://wooz.com/cgi-bin/scrpt.cgi" target="_blank">

<a href="your.html" target="_top">Leave Frames View</a>

Note: In HTML 4, the TARGET attribute value is case-insensitive, so that _top and _TOP both have the same meaning. However, most browsers treat the TARGET attribute value as case-sensitive and do not recognize _TOP as having the special meaning of _top.

13.7 CREATING BORDERLESS FRAMES

Whole Frameset

To hide all borders and ensure compatibility with most browsers, include the following two attributes. Options not applicable to a browser will simply be ignored.

```
<frameset cols="105,*" frameborder="0" framespacing="0">
   <frame src="toolbar.htm">
```

Contd....

```
<frame src="frames/info.htm">
</frameset>
```

Individual Frames not recommended.

This is a rarely used option, but to hide individual frame borders in frames sharing a common border with Ne., include the attributes, as above, but add them to the <frame> tags. IE will still show a fine border.

```
<frameset cols="105,*">
    <frame src="toolbar.htm" frameborder="0" framespacing="0">
    <frame src="frames/info.htm" frameborder="0" framespacing="0">
</frameset>
```

13.8 GUIDE TO FRAMES USAGE

13.8.1 Frames design guidelines: automatic no-frames content

An important aspect of any site using frames is to make sure the site can still be used when the visitor has frames support disabled or uses a browser that does not support them at all. The NOFRAMES element is used for this purpose.

13.8.2 Problem: duplicating content

Usually, a site using frames will still have several "ordinary" HTML documents. These are loaded in the frames, as set up by the initial frame set document. However, this initial document must have alternative content; otherwise, nothing in the site is accessible for people who do not see the frames. A simple approach is to cut & paste the "starting" document into the noframes section of the frame set document. The disadvantage is obvious: you now have to update two documents.

13.8.3 Solution: server-side includes (SSI) or preprocessing

If your server supports server-side include, you can use those to include the text into both the frame document and the noframes section of the initial document. Additionally, you can include the table of contents or links frame in the same way, so no navigational information is lost.

Imagine a site that has a table of contents and several text documents. The table of contents is found in "toc.html", and the starting document is "a.html". To properly use server-side includes in the manner described above, the text of these documents has to be put in a different document, so, it can be included in multiple places. Let's assume this is done by putting them in "toc.txt" and "a.txt" respectively. The various documents that use these then look like this:

index.html - main index for the site

```
<FRAMESET COLS="30%, *">
<FRAME SRC="toc.html" NAME=toc>
<FRAME SRC="a.html" NAME=content>
<NOFRAMES>
<!—#include-file "a.txt"—>
<!—#include-file "toc.txt"—>
</NOFRAMES>
</FRAMESET>
```

a.html - content document

```
<HEAD>
<TITLE>Title of document</TITLE>
<!— other header stuff —>
</HEAD>
<BODY>
<!—#include-file "a.txt"—>
</BODY>
```

toc.html - table of contents

```
<BODY>
<!--#include-file "toc.txt"-->
</BODY>
```

Note: The content documents have a <HEAD> section, but the table of contents does not. This is done because the table of contents is never loaded as a stand-alone document. You can get fancy with tables to get the original column-based layout.

The syntax for server-side includes depends on the server. Check your server's documentation for the correct syntax, if the above does not work. This approach requires that server-side includes are used for each document that can be used this way.

EXERCISE

Objective Type Questions

1. A file that specifies how the screen is divided into frames is called a ____________ .

   (A) tablelink

   (B) frameset

   (C) frametable

2. In the code <frameset cols="120,*"> the following would be true.

   (A) Top frame would be 120 pixels high

   (B) Left frame would be 120 inches wide

   (C) Left frame would be 120 pixels wide

3. You can add names to each frame window using which setting?

   (A) src

   (B) ur

   (C) name

4. If you don't want the frame windows to be resizeable, simply add what to the <frame> lines?

   (A) save

   (B) dontresize

   (C) noresize

5. Adding _top to a link within a frameset does what?

   (A) loads page in parent frame

   (B) loads the page into the current window

   (C) cancels all frames, loads in full browser window

6. Which is not valid HTML?

   (A) <frameset columns="16%,84%">

   (B) <frameset cols="100,150">

   (C) <frameset rows="16%,84%">

7. When making a 2 window frameset, you must name the windows "menu" and "main"?

   (A) False

   (B) True no matter what the frames actually consist of

   (C) True if the frames consist of a menu and a main area

8. Which of the following is not used to make your frame borders invisible?

   (A) col="0"

   (B) border="0"

   (C) framespacing="0"

9. If you leave out the setting for scrolling what will happen?

   (A) A scrollbar will always be present, needed or not

   (B) A scrollbar will appear if needed

   (C) No scrollbar will appear even if needed

10. Which attribute defines default pages to your frames?

   (A) def

   (B) a href

   (C) src

Review & Discussion Questions

1. Why do we need to specify NAME attribute within a FRAME tag?
2. Write HTML code to load a page named "logo.html" into a frame named "header" with a height of 20%.
3. Write HTML code to load a page named "FOOTER.html" into a frame named "FOOTER" with a height of 20%.
4. What is Frame? How will you divide you web browser screen using FRAME tag?
5. Write an HTML code to generate the study centre name, study centre coordinator, place and the state where you are studying your IT programmed. Use frame based approach. Make necessary assumptions and indicate them.
6. Design a home page for any movie theatre. Use frame-based approach. Assumptions can be made wherever necessary.
7. Draw the output for the following code:

```
<HTML>
<HEAD>
<TITLE>frame definition</TITLE>
</HEAD>
<FRAMESET COLS="20%, *, 20 %">
<FRAME SRC= "content1.html" NAME="1">
<FRAMESET ROWS="20%, *">
<FRAME SRC= "content2.html" NAME="2">
<FRAMESET COLS="50%, *">
<FRAMESET ROWS="50%, *">
<FRAME SRC= "content4.html" NAME="4">
<FRAME SRC= "content5.html" NAME="5">
</FRAMESET>
<FRAME SRC= "content3.html" NAME="3">
</FRAMESET>
</FRAMESET>
<FRAME SRC= "content9.html" NAME="9">
</FRAMESET>
</HTML>
```

8. Which tag is used to create inline frame?
9. List any two problems occurs using frame.
10. What do you mean by FRAME? How these can be created in web page?
11. Explain the <FRAME>, <FRAMESET> tags.
12. What is frame? Explain FRAME tag.
13. Explain FRAMESET tag with example.
14. Which are disadvantages of frame?
15. Which are advantages of frame?
16. Explain different attributes of FRAMESET tag.

CHAPTER 14

Cascading Style Sheets

CHAPTER OBJECTIVES

This chapter discusses the overall layout, text size, style and formatting, table formatting, link properties, and more that can be used for Web pages and the use of Cascading Style Sheets to control typography. There are CSS style blocks commonly referred to as rules that can be embedded into an individual HTML page or placed in an external file that will control many individual pages on your website.

CHAPTER OUTLINES

14.1 INTRODUCTION

CSS stands for Cascading Style Sheets, created by Hakon Wium Lie of MIT in 1994. It is a markup language used to directly effect the "look" of web pages. This includes overall layout, text size, style and formatting, table formatting, link properties, and more. CSS style blocks are also commonly referred to as rules. These rules can be embedded into an individual HTML page or placed in an external file that will control many individual pages on your website. Thus changing a property in one place in the linked style sheet will immediately make that change on every web page that is linked to it. When used correctly, CSS allows one to define the look of an entire site in one single document. It provides a means for authors to specify how they wish documents written in a markup language such as XML or HTML to be formatted.

In short Cascading Style Sheets:

- Styles define how to display HTML elements; styles are normally stored in Style Sheets.
- "Cascading" refers to the fact that each different style declaration can be "cascaded" under the one above it, forming a parent-child relationship between the styles.

14.2 CSS WEB TEMPLATE

"CSS Web Template" is a website design created using Cascading Style Sheets (CSS) technology. Cascading style sheets provide web developers an easy way to format and to style web pages. CSS will be used even more because it is seen the same way by all browsers, making it the best option during the browser wars.

CSS templates allow enhanced browser and platform compatibility (CSS supporting browsers are used by 99.98% of existent web surfers). Your website will look perfect in Windows, UNIX and MAC browsers. The template is primarily tested on multiple platforms to ensure better requirements compliance.

Style Sheets are the easiest way to provide a default font styling for HTML. Therefore, you can modify the whole text and link colors on every page by editing just a single CSS file! CSS also makes your coding much easier because you don't have to repeat the many formatting tags. This streamlined code equals faster download time and reduced bandwidth usage.

CSS templates show 100% compatibility with Macromedia Dream weaver and MS Front Page. Other web editors also handle this technology easier than the usual HTML code.

CSS technology is a great step forward in web development. Separated content and presentation adds more flexibility to your website. And, you'll have no problems with future modification of your website. All templates are based on w3c.org technologies and standards that make your website much more user-friendly.

14.3 W3C CSS RECOMMENDATIONS

CSS was first developed in 1997, as a way for Web developers to define the look and feel of their Web pages. It was intended to allow developers to separate content from design so that HTML could perform more of the function that it was originally based on the markup of content, without worry about the design and layout.

CSS didn't gain in popularity until around 2000, when Web browsers began using more than the basic font and color aspects of CSS. And, now all modern browsers support all of CSS Level 1, most of CSS Level 2, and some aspects of CSS Level 3.

14.3.1 Level 1 (CSS1), 17 Dec., 1996 (Rev. 11 Jan., 1999)

On Dec 17, 1996, W3C wrote the recommendation for CSS to be included in the HTML standard. CSS1 level 1 is a simple style sheet mechanism that allows authors and readers to attach style (e.g., fonts, colors and spacing) to HTML documents. The CSS1 language is human readable and writable, and expresses style in common desktop publishing terminology.

For more detail visit: http://www.w3.org/TR/REC-CSS1

14.3.2 Level 2 (CSS2), 12 May, 1998

Cascading Style Sheets level 2 is the second level of CSS. It provides more support for accessibility and positioning. CSS2 is a lot more flexible than CSS1, but that means that there is more to learn such as different media types i.e., paged media (for printing), aural style sheets (for speech synthesis). It allows you to extended selection mechanism, generated content, automatic numbering, formatting of tables and so on.

For more detail visit: http://www.w3.org/TR/REC-CSS2

14.3.3 Level 3 (CSS3), ongoing work; split in May 2001 into 26 modules.

Cascading Style Sheets level 3 is the most recent iteration of CSS. In it, CSS will be modularized to clarify the connections between the different parts of the specification as well as to make it more streamlined.

For more detail visit: http://www.w3.org/TR/css3-roadmap

14.4 WHY STYLE SHEETS?

There are two answers to this:

1. HTML is not designed for styling documents. When you write an HTML document, you are specifying only the content that the element contains. If you wished to state that you want your headings to be yellow Helvetica, then you could have <H1><FONT color="yellow" face="Helvetica">A heading</FONT></H1>, but this is bad for several reasons:
   - You have to add that piece of code to each heading that you want styled - this is time-consuming, prone to error and makes files excessively bloated (a typical page styled using HTML will be 1/3rd formatting tags).
   - If you want to change those headings to pink Arial, then you will have to change each heading individually - a prohibitively laborious task on a large site.
2. HTML simply doesn't offer sufficient control over document formatting important formatting effects such as leading (the space between lines), text shadows, and many other effects just can't be done using HTML. Style Sheets helps in cost reduction, but also the download speed will increase for viewers of your pages.

14.5 ADVANTAGES OF USING STYLE SHEETS

CSS was a revolution in the world of web design. The concrete benefits of CSS include:

- Separate content from formatting.
- Control layout of many documents from one single style sheet.
- Give far more control over formatting than HTML - such features as background.
- Apply different layout to different media-types (screen, print, etc.).
- Numerous advanced and sophisticated techniques.
- Images and colors on all elements - not just the whole document, etc.
- Reduce download time by removing formatting information from documents.
- Ensure a consistent appearance across a site.

14.6 HOW DOES CSS WORK?

In this lesson, you will learn how to make your first style sheet. You will get to know about the basic CSS model and which codes are necessary to use CSS in an HTML document. Many of the properties used in Cascading Style Sheets (CSS) are similar to those of HTML. Thus, if you are used to use HTML for the layout, you will most likely recognize many of the codes. Let us look at a concrete example.

The basic CSS syntax:

Let's say we want a nice red color as the background of a webpage:

Using HTML, we could have done it like this:

```
<body bgcolor="#FF0000">
```

With CSS the same result can be achieved like this:

```
body {background-color: #FF0000;}
```

As you will note, the codes are more or less identical for HTML and CSS. The above example also shows you the fundamental CSS model.

14.7 CSS RULES AND STYLE SHEETS

Rule: A rule or rule set is a statement about one stylistic aspect of one or more elements.

It's a set of instructions that a browser can follow to alter the appearance of HTML elements based on the presentational values you supply. A CSS rule consists of a few component parts, shown in Figure 14.1.

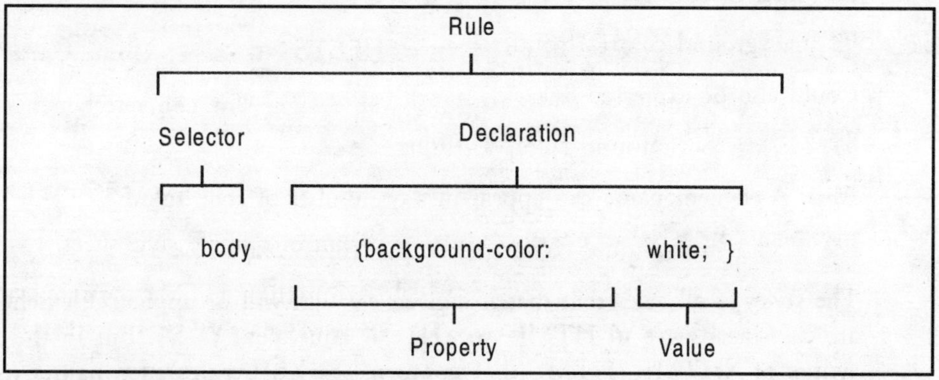

Figure 14.1 ♦ CSS Rules and Style Sheets

14.7.1 CSS Selectors

The CSS selector is the part of the rule that targets an element that will be styled. In their simplest form, selectors consist of a tag name. Selectors specify how to apply a given style to the HTML document. Possible scopes that affecting elements are:

All of the elements	td {color:#333399;}
Some of the elements	td.some {color:#333399;}
One of the elements	td#one {color:#333399;}

While applying to elements, the affected elements are coded as:

```
<TD class="some">
<TD id="one">
```

Some common rules for selector:

- A selector token can also match to any element
- The id attribute is used to match a single token
- You can also use a psuedoclass (represents a special characteristic of an element)

Examples: (The components of the anchor element where the link has been visited)

```
.danger {color: red;}
a:link {color: green;}
a:visited {color: red;}
```

14.7.2 Grouping Selectors

Multiple element names can be specified by separating them with a comma (","). This is known as grouping. So the following rules:

```
h1 {background-color: #ffff00}
h2 {background-color: #ffff00}
h3 {background-color: #ffff00}
```

Could also be expressed as:

```
h1, h2, h3 {background-color: #ffff00}
```

Note: A element name can appear in any number of style rules.

```
h1, h2, h3 {background-color: #ffff00}h1 {color: red}
```

The styles of all rules that match a given element will be applied. Element names are case-insensitive in HTML, so <H1> is equivalent to h1. But in the stricter syntax of XHTML (HTML that conforms to XML rules), tag names must be lowercase. Therefore, it's good practice to use lowercase tag names in your style sheets.

14.7.3 Selector Types

A selector, as its name implies, selects an element in your HTML document. A few different types of selectors are available, with varying levels of specificity to target a large number of elements or just a few.

A Selector is the portion of a Rule-Set that comes before the style Declaration Block embedded within curly braces ('{' and '}'.) Selector syntax in CSS2 can look for matches using five different contexts: elements, attributes, special HTML attributes, Pseudo-Classes and Pseudo-Elements.

Syntax

A Selector is composed of a series of one or more selector components separated by spaces and/or the ">" and "+" selector combining symbols. The components of a selector are described and linked below. Selector Component = ("*" | [Element Selector])? ([Attribute Selector] | [ID Selector] | [Class Selector] | [Pseudo-Class] | [Pseudo-Element])*

Element Selectors

These Selectors specify a portion of the document tree based upon its context with relation to other elements.

Attribute Selectors

These Selectors specify a portion of the document tree based upon its context with relation to attribute values for elements.

Special HTML Selectors

These Selector syntax forms existed in CSS1 and were specifically meant to target HTML, although at least the ID syntax could be generalized for use with other languages as well.

Pseudo-classes

The original pseudo-classes defined dynamic states of an element that are entered and exited over time, or through user intervention. CSS2 expanded on this concept to include virtual conceptual document components or inferred portions of the document tree (Netscape 6 has really expanded the use of this latter type of pseudo-class.)

The CSS specs do not always define, which elements may be in a pseudo-class dynamic state, or the method in which the state is entered or exited. CSS2 DOES state that a browser is not required to re-render a document because of pseudo-class state transitions however.

Unlike Pseudo-elements, Pseudo-classes are allowed anywhere in CSS selectors.

PSEUDO-CLASS	
:active	Adds special style to an activated element.
:focus	Adds special style to an element while the element has focus.
:hover	Adds special style to an element when you mouse over it.
:link	Adds special style to an unvisited link.
:visited	Adds special style to a visited link.
:first-child	Adds special style to an element that is the first child of some other element.
:lang	Allows the author to specify a language to use in a specified element.

Example

```
a:visited {font-size: 10pt; color: purple}
a:link {font-size: 14pt; text-decoration: underline; color: blue}
a:active {color: green}
a.test:hover {color: red}
a:focus img {border: thin solid green}
```

Pseudo-elements

Pseudo-elements allow logical elements to be defined which are not actually in the document element tree. Logical elements allow implied semantic structure to be addressed in CSS selectors, giving more power to the CSS author. Pseudo-elements can also address generated content that is not in the source document (with the 'before' and 'after' pseudo-elements.) Pseudo-elements may only be applied to external and document-level contexts - not to in-line styles.

CSS2 notes a few syntax caveats about pseudo-elements:

- They may only appear after the subject of the selector for a CSS rule. (e.g., After other classes and pseudo-classes - blockquote.foo:first-letter {color: red}) (e.g., Within a contextual selector - body p:first-line {margin-left: 2.0cm})
- Only one Pseudo-Element can be specified per selector. To address multiple pseudo-elements on a single element structure, multiple style Selector/ Declaration statements must be made. (e.g., blockquote.foo:first-letter {color: red} blockquote.foo:first-line {margin-left: 0.5in})
- Browsers are allowed to support only a subset of CSS properties for the: first-line and: first-letter pseudo-elements and still be considered legally 'conformant'.
- Browsers are also allowed to ignore the :first-line and :first-letter pseudo-elements completely in CSS selectors and still be considered legally 'conformant'.

PSEUDO-ELEMENT	
:first-letter	Adds special style to the first letter of a text
:first-line	Adds special style to the first line of a text
: before	Inserts some content before an element
:after	Inserts some content after an element

Example

```
em:before {content: url ("ding.wav")}
table:after {content: END OF TABLE}
div:first-letter {font-size: xx-large}
p:first-line {margin-left: 0.5in}
```

14.7.4 Table Format of Selector Types

SELECTOR TYPES		
Name	**Description**	**Example**
Universal	Any element.	* {font: 10px arial;}
Type	Any element of that type.	h1 {text-decoration: underline;}
Grouping	Multiple elements of different types.	h1, h2, h3 {font-family: verdana;}
Class	Multiple elements of different types where you don't want to affect all instances of that type.	.sampleclass { text-decoration: underline; }
Id	A single element type when you don't want to affect all instances of that type.	#sampleid { text-decoration: underline; }
Descendant	An element that is below (in the document tree) another element-no matter how many levels below.	#gallery hl { text-decoration: underline; }
Child	An element that is directly below (In the document tree) another element.	#title > p { font-weight: bold; }
Sibling	All elements of a type that share the same parent.	hl + p { font-style: Italic; }

Attribute	An element with that matches the attribute listed.	optlon[selected] { color: #ffOOOO; }
		Input[type="pass") { color: #ccc; }
		Img[src="sm.glf "] { border: lpx solid #000; }
		a[rel~="next"] { color: #fff; }
		*[langl="en"] { color: red; }

14.7.5 Selector Patterns

Selectors are not limited to just tag names however. In fact, rules are applied to elements using pattern matching between the selector and various aspects of an element. These can include its attributes and its relation to other elements in the document.

SELECTOR PATTERNS	
*	Any element.
E	An element of type E.
E[foo]	An E element with a "foo" attribute.
E[foo="bar"]	An E element whose "foo" attribute value is exactly equal to "bar".

Contd...

E[foo~="bar"]	An E element whose "foo" attribute value is a list of space-separated values, one of which is exactly equal to "bar".
E [hrenang I = "en"]	An E element whose "hrenang" attribute has a hyphen-separated list of values beginning (from the left) with "en".
E:first-child	An E element, first child of its parent.
E:link **E:visited**	An E element being the source anchor of a hyperlink of which the target is not yet visited (:link) or already visited (:visited).
E:active **E:hover** **E:focus**	An E element during certain user actions.
E:lang(fr)	An element of type E in language "fr" (the document language specifies how language is determined).
E::first-line	The first formatted line of an E element.
E::first-letter	The first formatted letter of an E element.
E::before	Generated content before an E element.
E::after	Generated content after an E element.
E.warning	An E element whose class is "warning" (the document language specifies how class Is determined).
E#myid	An E element with ID equal to "myId".
EF	An F element descendant of an E element.
E>F	An F element child of an E element.
E+F	An F element Immediately preceded by an E element.

Note: Internet Explorer currently does not support many of these selector patterns. It's recommended that you use a current version of Netscape or even Opera (which supports more than IE but still less than Netscape).

14.8 CSS DECLARATION

A CSS declaration represents the effect to be applied to the element(s) and it consists of two more parts: a property and a value. The property is that aspect of an element's presentation that is being modified, such as its color, its width, or its placement on the page. Dozens of properties are available in the CSS language, and you'll become familiar with many of them in the pages of this book.

The declaration block, denoted by the curly braces ("{","}"). Within this block are zero or more declarations. While defining multiple declarations, it must be separated by a semicolon (";").

Each declaration consists of a property and a value, separated by a colon (":"). Properties are identifiers, such as font-size, background-color, etc. The values permitted depend on the individual property. Whitespace may be used around any of these tokens, so you can format them for easy reading. You can also insert comments anywhere whitespace is permitted.

14.9 CSS PROPERTIES

The property value delivers the specific style that should be applied to the selected element. The values accepted depend on the particular property, and some properties accept multiple values, separated by spaces.

A Property is an identifier. Every property has its own syntax and constraints on the values it accepts. Property values also often indicate measurement units to aid in rendering to the specified media.

14.9.1 Font Properties

A font is a set of glyphs, which map to known characters in one or more languages. The glyphs within a font usually all share common characteristics such as size, style, and design. The Font properties allow control over many different font criteria such as boldness, italics, size, and specific or generic font name.

In CSS1, fonts were identified only by their name. If none of the fonts an author specified were available, the browser had to resort to using default fonts. This is clearly not the best solution when documents are available in an environment as heterogeneous as the web.

CSS2 font selection greatly expands the capabilities of browsers with respect to matching fonts when the intended font is not available. Dozens of "font descriptors" have been introduced which break down a desired font's characteristics. When a desired font is not present, all of these descriptors can be used to make an intelligent "best-choice" for an alternate font match. In the event a best match cannot be generated, fonts may even be generated on the fly or downloaded as needed over the web.

FONT	
font	font-style font-variant font-weight font-size/line-height font-family caption I icon I menul message-box I small- caption I status-bar
font-family	family-name generic-family
font-size	xx-small I x-small I small I medium I large I x-large I xx-large I smaller I larger length %

Contd...

font-size-adjust	None Number
font-stretch	normal I wider I narrower I ultra-condensed I extra- condensed I condensed I semi-condensed I semi- expanded I expanded I extra-expanded I ultra-expanded
font-style	normal I italic I oblique
font-variant	normal I small-caps
font-weight	Normal I bold I bolder I lighter I 100 I 200 I 300 I 400 I 500 I 600 I 700 I 800 I 900

Example

```
P {font: 12pt/14pt sans-serif}
P {font: 80% sans-serif}
P {font: x-large/110% "new century schoolbook", serif}
P {font: bold italic large Palatino, serif}
P {font: normal small-caps 120%/120% fantasy}
```

14.9.2 Text Properties

These properties control the visual appearance and presentation of text content (characters, words, blocks and the spacing between them.) Some of the special physical formatting effects from HTML have found their home in the Text properties.

TEXT	
color	Color
direction	ltr I rtl
letter-spacing	normal length
text-align	left I right I center I justify
text-decoration	none I underline I overline I line-through I blink
text-indent	length %
text-shadow	none color length
text-transform	none I capitalize I uppercase I lowercase
unicode-bidi	normal I embed I bidi-override
white-space	normal I pre I nowrap
word-spacing	normal length

Example

```
H1 {word-spacing: 1em}
BLOCKQUOTE {letter-spacing: 0.1em}
BLOCKQUOTE {letter-spacing: 0}
BLOCKQUOTE {letter-spacing: 0cm}
A:link, A:visited, A:active {text-decoration: underline}
H1 {text-transform: uppercase}
DIV.center {text-align: center}
P {text-indent: 3em}
DIV {line-height: 1.2; font-size: 10pt}      /* number */
DIV {line-height: 1.2em; font-size: 10pt}    /* length */
DIV {line-height: 120%; font-size: 10pt}     /* percentage */
```

14.9.3 Outline Properties

New properties in CSS2 allow outlines to be created for an element to help it stand out from other elements. CSS Outlines are very similar to borders except for several subtle differences:

- Border sides can be independently controlled, Outline sides cannot. The visual effects for an outline are uniform for all sides.
- Outlines may be non-rectangular.
- Outlines do not take up space in the box-rendering model; they are rendered on "top" of the element's box. An outline does not affect the position or size of the rendering box.

OUTLINE	
Outline	Outline-color outline-style outline-width
outline-color	color invert
outline-style	none I dotted I dashed I solid I double I groove I ridge I inset I outset
outli ne-width	thin I medium I thick length

Example

```
BUTTON {outline-width: thick}
focus  {outline: thick solid black}
:active {outline: thick solid red}
```

14.9.4 List Properties

Lists are used to organize and render one or more data items with some relationship to each other. With a list structure, extra information is used to give some indication of the degree of relationship between the items.

However, this extra information is not actually stored in the document itself, it is generated automatically when it is rendered. List structures generate two blocks for each item of rendered data - a box for each data item, along with a separate marker box for the visual list iteration object (such as a bullet, number, or image) that is created by the system. The list properties control the type and placement of the marker box in list contexts.

LIST & MARKERS	
list-style	list-style-type list-style-position list-style-image
list-style-image	none url
list-style-position	inside I outside
list-style-type	none I disc I circle I square I decimal I decimal-leading- zero I lower-roman I upper- roman I lower-alpha I up- per-alpha I lower-greek I lower-latln I upper-latin I hebrew I armenian I geor- gian I cjk-ideographic I hiragana I katakana I hira- gana-iroha I katakaa-iroha
ma rker-offset	auto length

Example

```
UL {list-style: upper-roman inside}
UL UL {list-style: circle outside}
LI.square {list-style: square}
OL.alpha  {list-style: lower-alpha}
UL  {list-style: disc}
UL {list-style: url (http://png.com/ellipse.png) disc}
```

14.9.5 Generated Content Properties

The basic aim of CSS is to offer hints and aids for the direct translation of a document and its elements to differing physical media. There are times when the information contained in a document's structure is not enough to display the intended content. In HTML, the various list structures are a perfect example - the bullets and iterative/hierarchical numbers that are rendered before the items in the list are not explicitly present in the source document. This content is automatically generated by the browser when rendering an element from the source document.

CSS2 extends this concept of automatic content generation to allow content (strings, quotes, list generators or objects) to be rendered before or after any element. Generated content includes aural rendering as well; auditory icons can offer powerful usability enhancements for a listener.

GENERATED CONTENT	
content	String url counter (name) counter (name, list-style- type) counters (name, string) counters (name, string, list- style-type) attr (X) open-quote I close-quote I no-open-quote I no-close- quote
counter-increment	None identifier number
counter-reset	None identifier number
quotes	None string string string string

Example

```
BLOCKQUOTE P:before      {content: open-quote}
BLOCKQUOTE P:after       {content: no-close-quote}
BLOCKQUOTE P.last:after {content: close-quote}
[LANG|=fr] > *  {quotes: "«" "»" "\2039" "\203A"}
[LANG|=en] > *  {quotes: "\201C" "\201D" "\2018" "\2019"}
[LANG|=fr] > * {quotes: "«" "»" "‹" "›"}
[LANG|=en] > * {quotes: "“" "”" "‘" "’"}
H1:before {
   content: "Chapter " counter (chapter) ". ";
   counter-increment: chapter;  /* Add 1 to chapter */
   counter-reset: section;      /* Set section to 0 */
}
```

Contd....

```
H2:before {
    content: counter (chapter) "." counter (section) " ";
    counter-increment: section;
}
H1 {counter-reset: section -1}
H1 {counter-reset: imagenum 99}
OL {counter-reset: item}
LI {display: block}
LI:before {content: counter (item) ". "; counter-increment: item}
```

14.9.6 Margin Properties

In CSS, the fundamental visual rendering model places all components of the document tree in physical and virtual rectangular boxes, each having a specific height and width. An element's rendering box consists primarily of an element's content at the center (text, images, etc.) Surrounding the element's content (moving outward in rectangular layers/strips) are optional padding, surrounded by any optional border effects, surrounded in turn by any optional margin values that may be specified.

The margin properties allow the author to specify how much space will be inserted between other exterior elements and the current element border. Negative values may be used with margin properties to create overlapping content.

Each side of the margin dimensions (top, right, bottom and left) can be addressed and controlled, independently using separate properties, or a convenient shorthand notation may be used that controls multiple sides at once.

MARGIN	
margin	margin-top margin-right margin-bottom margin-left
margin-bottom	auto length %
margin-left	auto length %
margin-right	auto length %
margin-top	auto length %

Example

```
BODY {margin: 2em} /* all margins set to 2em */

BODY {margin: 1em 2em} /* top & bottom = 1em, right & left = 2em */

BODY {margin: 1em 2em 3em} /* top=1em, right=2em, bottom=3em, left=2em
*/

BODY {
  margin-top: 1em;
  margin-right: 2em;
  margin-bottom: 3em;
  margin-left: 2em;        /* copied from opposite side (right) */
}

H1 {margin-top: 2em}

H1 {margin-right: 12.3%}

H1 {margin-bottom: 3px}
```

14.9.7 Border Properties

In CSS, the fundamental visual rendering model places all components of the document tree in physical and virtual rectangular boxes, each having a specific height and width. An element's rendering box consists of an element's content at the center (text, images, etc.) Surrounding the element's content (moving outward in rectangular layers/strips) are optional padding, surrounded by any optional border effects, surrounded in turn by any optional margin values that may be specified.

The border properties allow an author to specify the width, color, and style of the border area (between any specified padding and margins) of an element's rendering box. While the capability to create simple line effects has been available in HTML via tables, the CSS border properties give authors much more power in creating such effects and allow them to be applied to any element.

Each side of the border dimensions (top, right, bottom and left) can be addressed and controlled, independently using separate properties, or a convenient shorthand notation may be used that controls multiple sides at once.

BORDER	
border	border-width border-stye border-color
	border-bottom-width

Contd....

border-bottom	border-style border-color
border-bottom-color	border-color
border-bottom-style	border-style
border-bottom-width	thin I medium I thick length
border-color	color
border-left	border-left-width border-style border-color
border-left-color	border-color
border-left-style	border-style
border-left-width	thin I medium I thick length

Example

```
P {border: solid red}
P {
  border-top: solid red;
  border-right: solid red;
  border-bottom: solid red;
  border-left: solid red
}
H1 {border-bottom: thick solid}
H1 {border-bottom: thick solid red}
H1 {border-width: thin}                  /* thin thin thin thin */
H1 {border-width: thin thick}            /* thin thick thin thick */
H1 {border-width: thin thick medium}     /* thin thick medium thin */
H1 {border-width: thin thick medium thin} /* thin thick medium thin */
```

14.9.8 Padding Properties

In CSS, the fundamental visual rendering model places all components of the document tree in physical and virtual rectangular boxes, each having a specific height and width. An element's rendering box consists of an element's content at the center (text, images, etc.) Surrounding the element's content (moving outward in rectangular layers/strips) are optional padding, surrounded by any optional border effects, surrounded in turn by any optional margin values that may be specified.

The padding properties allow the author to specify how much space will be inserted between the element border and the element content. Negative values are not allowed.

Each side of the padding dimensions (top, right, bottom and left) can be addressed and controlled, independently using separate properties, or a convenient shorthand notation may be used that controls multiple sides at once.

PADDING	
Padding	padding-top padding-right padding-bottom padding-left
padding-bottom	length %
padding-left	length %
padding-right	length %
padding-top	length %

Example

```
BLOCKQUOTE {padding-top: 0.3em}
BLOCKQUOTE {padding-left: 20%}
BLOCKQUOTE {padding-bottom: 2em}
H1 {background: white;
  padding: 1em 2em;
}
```

14.9.9 Positioning Properties

When an element is called 'positioned' in the visual formatting model, it may or may not be rendered immediately after the previous element in the document tree. An element that is positioned ('position' property) has its rendering offset from the canvas origin or from its normal flow position via the 'top', 'right', 'bottom', and 'left' properties.

In addition to determining position offsets, positioning properties also specify the the visible display area of an element's rendering box ('clip') and directives indicating what should happen when an element's content falls outside the rendering box ('overflow'.)

But, positioning in CSS is not just about rendering in 2-dimensions. It also allows for placement and overlap of elements in an imaginary third dimension perpendicular to the screen ('z-axis'.)

The final property included in this category, 'vertical-align', is not involved with "CSS positioning" per se, but it does involve vertical positioning of content within a rendered line box.

Many of these properties were first introduced prior to CSS2 in the W3C Working draft "Positioning HTML Elements with Cascading Style Sheets"(http://www.w3.org/TR/WD-positioning, Robert Stevahn, Scott Furman, Scott Isaacs, et.al., 19 August, 1997).

POSITIONING	
bottom	auto % length
clip	shape auto
left	auto % length
overflow	visible I hidden I scroll I auto
position	static I relative I absolute I fixed
right	auto % length
top	auto % length
vertical-align	baseline I sub I super I top I text-top I middle I bottom I text-bottom length %
z-index	auto number

Example

```
BODY {height: 8.5in} /* Required for percentage heights below */
   #header {
     position: fixed;
     width: 100%;
     height: 15%;
    top: 0;
```

Contd....

```
    right: 0;
    bottom: auto;
    left: 0;
  }
  #sidebar {
    position: fixed;
    width: 10em;
    height: auto;
    top: 15%;
    right: auto;
    bottom: 100px;
    left: 0;
  }
  #main {
    position: fixed;
    width: auto;
    height: auto;
    top: 15%;
    right: 0;
    bottom: 100px;
    left: 10em;
  }
  #footer {
    position: fixed;
    width: 100%;
    height: 100px;
top: auto;
    right: 0;
    bottom: 0;
    left: 0;
  }
```

14.9.10 Classification Properties

The classification properties serve to classify elements and select which layout models will be used in their display. In the visual media-formatting model, an element's rendering is based heavily upon, among other things, the positioning method specified (floating, positioned or normal flow positioning) and the classification type of the element's box (the 'display' property).

CLASSIFICATION	
clear	left I right I both I none
cursor	url auto I crosshair I default I pointer I move I e-resize I ne-resize I nw-resize I n-resize I se-resize I sw-resizel s-resize I w-resize I text I wait I help
display	none I inline I block I list- item I run-in I compact I marker I tabie I in line-tablel table-row-group I table- header-group I table-footer- group I table-row I table-column-group I table- column I table-cell I table caption
float	left I right I none
position	static I relative I absolute I
visibility	visible I hidden I collapse

Example

```
P {display: block}
EM {display: inline}
LI {display: list-item}
IMG {display: none}
```

More Practical Example

```
<!DOCTYPE HTML PUBLIC "-//W3C//DTD HTML 4.0//EN">
<HTML>
<HEAD>
<STYLE type="text/css">
<!—
   #container1 {position: absolute;
              top: 2in; left: 2in; width: 2in}
   #container2 {position: absolute;
              top: 2in; left: 2in; width: 2in;
```

Contd....

```
            visibility: hidden;}
—>
</STYLE>
</HEAD>
<BODY>
<P>Choose a suspect:</P>
<DIV id="container1">
  <IMG alt="Al Capone"
       width="100" height="100"
       src="suspect1.jpg">
  <P>Name: Al Capone</P>
  <P>Residence: Chicago</P>
</DIV>
<DIV id="container2">
  <IMG alt="Lucky Luciano"
       width="100" height="100"
       src="suspect2.jpg">
  <P>Name: Lucky Luciano</P>
  <P>Residence: New York</P>
</DIV>
<FORM method="post"
     action="http://www.bpkm.org.in/process-bums">
  <P>
  <INPUT name="Capone" type="button"
       value="Capone"
         onclick='show ("container1"); hide ("container2")'>
  <INPUT name="Luciano" type="button"
       value="Luciano"
         onclick='show ("container2"); hide ("container1")'>
</FORM>
</BODY>
</HTML>
```

14.9.11 Dimension Properties

In CSS, the fundamental visual rendering model places all components of the document tree in physical and virtual rectangular boxes, each having a specific height and width. The dimension properties describe the details influencing the calculation and visual rendering of an element's line, in-line and block box dimensions. The actual values for an element's visually rendered height and width are dependent on many criteria, including the intrinsic type of the current element and the dimensions of the element's containing block.

DIMENSION	
height	auto length %
line-height	normal number length %
max-height	none length %
max-width	none length %
min-height	length %
min-width	length %
width	auto % length

14.9.12 Color/Background Properties

Color and Background properties allow color control of both the foreground and background of an element's rendering box. The background properties also allow sophisticated placement and control of images to create background textures. The color and background capabilities behaviors originally available in HTML have been absorbed in to these CSS properties and greatly expanded.

background	background-color background-image background-repeat background-attachment background-position
background-attachment	scroll I fixed

Contd....

background-color	color-rgb color-hex color-name Transparent
background-image	url None
background-position	top left I top center I top right I center left I center center I center right I bottom left I bottom center I bottom right x-%y-% x-pos y-pos
background-repeat	repeat I repeat-x I re- peat-y I no-repeat

Example

```
EM {color: red}              /* natural language */
EM {color: rgb (255,0,0)}       /* RGB range 0-255    */
H1 {background-color: #F00}
BODY {background-image: url (marble.gif)}
P {background-image: none}
BODY {background: red url (pendant.gif);
  background-repeat: repeat-y;
}
BODY {background: red url (pendant.gif);
  background-repeat: repeat-y;
  background-attachment: fixed;
}
BODY {background: url (banner.jpeg) right top}      /* 100% 0% */
BODY {background: url (banner.jpeg) top center}    /* 50% 0% */
BODY {background: url (banner.jpeg) center}        /* 50% 50% */
BODY {background: url (banner.jpeg) bottom}         /* 50% 100% */
BODY {background-image: url (logo.png);
  background-attachment: fixed;
  background-position: 100% 100%;
}
BODY {background: red}
P {background: url (chess.png) gray 50% repeat fixed}
```

14.9.13 Units of Measure

CSS is used to render information to a device. These devices exist in the real world and have dimensions and capabilities that are measurable. Therefore, CSS provides a way for document content to explicitly specify how it will be mapped to a physical device. If a property value contains an illegal unit measure, the entire style rule should be ignored.

UNITS of MEASUREMENT	
%	Percentage
cm	Centimeter
em	1em = current font size of current element
ex	lex = 1/2 current size of current element
in	Inch
mm	Millimeter
pc	pica (= 12 points)
pt	point (= 1/72 inch)
Px	Pixel
COLORS	
Color name	Red, blue, green, dark green
rgb(x,y,z)	Red = rgb (255,0,0)
rgb(x%,y%,z%)	Red = rgb(100%,0,0)
#rrggbb	Red = #00000 (or shorthand =#f00)

14.10 CSS COMMENTS

You can add comments to your style sheets for the same reasons you might use comments in HTML: to make notes, to pass along instructions to other web developers, or to temporarily hide or disable parts of the style sheet during testing. A comment in CSS begins with /* and ends with */, and anything between those markers won't be interpreted by the browser. Just like comments in HTML, CSS comments can span multiple lines.

```
/* These base styles apply to all heading levels. */
h1, h2, h3, h4, h5, h6 {color: red; margin-bottom: .5em;}

/* Adjust the size of each. */
h1 {font-size: 150%;}
h2 {font-size: 130%;}
h3 {font-size: 120%;}

/* Temporarily hiding these rules
```

```
h4 {font-size: 100%;}

h5 {font-size: 90%;}

h6 {font-size: 80%;}

End hiding */
```

14.11 STYLE SHEETS

A style sheet is a set of one or more rules that apply to an HTML document. You can define a style sheet within an HTML page using a STYLE tag in the head of the document (between the <HEAD> and </HEAD> tags).

```
<style type="text/css">
...style rules...
</style>
```

Or, like JavaScript, style sheets can be defined in a separate file and referenced by a URL. An external style sheet is included in a page using the <LINK> element, again in the head of the document.

```
<link href="url" rel="stylesheet" type="text/css">
```

This is useful for sharing a common style sheet among several pages in a site. You can combine any number of <STYLE> and <LINK> elements within a single page, but as we'll see when we discuss conflicting styles, the order in which, they are placed can be important.

14.11.1 Different Ways to Implement CSS

There are four (4) different ways to use CSS in your Web pages: Inline CSS, Embedded CSS, Linked CSS and Importing CSS. They all provide advantages over normal HTML.

Inline CSS

This is the HTML specific style inclusion method, in which style information is directly attached to the HTML elements, they affect. A universal element attribute, called STYLE, may be specified for an HTML element, taking as a value one or more style Declarations.

Many of the powerful CSS syntax mechanisms (like Selectors) are not applicable in Inline CSS. This style specification method is most useful, when serving as an override on a case-by-case basis for style rules specified in an External or Embedded style sheet. Inline styles have higher cascade precedence than the other specification methods.

The simplest and most direct way of applying CSS to an element is to write it into the tag itself as a style attribute style="...". CSS styles applied this way have the highest priority over other style definitions, i.e., they will overwrite existing styles.

Syntax:

```
<[element name] STYLE="[CSS property]:[property value]">
```

Example

```
<p style="border:2px solid #8dc919">
```

Using HTML Code:

<p><font face= "Arial" color= "#000000" size="3">Boy do I love Saturdays. Nothing like sleeping 'til 10 and not waking up for work.</font></p>

Using inline CSS: (this above same paragraph could be coded like)

<p style="font-family:Arial; color:#000000; font-size:12px;"> Boy do I love Saturdays. Nothing like sleeping 'til 10 and not waking up for work.</p>

Usage Guidelines:

1. Use as little as possible: Remember that we're trying to separate content from presentation. Inline styles are the exact opposite. They're inefficient because they'll indulge up your code and are difficult to maintain. Only use them for some quick testing of CSS styles or for exceptions, where a style is only used at a particular place and nowhere else on the homepage.
2. Don't use double quotes: Because double quotes are already used for marking the start and end of the style attribute, having another double quote in-between would abruptly terminate the CSS instructions. Use single quotes instead.

Example

<p style="font-family:'trebuchet ms'">...</p> is ok but not <p style= "font family:"trebuchet ms"">...</p>.

CSS offers, Web designers more precise control over the look of their pages. With inline CSS, we can specify the exact pixel size of a font. In comparison, <font> tags limit us to numbers (-7,-6,-5,-4-3,-2,-1, 1,2,3,4,5,6...). These numbers correspond to the font settings in the user's browser, and thus eliminate the control you have over the final size of a font.

Apart from this small improvement in the control of our font size, inline CSS does not really reduce the amount of code needed to format text. It just accomplishes a similar result in a different way. This leads us to a slightly better method of CSS implementation.

[See complex HTML example using Inline Style Sheets]

```
<html>
    <head>
        <title>Document Title</title>
    </head>
    <body LINK="#ff8080" VLINK="#ff0000" ALINK="a05050"
STYLE="background: #000000; color: #80c0c0">
 <h1 ALIGN="center" STYLE="background: #000080; font: 36pt/40pt courier;
font-variant: small-caps; border: thick dashed blue">Welcome to my home page!</
h1>
     <br><br>
 <p><span STYLE="margin-left: 25px">Hi there! If you are reading this then you
have found my home page! Congratulations! </span>
    I know it can be hard to find my pages, but I bet that you feel lucky now. Now
that you are here, please take a look at my page of links to <a HREF="http://
www.mysite.com/coolsites.html">cool sites</a> or sign my <a HREF="http://
www.mysite.com/guestbook.html">guest book</a></p>
 <div><div STYLE="font-weight: bold; margin-left: 30px">
<span STYLE="font-size: x-large; color: #ffffff">M</span>y wonderful poetry</
div> is available if you are REALLY bored. Why not give it a spin? </div>
 <h2 STYLE="background: #000080; color: green; line-height: 50px; font-size:
40px">
 The Best Poetry I <em STYLE="font-weight: 900">NEVER</em> Wrote</h2>
    <ul>
       <li>'There Once Was A Man From Nantucket' -
          <span STYLE="font-family: 'comic sans ms', fantasy; color: rgb (100%,
100%, 0%)">Anonymous</span></li>
       <li>'Cool In Fur' -
          <span STYLE="font-family: 'comic sans ms', fantasy; color: rgb (100%,
100%, 0%)">Harry B. Foot</span></li>
       <li>And My All Time Fave:
       <ul>
        <li STYLE="font-size: x-large; font-style: italic"> 'A Toast To My Toaster' -
          <span STYLE="font-family: 'comic sans ms', fantasy; color: rgb (100%,
100%, 0%)">Me!</span></li>
       </ul>
```

Contd....

```
</li></ul>

<blockquote STYLE="background: #000080; color: #00ff00; margin-left: 2cm">Brought to you by the letter

<span STYLE="font-family: 'comic sans ms', fantasy; color: rgb(100%, 100%, 0%)">&quot;H&quot;</span>

and <span STYLE="Padding: 20px; border: 20px groove #ffffff">Joe Shmoe</span> </blockquote>

<div STYLE="background: #000080; font-weight: bold; margin-left: 30px">

<span STYLE="font-size: x-large; color: #ffffff"> W</span>hen you are done looking through these masterpieces, I encourage you to visit my proud sponsor!! </div>

<p STYLE="font: 12pt/14pt sans-serif; margin: 5px 0px 2px 25px; border: medium dashed #ff0000; background: white url (http://www.foo.com/image.gif) repeat-x fixed top right}">

<span STYLE="font: 36pt/40pt courier; font-variant: small-caps; border: thick dashed blue}"> ADVERTISEMENT:</span>

Buy Navel Lint Contemplator! It's a browser and it's a sandwich spread! Go to our <a HREF="http://www.navellint.com">home page</a> without delay! Why? Because shelf life is only 8 hours unless refrigerated. We know that makes it hard to browse, but it promotes frequent upgrading to the latest and greatest version. </p>

<h6 STYLE="font-size: xx-small! important; color: red! important">All standard disclaimers apply. Your life depends on NOT copying this document in any way. This tape will

<a HREF="http://www.mysite.com/selfdestruct.html">self destruct</a> in 10 seconds...</h6>

</body>

</html>
```

Inline Styles Are Not Best Practice

Inline styles, while they have a purpose, are not the best way to maintain your Web site. They go against every one of the above benefits:

- ***Inline styles don't separate content from design:*** In fact, inline styles are exactly the same as embedded font tags and other design tags that we're trying to stop using. The styles only affect the exact tag they are applied to, and while that might give you more control, it makes other aspects of your design and development more difficult.

- ***Inline styles cause more maintenance headaches:*** When you're working with style sheets, it can sometimes be very difficult to figure out where a style is being set. When you add a mixture of inline, embedded, Linked CSS and Importing CSS and you have even more locations to look. Again, if you work on a Web design team or have to redesign or maintain a site built by someone else, then you're going to have even more trouble. Then, once you find the style and get rid of it, you'll have to get rid of it on every element on every page where it's been placed, which can increase your maintenance work astronomically.
- ***Inline styles are not as accessible:*** While a screen reader or other assistive device might be able to handle the attributes and tags effectively, some of the older devices don't and can result in some strange Web pages. In addition, the extra characters and text can affect how your page is viewed by a robot such as a search engine, so your page optimization would not do as well as a page with external style sheets.
- ***Inline styles make your pages bigger:*** If you set a style on every paragraph on your site, you can do it once with like 6 lines of code and an external style sheet. However, if you do it with an inline style, you'll have to add those styles to every paragraph of your site. If you have, 5 lines of CSS that's 5 lines are multiplied by every paragraph on your site. That bandwidth can add up in a hurry.

Embedded CSS or Internal Styles

When applying internal CSS you put all your CSS rules in the <head>...</head> part of your HTML document and enclose it with <style type="text/css">...</style> tags. This CSS style specification method is only used with HTML. An entire style sheet can be embedded in an HTML document using the <STYLE> element contained within the <HEAD> block. The complete range of CSS syntax is not explicitly tied directly to the document's elements, so Selector syntax is used to specify what styles attach to which portions of the document tree (the same as with External Style Sheets, but in this case the style sheet is contained within the document itself).

Unlike external style sheets, this method can only specify style information for the current document. If equivalent style rules are specified in an external and embedded style sheet, the embedded style sheet rule will have higher precedence.

Syntax:

```
    <style TYPE="text/css">
<!--
[CSS Style Sheet]
-->
</style>
```

Example

```
<!DOCTYPE html PUBLIC "-//W3C//DTD XHTML 1.0 Strict//EN" "http://
www.w3.org/TR/xhtml1/DTD/xhtml1-strict.dtd">
<html xmlns="http://www.w3.org/1999/xhtml" xml:lang="en" lang="en">
  <head>
    <meta http-equiv="content-type" content="text/html; charset=utf-8" />
    <title>Internal CSS styles</title>
    <style type="text/css">
      p {border:2px solid #8dc919}
    </style>
  </head>
  <body>
    <p>1st pragraph ...</p>
    <p>2nd pragraph ...</p>
  </body>
</html>
```

Usage Guidelines:

1. ***Avoid if possible:*** Really, there's not much point using internal CSS styles. You might as well take all those CSS rules and put them into an external .css file so it can be re-used in other pages.

[See complex HTML example using Internal Style Sheets]

```
<html>
    <head>
          <title>Document Title</title>
     <style TYPE="text/css">
     <!—
     body {
            background: black;
            color: #80c0c0}
     a:link {color: #ff8080}
     a:visited {color: #ff0000}
```

Contd....

```
a:active {color: #a05050}
a.case1:link {background: green}
p:first-line { margin-left: 25px }
div.foo:first-line {
        font-weight: bold;
        margin-left: 30px}
div:first-letter {
        font-size: x-large;
        color: #ffffff}
ul ul li {
        font-size: x-large;
        font-decoration: italic}
h2 em {font-weight: 900}
h2.ex1 {
        color: green;      /* This type of heading MUST be Green and Large! */
        line-height: 50px;
        font-size: 40px}
.funkyclass {
        font: 36pt/40pt courier;
        font-variant: small-caps;
        border: thick dashed blue}
#tagid1 {
        padding: 20px;
        border: 20px groove #ffffff}
.class1, #tagid2 {font-family: 'comic sans ms', fantasy; color: rgb
(100%,100%,0%)}
h1, h2, div.class5, blockquote {background: #000080}
p.special {
        font: 12pt/14pt sans-serif;
        margin: 5px 0px 2px 25px;
        border: medium dashed #ff0000;
```

Contd....

```
background: white url (http://www.foo.com/image.gif) repeat-x fixed top right}
    blockquote {
            margin-left: 2cm;
            color: #00ff00}
    .part1 {
            font-size: xx-large;
            color: #808000}
    h6 {
            font-size: xx-small ! important;
            color: red ! important}
    —>
    </style>
    </head>
 <body>
 <h1 CLASS="funkyclass" ALIGN="center">Welcome to my home page!</h1>
    <br><br>
 <p>Hi there! If you are reading this then you have found my home page! Congratulations! I know it can be hard to find my pages, but I bet that you feel lucky now. Now that you are here, please take a look at my page of links to <a HREF="http://www.mysite.com/coolsites.html">cool sites</a> or sign my <a HREF="http://www.mysite.com/guestbook.html">guest book</a></p>
 <div CLASS="foo"> My wonderful poetry <br> is available if you are REALLY bored. Why not give it a spin?</div>
 <h2 CLASS="ex1"> The Best Poetry I <em>NEVER</em> Wrote</h2>
    <ul>
 <li>'There Once Was A Man From Nantucket' - <span CLASS="class1"> Anonymous</span></li>
        <li>'Cool In Fur' - <span CLASS="class1">Harry B. Foot</span></li>
            <li>And My All Time Fave:
            <ul>
        <li> 'A Toast To My Toaster' - <span CLASS="class1">Me!</span></li>
            </ul>
    </li></ul>
```

Contd....

```
<blockquote>Brought to you by the letter <span ID="tagid2">&quot;H&quot;</span> and <span ID="tagid1">Joe Shmoe</span> </blockquote>

<div CLASS="class5"> When you are done looking through these masterpieces, I encourage you to visit my proud sponsor!! </div>

<p CLASS="special"><span CLASS="funkyclass">ADVERTISEMENT:</span> Buy Navel Lint Contemplator! It's a browser and it's a sandwich spread! Go to our <a HREF="http://www.navellint.com">home page</a> without delay! Why? Because shelf life is only 8 hours unless refrigerated. We know that makes it hard to browse, but it promotes frequent upgrading to the latest and greatest version. </p>

<h6>All standard disclaimers apply. Your life depends on NOT copying this document in any way. This tape will <a HREF="http://www.mysite.com/selfdestruct.html" CLASS="case1">self destruct</a> in 10 seconds...</h6>

    </body>

    </html>
```

External Style Sheets/Linked CSS

The true power of this CSS specification mechanism is separating presentation from content. External Style Sheets are the tool for doing exactly this by putting all your CSS rules into a separate .css file (a simple text file) you can reuse them for all your pages without rewriting. All your styles are in a centralized place making it easy to maintain and change the look of your website.

This is the most powerful of all the CSS attachment methods, as it allows a single style sheet to control the rendering of multiple documents. These results in a timesaving for the author, a savings of space for the web server, and less download time for the user. In addition, this method can be used in both HTML and XML.

An External Style Sheet is a file containing only CSS syntax (no document content or elements) and should carry a MIME type of "text/css". The style information is not explicitly tied directly to the document's elements, so Selector syntax is used to specify what styles attach to which portions of the document tree. The full range of CSS syntax is allowed in this method.

Syntax:

```
<link REL="STYLESHEET" TYPE="text/css" HREF="[Style sheet URL]">
```

LINK Attribute	Description
type:	This is the MIME content-type and should always be set to text/css for stylesheets.
rel:	This attribute describes the relationship between the actual document and the one you're linking to. In this case, it's always stylesheet.

Contd....

media:	You might want to provide more than one stylesheet for different presentations of your website. For example a normal one, a high-contrast one for people with reading difficulties, a printer-friendly one for printing and so on. If the client supports this, it will use the appropriate stylesheet. If you just have a single stylesheet for everything, you can omit this attribute or use all.
href:	This is the link to your stylesheet.

Usage Guidelines:

1. *Use as much as possible:* Try to put all your CSS styles into stylesheets and minimize your inline CSS and internal CSS.
2. *Use a logical structure:* As a CSS beginner you probably won't care much about the order in which you write your CSS rules, because your stylesheets will be relatively small. As they get bigger, though, it can help having a logical structure in your stylesheet. For example you could group general selectors such as <BODY>, <A>, <P>, <IMG>, <H1>, ... at the beginning and then follow with contextual selector rules. Or group CSS styles together, which belong to a certain layout part of the page such as the header, sidebar, footer and so on.
3. *Naming your stylesheet:* It's an unofficial naming convention that the main stylesheet is called style.css. It can't hurt adopting this yourself.
4. *Use F5 to display recent changes:* When you're making changes to your stylesheets you have to press the F5 key to force the web browser to load the newest version instead of using the cached one.

Creation of .css File

Let us get started by making that external CSS file. Open up notepad.exe or any other plain text editor and type the following CSS code.

CSS Code: (test.css)

```
body{background-color: gray}
p {color: blue;}
h3{color: white;}
```

Now save the file as a CSS (.css) file. Make sure that you are not saving it as a text (.txt) file, as notepad likes to do by default. Name the file "test.css" (without the quotes). Now create a new HTML file and fill it with the following code.

HTML Code: (index.htm)

```
<html>
<head>
<link rel="stylesheet" media="all" type="text/css" href="test.css" />
```

Contd....

```
</head>
<body>
<h3> A White Header </h3>
<p> This paragraph has a blue font.
The background color of this page is gray because
we changed it with CSS! </p>
</body>
</html>
```

Save this file as "index.htm" (without the quotes) in the same directory as your CSS file. Now open your HTML file in your web browser and it should look something like…

Display:

[See complex HTML example using External Style Sheets]

External File: 'example.css'

```
    body {
            background: black;
            color: #80c0c0}
    a:link {color: #ff8080}
    a:visited {color: #ff0000}
    a:active {color: #a05050}
    a.case1:link {background: green}
    p:first-line {margin-left: 25px }
    div.foo:first-line {
            font-weight: bold;
            margin-left: 30px}
    div:first-letter {
            font-size: x-large;
            color: #ffffff}
    ul ul li {
            font-size: x-large;
            font-decoration: italic}
```

Contd....

```
h2 em {font-weight: 900}
h2.ex1 {
        color: green;       /* This type of heading MUST be Green and Large! */
        line-height: 50px;
        font-size: 40px}
.funkyclass {
        font: 36pt/40pt courier;
        font-variant: small-caps;
        border: thick dashed blue}
#tagid1 {
        padding: 20px;
        border: 20px groove #ffffff}
.class1, #tagid2 {font-family: 'comic sans ms', fantasy; color: rgb
(100%,100%,0%)}
h1, h2, div.class5, blockquote {background: #000080}
p.special {
        font: 12pt/14pt sans-serif;
        margin: 5px 0px 2px 25px;
        border: medium dashed #ff0000;
        background: white url (http://www.foo.com/image.gif) repeat-x fixed
top right}
blockquote {
        margin-left: 2cm;
        color: #00ff00}
.part1 {
        font-size: xx-large;
        color: #808000}
h6 {
        font-size: xx-small ! important;
        color: red ! important}
```

Main Document: 'example.htm'

```
<html>
```

Contd....

```
<head>
    <title>Document Title</title>
    <link REL="StyleSheet" TYPE="text/css" HREF="example.css">
</head>
<body>
<h1 CLASS="funkyclass" ALIGN="center">Welcome to my home page!</h1>
    <br><br>
<p>Hi there! If you are reading this then you have found my home page! Congratulations! I know it can be hard to find my pages, but I bet that you feel lucky now. Now that you are here, please take a look at my page of links to <a HREF="http://www.mysite.com/coolsites.html">cool sites</a> or sign my <a HREF="http://www.mysite.com/guestbook.html">guest book</a></p>
<div CLASS="foo"> My wonderful poetry <br> is available if you are REALLY bored. Why not give it a spin?</div>
<h2 CLASS="ex1"> The Best Poetry I <em>NEVER</em> Wrote</h2>
    <ul>
            <li>'There Once Was A Man From Nantucket' - <span CLASS="class1">Anonymous</span></li>
        <li>'Cool In Fur' - <span CLASS="class1">Harry B. Foot</span></li>
            <li>And My All Time Fave:
            <ul>
                <li> 'A Toast To My Toaster' - <span CLASS="class1">Me!</span></li>
            </ul>
    </li></ul>
<blockquote>Brought to you by the letter <span ID="tagid2">&quot;H&quot;</span> and <span ID="tagid1">Joe Shmoe</span> </blockquote>
<div CLASS="class5"> When you are done looking through these masterpieces, I encourage you to visit my proud sponsor!! </div>
<p CLASS="special"><span CLASS="funkyclass">ADVERTISEMENT:</span> Buy Navel Lint Contemplator! It's a browser and it's a sandwich spread! Go to our <a HREF="http://www.navellint.com">home page</a> without delay! Why? Because shelf life is only 8 hours unless refrigerated. We know that makes it hard to browse, but it promotes frequent upgrading to the latest and greatest version. </p>
```

Contd....

```
<h6>All standard disclaimers apply. Your life depends on NOT copying this document in any way. This tape will <a HREF="http://www.mysite.com/selfdestruct.html" CLASS="case1">self destruct</a> in 10 seconds...</h6>
    </body>
    </html>
```

Benefits of External CSS

- It keeps your website design and content separate.
- It's much easier to reuse your CSS code if you have it in a separate file. Instead of typing the same CSS code on every web page you have, simply have many pages refer to a single CSS file with the "link" tag.
- You can make drastic changes to your web pages with just a few changes in a single CSS file.
- Help to achieve the consistency in the styles through out the pages.

Limitation of External CSS

If the user downloads the page and if he forgot to download the Linked CSS then he/she will not be able to view the page with all the styles.

Importing Style Sheets

The @import rule thus allows you to keep some things the same while having others different.

Syntax:

```
@import url (nameoffile.css)
```

It must come at the start of the style sheet, before any rulesets (a ruleset is something like P {color: red}). Alternatively, it can be specified as:

Syntax:

```
@import "nameoffile.css"
as @import url ("nameoffile.css")
or as @import 'nameoffile.css'
```

However, Internet Explorer only supports the url() formats, not the " and ' formats.

14.12 LIMITATIONS OF CSS

- Limited transcription capabilities
  - ❖ Limited transposition of elements (float:left/right)
  - ❖ Calls of parameterised formatting tasks the major transcription type supported

- In CSS1 context specification limited:
    - ❖ No sibling or parent/child relationships
    - ❖ Limited use of attributes (CSS1: only class)
    - ❖ CSS2 more powerful,
        - ♦ But no access to element's children or content
        - ♦ Unable to access targets of cross references (?)
- Non-programmable
    - ❖ No decision structures
    - ❖ Unable to store calculated quantities
    - ❖ Non-extensible
    - ❖ Relatively simple
- ❖ Western-language orientation (left-to-right)
- ❖ XSL allows unrestricted transformations of the document to precede a CSS-like formatting

14.13 ADVANTAGES OF CSS

- Workflow
    - ❖ Faster downloads
    - ❖ Streamlined site maintenance
    - ❖ Global control of design attributes
    - ❖ Precise control (Advanced)
        - ♦ Positioning
        - ♦ Fluid layouts
- Cost Savings
    - ❖ Reduced Bandwidth Costs
        - ♦ One style sheet called and cached
    - ❖ Higher Search Engine Rankings
        - ♦ Cleaner code is easier for search engines to index
        - ♦ Greater density of indexable content
- Faster download = better usability
    - ❖ Web usability redesign can increase the sales/conversion rate by 100% (source: Jakob Nielson)

- CSS requires less code
- Tables require spacer images
- Entire table has to render before content
- CSS can control the order that elements download (content before images)

- Increased Reach
  - CSS website is compatible with many different devices
  - In 2008 an est. 58 Million PDA's will be sold (Source: eTForecast.com) 1/3 of the world's population will own a wireless device by 2010

Cascading Style allows obtaining the full control under HTML tagging. CSS allows easily redefining the all default properties of any HTML tag. Using CSS, you will open new unique opportunities missing in common HTML.

EXERCISE

Objective Type Questions

1. What does CSS stand for?

   (A) Creative Style Sheets (B) Colorful Style Sheets

   (C) Cascading Style Sheets (D) Computer Style Sheets

2. What is the correct HTML for referring to an external style sheet?

   (A) <stylesheet>mystyle.css</stylesheet>

   (B) <style src="mystyle.css">

   (C) <link rel="stylesheet" type="text/css" href="mystyle.css">

3. Where in an HTML document is the correct place to refer to an external style sheet?

   (A) In the <head> section

   (B) At the top of the document

   (C) At the end of the document

   (D) In the <body> section

4. Which HTML attribute is used to define inline styles?

   (A) class (B) styles

   (C) style (D) font

5. Which is the correct CSS syntax?

   (A) {body;color:black} (B) body {color: black}

   (C) body:color=black (D) {body:color=black(body}

6. How do you insert a comment in a CSS file?

   (A) // this is a comment (B) // this is a comment //

   (C) ' this is a comment (D) /* this is a comment */

7. Which property is used to change the background color?

   (A) background-color

   (B) color

   (C) bgcolor

8. How do you add a background color for all <h1> elements?

   (A) all.h1 {background-color:#FFFFFF}

   (B) h1.all {background-color:#FFFFFF}

   (C) h1 {background-color:#FFFFFF}

9. How do you change the text color of an element?

(A) fgcolor (B) color

(C) text-color (D) text-color

10. Which CSS property controls the text size?

(A) font-size (B) font-style

(C) text-style (D) text-size

11. What is the correct CSS syntax for making all the <p> elements bold?

(A) <p style="font-size:bold"> (B) p {text-size:bold}

(C) p {font-weight:bold} (D) <p style="text-size:bold">

12. How do you display hyperlinks without an underline?

(A) a {text-decoration:no underline}

(B) a {text-decoration:none}

(C) a {underline:none}

(D) a {decoration:no underline}

13. How do you make each word in a text start with a capital letter?

(A) You can't do that with CSS

(B) text-transform:uppercase

(C) text-transform:capitalize

14. How do you change the font of an element?

(A) font=

(B) font-family:

(C) f:

15. How do you make the text bold?

(A) font:b

(B) style:bold

(C) font-weight:bold

16. How do you display a border like this:

The top border = 10 pixels

The bottom border = 5 pixels

The left border = 20 pixels

The right border = 1pixel?

(A) border-width:10px 20px 5px 1px

(B) border-width:5px 20px 10px 1px

(C) border-width:10px 5px 20px 1px

(D) border-width:10px 1px 5px 20px

17. How do you change the left margin of an element?

(A) margin: (B) text-indent:

(C) indent: (D) margin-left:

18. How do you make a list that lists its items with squares?

(A) type: 2 (B) type: square

(C) list-type: square (D) list-style-type: square

19. Where in an HTML document is the correct place to refer to an external style sheet?

(A) In the <body> section

(B) At the end of the document

(C) At the top of the document

(D) In the <head> section

(E) Between head and body

20. Which HTML tag is used to define an internal style sheet?

(A) css (B) text/style

(C) style (D) script

21. Which is the correct CSS syntax?

(A) body {color: black} (B) body:color=black

(C) {body:color=black(body} (D) {body;color:black}

22. Which property is used to change the background color?

(A) bgcolor:

(B) background-color:

(C) color:

23. How do you add a background color for all "<h1>" elements?

(A) all.h1 {background-color:#FFFFFF}

(B) h1.all {background-color:#FFFFFF}

(C) h1 {background-color:#FFFFFF}

24. Which CSS property controls the text size?

(A) font-style (B) text-style

(C) font-size (D) text-size

25. How do you display hyperlinks without an underline?

(A) a {decoration:no underline}

(B) a {text-decoration:no underline}

(C) a {underline:none}

(D) a {text-decoration:none}

26. How do you make each word in a text start with a capital letter?

(A) text-transform:uppercase

(B) text-transform:capitalize

(C) You can't do that with CSS

27. How do you change the font of an element?

(A) fon-face: (B) font-family:

(C) f: (D) font-style:

28. How do you make the text bold?

(A) font:b

(B) style:bold

(C) font-weight:bold

29. How do you display a border like this: The top border = 10 pixels, The bottom border = 5 pixels, The left border = 20 pixels, The right border = 1pixel?

(A) border-width:10px 20px 5px 1px

(B) border-width:10px 1px 5px 20px

(C) border-width:10px 5px 20px 1px

(D) border-width:5px 20px 10px 1px

30. How do you change the left margin of an element?

(A) padding: (B) indent:

(C) margin: (D) text-indent:

(E) margin-left:

31. To define the space between the element's border and content, you use the padding property, but are you allowed to use negative values?

(A) Yes (B) No

32. How do you make a list that lists its items with squares?

(A) type: square (B) list-style-type: square

(C) list-type: square (D) style-list: square

33. What is the correct HTML for referring to an external style sheet?

(A) <link rel="stylesheet" type="text/css" href="mainstyle.css">

(B) <style src="mainstyle.css">

(C) <stylesheet>mainstyle.css</stylesheet>

(D) <link url="stylesheet" type="text/css" href="mainstyle.css">

34. Which HTML tag is used to define an internal style sheet?

(A) <script> (B) <css>

(C) <stylesheet> (D) <style>

35. How do you make each word in a text start with a capital letter?

(A) text-transform:capitalize

(B) ext-transform:uppercase

(C) You can't do that with CSS

36. How do you change the left margin of an element?

(A) left-margin: (B) margin:

(C) margin-left: (D) text-indent:

37. What are the three methods for using style sheets with a web page

(A) Dreamweaver, GoLive or FrontPage

(B) Inline, embedded or document level and external

(C) Handcoded, Generated or WYSIWYG

38. Which of the following styles is recommended?

(A) In-Line styles (B) External styles

(C) Embedded styles (D) Multiple styles

39. In what form are style rules presented?

(A) selector { property: value } (B) selector { property= value }

(C) selector (property: value) (D) selector (property= value)

40. Which property applies a color to text?

(A) text-color (B) foreground-color

(C) background-color (D) color

41. Which values for font-family property is valid?

(A) Times New Roman, serif (B) "Times New Roman", serif

(C) Times New Roman; serif; (D) "Times New Roman"; "serif";

42. What does the ID selector do?

(A) Apply the style to a specific element

(B) Apply the style to all the elements

(C) Apply the style to a group of elements

(D) Apply the style to elements of the same type

43. What selector should you use when applying a style to multiple elements?

(A) ID (B) Class

(C) Type (D) Any of the above

44. How to apply a style to several specific element types?

(A) Use the type selector with, delimiter

(B) Use the type selector with. delimiter

(C) Use the ID selector with; delimiter

(D) Use the ID selector with > delimiter

45. One of the following rules will display text colored bright red. Which one?

(A) color: #f00;

(B) color: #0f0;

(C) color: #fff000;

46. CSS Zengarden is a website created by

(A) Dave Shea

(B) Doug Bowman

(C) Jeffrey Zeldman

47. Rule font-size:small will display significantly larger text than usually in one of the following browsers. Which one?

(A) FireFox 1 Mac

(B) Opera 8 Win

(C) IE5 Win

48. Which one of the following CSS examples is so-called Box Model Hack?

(A)
```
div.content {
    width:400px;
    voice-family: "\"}\"";
    voice-family:inherit;
    width:300px;
}
```

(B)
```
div.content {
    width:400px;
    w/idth:300px;
}
```

(C)
```
div.content {
    width:400px !important;
    width:300px;
}
```

49. A hypertext document is thought to make of three layers. General terms for these layers are

(A) code, style and data

(B) structure, presentation and behavior

(C) HTML, CSS and JavaScript

50. A technique widely known as Sliding Doors is used to create

(A) a pretty JavaScript effect that displays an image "sliding" it on top of another

(B) a 2-column layout where right-side column comes first in the markup

(C) an element that is styled with CSS to grow as the content of the elemer grows

51. CSS rule known as Be Nice To Opera could be marked as:

(A)
```
html>body .content {
    width:300px;
}
```

(B)
```
#wrap .content {
    width:300px;
```

}

(C) html body .content {

width:300px;

}

52. Which one of the following CSS selectors has the highest specificity value?

(A) html body div

(B) html body.home div.normal

(C) html body div#content

53. :focus pseudoclass is part of which CSS specification?

(A) CSS1

(B) CSS2

(C) CSS1.1

54. What is the correct XHTML markup for referring to an external style sheet?

(A) <link rel="stylesheet" type="text/css" href="style.css">

(B) <link rel="stylesheet" type="text/css" href="style.css" />

(C) <link rel="stylesheet" type="application/css" href="style.css" />

55. Instead of using different selectors for each list-style you can specify them all at once using the what?

(A) list-style type property

(B) list-style position property

(C) list-style property

56. <SPAN>, <B> and <I> are examples of what kind of tags?

(A) Inline tags

(B) Block tags

(C) Price tags

57. Which of the following can NOT be changed with the text-decoration property?

(A) Overline

(B) Capitalization

(C) Underline

58. Which of the following is NOT a valid value for the visibility property?

(A) Middle

(B) Hidden

(C) Visible

59. Selectors that will only work in certain contexts are called?

(A) Context Dependent Selectors

(B) Hyper Text Markup Selectors

(C) Grouped Selectors

60. Which would you NOT be able to do with CSS?

(A) Add text

(B) Position the content

(C) Define the look of your pages in one place

61. When changing a style you must edit?

(A) All tags that refer to the style

(B) The style difnintion only

(C) The settings on your browser

62. When referring to a Class selector you simply add the class to what?

(A) HTML Tag

(B) Head

(C) Title

63. In CSS, the font-style property can make text what?

(A) Italic

(B) Different colors

(C) Bigger

64. Which of the following does NOT work on Netscape browsers prior to version 6?

(A) A:link

(B) A:visited

(C) A:hover

65. CSS can be defined for entire pages by simply adding what to the head section?

(A) Style definition

(B) Script

(C) Class structure

66. In CSS, A:link defines the style for?

(A) visited links

(B) normal unvisited links

(C) active links

67. Can you add a style in a single place on a page?

(A) Yes, with a global style definition that redefines the tag.

(B) No - CSS can only be defined for entire pages.

(C) Yes, with a style-definition written into the tag.

68. You can change the look of the entire site at once when CSS is defined where?

(A) With each block of text

(B) On your computer

(C) In an external file

69. In CSS, what is a definition of fonts, colors, etc. called?

(A) Style

(B) Font-family

(C) ID tag

70. Which of the following is NOT an advantage of CSS?

(A) Define the look of your pages in one place

(B) Easily change the look

(C) Works on version 4 browsers or newer

71. Selectors are the names that you give to?

(A) Tags

(B) Tables

(C) Styles

72. CSS can be defined for entire sites by simply writing the CSS definitions in a what?

(A) Plain text file

(B) Meta tag

(C) Table

73. Which of the following is NOT a valid CSS selector?

(A) HEAD selectors

(B) TAG selectors

(C) ID selectors

74. Which selectors are used when you want to redefine the general look for an entire HTML tag?

(A) ID

(B) HTML

(C) Class

75. Which selectors are used when you want to define a style that does not redefine an HTML tag entirely?

(A) None

(B) Class

(C) HTML

76. <DIV> is what kind of tag?

(A) Block tag

(B) Inline tag

(C) Font tag

77. What do you define in the style definition?

(A) Which browser the visitor is using

(B) How each selector should work

(C) Where to place each selector

78. When using CSS, you refer to selectors to activate what?

(A) IDs

(B) Styles

(C) Tags

79. Selectors that will share some of the same styles can be?

(A) Styled

(B) Grouped

(C) Defined as super selectors

80. CSS can be added to a page on how many levels?

(A) 2 - Head and External file

(B) 3 - Tag, Head and External file

(C) 4 - Tag, Head, External file and Meta tag

81. Can you add a style in a single place on a page?

(A) Yes, with a global style definition that redefines the tag

(B) No - CSS can only be defined for entire pages

(C) Yes, with a style-definition written into the tag

82. Why should your use of single tag CSS be limited?

(A) You will lose much of the power associated with CSS

(B) You will bore your visitors

(C) You will grow tired of reading it

83. With CSS where do you add the following: <style type="text/css">?

(A) Head section

(B) Body section

(C) Text document

84. CSS can be defined for entire sites by simply writing the CSS definitions where?

(A) Head section of each page

(B) Body section of each page

(C) Plain Text document

85. Which of the following is NOT an advantage of CSS defined for the entire site?

(A) Faster loading pages

(B) Flexibility to change styles for entire site

(C) Prettier colors

86. <link rel=stylesheet href="whatever.css" type="text/css"> is used for adding CSS to the entire site?

(A) No

(B) Only if written in the <body>-section of the page

(C) Yes - if present on all pages in the site

Review & Discussion Questions

1. What is CSS? How it is differ from HTML? Explain with suitable example.
2. What is CSS web template? List out the different level of CSS.
3. List out the advantages of CSS used in HTML.
4. Explain how CSS works.
5. Define Rule and Selectors. Explain various selector types with examples.
6. What do you mean by pseudo-classes? Give example.
7. What do you mean by pseudo-elements? Give example.
8. What is the meaning of class, id, child and attribute? Give example each.
9. What are Selector patterns? Explain with examples.
10. What do you mean by CSS declaration and CSS properties? Give examples.
11. What is class and grouping? Give example.
12. What is cascade? Define its order.
13. Can Style Sheets and HTML stylistic elements be used in the same document?
14. What is list and outline property? Give example.
15. Explain margin property with example.
16. What are the importances of using border property? Give example.
17. What are the importances of using classification property? Give example.
18. List out the different ways of implementing CSS.
19. What is inline CSS. What are its advantages and disadvantages?
20. What is embedded CSS? When it can be used? What are its advantages and disadvantages?
21. What is the power of external CSS? List out its advantages and disadvantages?
22. How will you import CSS?
23. List out the advantages and disadvantages of CSS.
24. Write a CSS code for bold, itaic and underline the text?

CHAPTER 15

Graphics

CHAPTER OBJECTIVES

In this chapter, covers the categories of graphic images that have been processed by a computer. Starting with bitmap graphics, the chapter goes on to discussion on vector images, web graphics format. This will help to learn how to design good images, scan images as well as reduce size.

CHAPTER OUTLINES

15.1 INTRODUCTION

To a computer, an image is just a set of numbers. The numbers specify the color of each pixel in the image. The numbers that represent the image on the computer's screen are stored in a part of memory called a frame buffer. Many times each second, the computer's video card reads the data in the frame buffer and colors each pixel on the screen according to that data. Whenever the computer needs to make some change to the screen, it writes some new numbers to the frame buffer, and the change appears on the screen a fraction of a second later, the next time the screen is redrawn by the video card.

Since it's just a set of numbers, the data for an image doesn't have to be stored in a frame buffer. It can be stored elsewhere in the computer's memory. It can be stored in a file on the computer's hard disk.

Graphic images that have been processed by a computer can usually be divided into two distinct categories. Such images are either bitmap files or vector graphics. If you work in prepress, you need a good comprehension on the advantages and disadvantages of both types of data. You can come up with your own way and thus, your own storage format. There are many possible ways you can express image data and create file formats.

15.2 BITMAPPED GRAPHICS

A bitmap is a collection of pixels that describes an image, in human terms, a complete picture. The image consists of a matrix of individual dots (or pixels) that all have their own color (described using bits, the smallest possible units of information for a computer). A bitmap can be of various bit depth and resolution. Basically, a bitmap is an array of pixels. Therefore, the quality and detail in these images is resolution dependent on the output device and specified as dpi or dots per inch. Scanned images are always bitmapped images. Extensive resizing of bitmapped images can result in a modish pattern. Graphics that contain a number of hard-edged lines will appear stair stepped or rough when saved in a bitmapped format.

Bit depth is the number of bits used to store information about each pixel. The higher the depth, the more colors are stored in an image. For example, the lowest bit-depth, 1 bit graphics are only capable of showing two colors, black & white. This is because there are only two combinations of numbers in one bit, 0 and 1. Four-bit color is capable of displaying 16 colors because there are 16 different combinations of four bits:

0000 0001 0010 0011 0100 0101 0110 0111 1000 1001 1010 1011 1100 1101 1110 1111

With 8-bit color, there are a total of 256 colors available. With 16-bit color, a total of 65536 is available. When you have 24 bit color, a total of 16777216 colors are available.

Bit depth might refer to the bit depth of an image, or the bit depth of a monitor. When it refers to the bit depth of a monitor, it means that your monitor is able to show a certain number of colors at one time. If it is meant as the bit depth of an image, it means that the image may contain the specified number of colors.

Resolution: Resolution in computer graphics, either refers to the number of pixels per inch or other unit of measure (centimeter for example) on a monitor or printer. It is also sometimes used to describe the total number of pixels on a monitor. Resolution is usually measured in pixels per inch or dots per inch (dpi).

Most monitors can display at 72 dpi. Monitors come in a variety of resolutions. They can get as small as 320 pixels by 200 pixels or as large as 1280 by 1024. Printers can also print at many different resolutions. The resolution can be as small as 128 dpi or less, to 300 dpi on inkjet printers, to 720 dpi on laser printer, and up to 2000 dpi on high quality typesetters. Let's take a look at a typical bitmap image to demonstrate the principle:

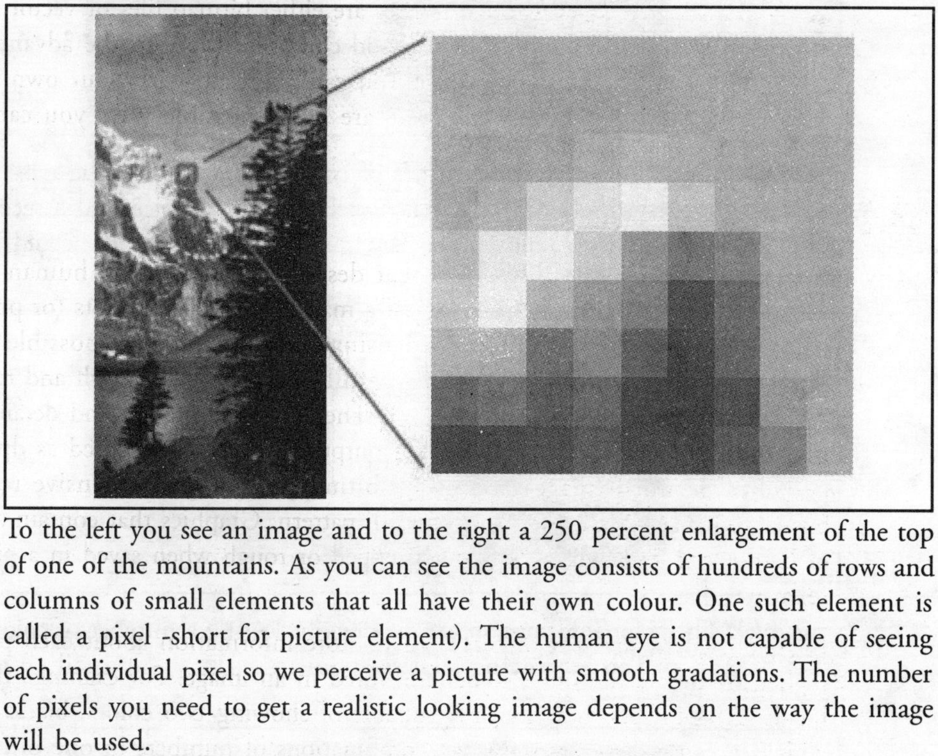

To the left you see an image and to the right a 250 percent enlargement of the top of one of the mountains. As you can see the image consists of hundreds of rows and columns of small elements that all have their own colour. One such element is called a pixel -short for picture element). The human eye is not capable of seeing each individual pixel so we perceive a picture with smooth gradations. The number of pixels you need to get a realistic looking image depends on the way the image will be used.

15.2.1 Types of Bitmap Images

Bitmap images can contain any number of colors but we distinguish between four main categories:

Line-art: These are images that only contain two colors, usually black and white. Sometimes these images are referred to as bitmaps because a computer has to use only 1 bit (on=black, off=white) to define each pixel.

Grayscale: These images, which contain various shades of grey, as well as pure black and white.

Multitones: Such images contain shades of two or more colors. The most popular multitone images are duotones, which usually consist of black and a second spot color (often an Pantone color). The example below contains black and Pantone Warm Red.

Full color: The color information can be described using a number of color spaces: RGB, CMYK or Lab for instance. These are discussed in more detail on this page (not yet available).

15.2.2 Characteristics of Bitmap Data

Large Size: Bitmap data can take up a lot of room. A CMYK A4-size picture that is optimized for medium quality printing (150 lpi) takes up 40 MB. Compression can reduce the size of the file.

Loose Sharpness: The image with the enlargement showed one of the main disadvantages of bitmap images: once they are enlarged too much, they look unnatural and blocky. But, reducing a picture too much also has a bad influence as it looses sharpness.

Fair Quality: Bitmaps are fairly simple to output, as long as your RIP or printer has sufficient memory. Old PostScript level 1 devices could get into trouble when images (especially line-art) were rotated but the newest hardware and software has enough processing power to handle any effect without troubles.

Not Easily Scalable: Bitmap-based files are more suitable for photo-realistic images that require complex color variations. They are, however, not easily scalable because each bitmap-based image is mapped to a non-flexible grid. If a bitmap-based image were to be enlarged, it would lose its sharpness. All edges within the image would appear to be jagged.

File names for bitmap-based images usually consist of extensions such as PSD, JPEG, GIF, TIF, BMP, EPS, PDF, PICT, and TIFF.

In general, bitmap-based files require more computer memory for file storage than vector-based files. The former contains all information for every single pixel of the image while the latter contains only the defining mathematical formulas for each element within the image.

Note: The above is not entirely true if the bitmapped image is compressed. Compression reduces the size of an image file by reducing the amount of information needed to replicate the image. A compressed file will download more quickly, because of its smaller size, but it needs to be decompressed before the image can be displayed. This decompression step means additional processing effort.

Bitmap based images, on the other hand, do not rely on mathematical formulas to define their various elements. Each bitmap-based image is mapped into a grid. The size of the grid is based on the image's resolution. For example, a bitmap-based image of 1 inch × 1 inch with a 600 dpi resolution would be defined by a grid of 600 × 600 pixels. Hence, a bitmap-based image is like a mosaic of pixels with each pixel holding a specific color value.

15.3 VECTOR GRAPHICS

A vector graphic file contains mathematical information that is used to redraw the image on the screen. When a computer displays a vector image file, it reads in the redrawing instructions and follows them. This might sound like a lot of unnecessary processing, but there is an important advantage to this approach: You can rescale the image to new sizes without loss of resolution because there's no fixed relationship between how its defined in the file and the pixel-by-pixel image on the screen. When you try to resize a bitmapped file, you often get a loss of resolution that detracts from the image.

Vector graphic formats are typically used for images with distinct geometric shapes. Computer Aided Design (CAD) drawings are examples of this type of image.

Vector-based files are more suitable for illustrations that require precise measurements. They are also easily scalable due to their mathematical nature. However, the vector-based file format has its drawbacks as well. It is not good for displaying photo-realistic images such as a photograph because images of this type generally do not contain well-defined shapes and curves.

Note: Some file formats combine the best of both bitmapped and vector graphics into what's called a metafile format. Windows metafiles (.WMF) are frequently used to store clip-art images that need to be resized often.

Vector-based images generally contain well-defined elements such as curves and shapes of various colors. These elements can be either pure graphics, western alphabets or Asian characters. Each element is defined mathematically by the computer. For example, if a vector-based image contains a red dot, then information such as the location of the circle's center point, the length of its radius, and the color, red, would be the essential information for this image file.

File names for vector-based images usually consist of extensions such as *.EPS, *.AI, *CDR, or *.DWG.

15.4 WEB GRAPHIC FORMATS

When you focus your attention on Web graphics, the vast number of usable graphic storage formats quickly reduces to two (GIF and JPEG). The Graphics Interchange Format, or GIF, was developed by CompuServe in 1987 to store graphics used over its network. The other format came about more recently and was named for the group that developed it: the Joint Picture Experts Group, or JPEG. Both formats are bitmapped formats. Currently, there is virtually no support for vector storage formats, except by means of browser plug-ins. The specifics of each of these formats, and instances when you would want to use one over the other, are discussed in the following sections.

15.4.1 Graphics Interchange Format (GIF)

CompuServe released the GIF standard in 1987 and updated it in 1989 and 1990. The current standard is 89a, and it supports 8-bit color. That is, a GIF image can contain up to 28, or 256 colors. Image data in a GIF file is organized into related blocks and sub blocks that provide information on how to paint screen pixels to reproduce the image. When transmitting a GIF image, a program called an encoder is used to produce a GIF data stream of control and data blocks that are sent along to the destination machine. There, a program called a decoder parses the data stream and assembles the image. GIF is a compressed format as well. GIF files employ the LZW compression scheme to reduce the amount of information needed to completely describe the image. The LZW scheme is best suited to simple images like line drawings or images with just a few unique colors. As the number of colors grows, LZW compression becomes less efficient, providing compression ratios of 2:1 or less.

Note: The LZW compression used with GIFs was actually conceived by the Unisys Corporation and not by CompuServe. CompuServe and Unisys were entangled in patent disputes for a while. The end result, was CompuServe's licensing of the GIF format. Fortunately, for them, the license agreement pertained only to software that was primarily used for accessing CompuServe. The downside was these developers still had to worry about licensing with Unisys as well. Unisys has yet to pursue this with any vigor though, and the GIF format continues to be one of the most popular formats on the Internet.

Transparent GIFs: GIF supports many effects that are desirable on Web pages. In a transparent GIF, you can designate one color to be the transparent color. Then, whenever the GIF is rendered on screen, pixels painted with the transparent color will actually be painted with the color of the page background. This gives the illusion of the pixels being transparent, since they allow what's behind them to show through. The advantage of transparent GIFs is that they make a graphic appear to float freely on a page.

Many graphics programs available today come with support for creating transparent GIFs. Lview Pro, a graphic utility discussed later in this chapter, makes it very easy to designate a transparent color in a GIF.

Interlaced GIFs: When you store a GIF in an interlaced format, non adjacent parts of the image are stored together and as the GIF is decoded, pixels from all over the image are filled in rather than being filled in row by row. The result is that the image appears to "fade on" to the page, as if it were being revealed from behind Venetian blinds. This permits the user to get a sense of the entire image right away instead of having to wait for the whole thing to be read in from top to bottom. It usually takes several passes for the image to fade in completely. Just as with transparency, most good graphic programs give you the option of saving a GIF, as interlaced. All three programs discussed in this chapter support interlaced GIFs.

Animated GIFs: The first animations that appeared on the Web required a great deal of effort. Using an approach introduced by Netscape called server push, you could create an animation by having a server literally push several images down an open HTTP connection. When presented in sequence on the browser screen, these images created the illusion of animation. Since most digital media graphic artists don't have knowledge of CGI programming, producing a Web animation often required collaboration between the artists and the server administrator. Then it occurred to someone that the GIF 89a standard supports multiple images stored in the same file. Further, you could place instructions in the file header that describe how the images should be presented. In short, the 89a standard gives you everything you need to produce an animation! The individual frames that comprise the animation can all be stored in one file, and you can specify in the file header parameters like how much delay before starting the animation and how many times the animation should repeat.

Note: Like many popular Web page components, a number of animated GIFs have been made publicly available for download at many sites. The result is that these GIFs quickly become overused. Placing such a GIF on your pages does nothing to distinguish them. If you really need an animated GIF on your page, create your own unique animation. Don't put a trite animated GIF on a page just for the sake of having one there.

15.4.2 Joint Picture Experts Group (JPEG)

JPEG actually refers to a set of formats that supports full-color and grayscale images and stores them in compressed form. JPEG stores color information at 24 bits per pixel, allowing an image to contain 2^24 or over 16.7 million colors! This makes it the format of choice for photographs, especially nature photographs, where a continuum of colors is in play. Photographs of naturally occurring objects are prime candidates for being stored as JPEGs. JPEG can handle so many colors while still keeping file sizes reasonable because it compresses the image data. You even have some control over how big or small the file ultimately is. You can specify a high level of compression to get a very small file, but the quality of the image on-screen will be reduced. When you decompress a JPEG image, there is always the some amount of loss, meaning that the image will not look the way it did originally. Fortunately, JPEG's compression/decompression scheme is such that the lost image data tends to be in the higher color frequencies, where it is harder for the human eye to detect the differences. In spite of this loss, you can still use JPEG to achieve compression ratios between 10:1 and 20:1 without appreciable change in the image. This means you've essentially reduced the amount of storage space per pixel from 24 bits to 1 or 2 bits--quite a savings! You can take the compression ratios even higher, but as noted above, the loss will become more detectable and image quality will suffer.

Note: Always do the conversion to JPEG as your very last step in creating a Web image. Resaving as a JPEG after each change can increase the amount of loss, since the image is recompressed each time.

Progressive JPEGs (p-JPEG): A p-JPEGs JPEG isn't as versatile a format as GIF when it comes to supporting desirable Web page effects. However, a relatively new type of JPEG, called a progressive JPEG or p-JPEG, provides an analogy to the interlaced GIF. A p-JPEG is stored as a series of scans that together comprise the entire image. When the first scan is read in, users see a blocky approximation of the whole image, so they can quickly get an idea of what they're ultimately going to see. As subsequent scans are read in, the image comes into sharper focus.

Note: People often ask if there will ever be transparent JPEGs. Unfortunately, the answer to this question is no. To understand why, recall that there is always some loss during JPEG compression/decompression. This means that some pixels are not colored with the same color they originally were.

Now suppose, you've specified a transparent color for the JPEG. If a pixel originally colored with the transparent color is assigned a new color due to the loss, then that pixel will no longer be transparent. Similarly, nontransparent pixels could be colored with the transparent color after compression/decompression, meaning that they will end up being transparent. Either way, you get the opposite of what you wanted and the on-screen results would be disastrous. Unless JPEG is changed to become a lossless format, there is little hope of there ever being transparent JPEGs.

15.4.3 When to Use GIF or JPEG

Given that you have the choice between two formats for Web graphics, you may find yourself wondering when to use one or the other. To help you answer that question, review some guidelines below.

You have to use a GIF if you want transparency or animation, since; it's the only format, which supports them. Beyond that, you should consider GIF for the following types of images:

- Black-and-white line art and text
- Images with a limited number of distinct colors
- Graphics with sharp or distinct edges (most menus, buttons, and graphs fit this category)
- Graphics that are overlaid with text

JPEG is better suited for the following situations:

- Scanned photographs and ray-traced renderings
- Images that contain a complex mixture of colors
- Any image that requires a palette of more than 256 colors

Because the compression computations work better with a continuum of color, the JPEG format is not well suited to images that have very sharp color changes.

15.4.4 Up and Coming: Portable Network Graphics (PNG)

GIF and JPEG are currently the two principal Web formats, but there's a new kid on the block that shows a great deal of promise. The Portable Network Graphics (PNG) format has been defined as a network standard by the World Wide Web Consortium (W3C).

PNG is described as "an extensible file format for the lossless, portable, well-compressed storage of raster (bitmapped) images. PNG provides a patent-free replacement for the GIF format and can also replace many common uses of the older TIFF format. Indexed-color, grayscale, and true color images are supported. PNG is designed to work well in online viewing applications, such as the World Wide Web, and so it is fully streamable with a progressive display option." Look for PNG graphics to become more prevalent on the Web as this new standard is adopted. It is already supported by Internet Explorer and Netscape Communicator.

On The Web: You can find out more about the PNG graphics format on the W3C Web site at http://www.w3.org/Graphics/PNG/.

15.4.5 Tagged Image File Format (TIFF)

The format was released in 1986 and was generally used to hold scanned white and black images (Tiff 3.0). Released in 1987, Tiff 4.0 got prevalence for it supported incompact color RGB images. Tiff 5.0 format, released in 1988, made possible to hold palette color images and support LZW compression algorithm (read more about LZW compression algorithm here). , Released in 1992, Tiff 6.0, supported CMYK and YcbCr color images and Jpeg compression algorithm (read more about Jpeg compression algorithm here).

The current Tiff (Tiff 6.0) is a rich and flexible file format, supported virtually by many programs such as paint, image editing & page layout application. The format is capable to record halftone images with different pixel intensity. So, it is considered to be a perfect format for graphic data storage and processing. Tiff format is one of the most multipurpose and integrated raster formats. It is easily ported among platforms and used for different purposes (besides Internet).

15.4.6 WMF (Microsoft Windows Metafile)

You can use WMF files to hold vector and halftone images in working memory or in disks with post output display. Windows Metafile format is a specific Windows format. So, it is supported by a lot of "non - Windows" applications for data exchange with Windows applications. Out of Microsoft Windows interface prevalence, WMF format is considered to be a general format for graphic applications and is supported by all platforms.

15.4.7 PCX (PC Paintbrush File Format)

PCX format is one of the most usable graphic formats. Originally, it was designed by Zsoft for PC Paintbrush MS-DOS. That is why, it is also known as PC Paintbrush format. Zsoft entered into a treaty with Microsoft. The latter was entitled to use PCX format with other products, including Microsoft Paintbrush for Windows (Microsoft Paintbrush program is delivered with each copy of MS Windows). As a result, the format became of great importance not only for computers, based on Intel processors, but also for the whole computer industry.

PCX files are used for graphic data storage and exchange in desktop publishing system.

Originally, the format was used to hold graphics and images, which contained not more than 16 colors. This limitation was conditioned by IBM EGA display construction (Enhanced Graphics). When IBM started to release VGA adapter (Virtual Graphics Array), PCX format was revised to hold graphics and images, which contained up to 256 colors.

The last PCX versions make possible to hold 24 bits color displays. Due to this fact, the format can be generally used for graphic data operating. Unfortunately, its compression algorithm is not effective enough to hold images with large pixel intensity. Image data are encoded with the help of one of the RLE algorithm variants (read more about this compression algorithm here). Using the RLE algorithms, it is difficult to foresee the end, for compressing factor is highly depended on image data and on the number of colors, used in the concrete. Generally, image data, which contain not more than 16 colors, decrease by 40-70% as compared with the original file size. While 64 or 256 color images, which were scanned or videoed, decrease only by 10-30%. Sometimes you can increase PCX file size via using compression algorithm for complex images.

15.5 SUMMARY OF IMAGE FORMATS

This table summarizes the key differences between the GIF, JPEG and PNG image formats.

GIF	JPEG	PNG-8	PNG-24
Better for clipart and drawn graphics with few colors, or large blocks of colour	Better for photographs with lots of colors or fine colour detail	Better for clipart and drawn graphics with few colors, or large blocks of colour	Better for photographs with lots of colors or fine colour detail
Can only have up to 256 colors	Can have up to 16 million colors	Can only have up to 256 colors	Can have up to 16 million colors
Images are "lossless" - they contain the same amount of information as the original (but with only 256 colors)	Images are "lossy" - they contain less information than the original	Images are "lossless" - they contain the same amount of information as the original (but with only 256 colors)	Images are "lossless" - they contain the same amount of information as the original
Can be animated	Cannot be animated	Cannot be animated	Cannot be animated
Can have transparent areas	Cannot have transparent areas	Can have transparent areas	Can have transparent areas

Format name	Extension	Type	Compression algorithm	Color depth	Platforms
JPEG (Joint Photographic Experts Group)	jpg, jpeg, jfif, jfl	bitmapped	JPEG (lossy)	24 bits	All
GIF (Graphics Interchange Format)	gif	bitmapped	LZW (lossless)	up to 8 bits	All

Contd....

Bitmap (Microsoft Windows Bitmap)	bmp, dib, rle	bitmapped	RLE (lossless), without compression	up to 32 bits	Windows, OS/
TIFF (Tagged Image File Format)	tif	bitmapped	CCITT-RLE, CCITT-FAX3, CCITT-FAX4, LZW, OJPEG, JPEG, CCITT-RLEW, Packbits, Deflate	up to 48 bits	All
WMF (Microsoft Windows Metafile)	wmf	metafile	24 bits		All
PCX (PC Paintbrush File format)	pcx	bitmapped	, without compression	1, 4, 8, 24 bits	All

15.6 MAKING GOOD USE OF IMAGES

While it is true that a properly designed image can enhance a document, a poorly designed image can detract from it. Graphic images certainly have their place in Web documents, and in fact, they are expected in many places by users. The next few sections look at the types of graphics commonly found on the Web and give you some tips on how to maximize the effectiveness of each kind.

- *Main Page Graphics:* If you've visited many Web sites, you've very likely noticed the tendency to put a large graphic on the main page of a site that lets a visitor navigate to all of the major sections of the site. Such a graphic is a good idea for many reasons. It lets the user know right away, what major content sections are available. Additionally, it lets the site designer establish a visual look for each section, which can be helpful to users later as they navigate through the site. But, there are pitfalls to this type of image. Here are some things to think about:

- *Keep the file size small:* Forcing users to wait a long time for a large image to load can prompt them to interrupt the loading and move on to another site. Make sure that your main-page graphics are a reasonable size--somewhere between 50K and 100K, if possible.

- *Be consistent:* Use the graphics elements (color, icons, headings) that you associate with each content section consistently throughout the site. This gives visitors a better chance of figuring out where they are and how to get to where they want to go.

- *Provide a text-based alternative:* Users with text-only browsers, or who have image loading turned off, won't be able to see your main-page graphic at all. Be sure to include a set of hypertext links that these users can use to navigate to the major areas of your site.

Your main-page graphic is the first thing users will see when visiting your site and sets the tone for the rest of their time there. The best rule of thumb for this kind of graphics is to make sure it is eye-catching and distinctive, without falling prey to one of the issues above.

- *Icons:* Icons are small graphics that are meant to represent a certain content section or piece of information on your site. Commonly used icons include a question mark for Help and Frequently Asked Questions (FAQ) sections or a magnifying glass for a search engine.

Because icons are small, file size is usually not a problem. Icons download quickly and, once they are in a user's cache, can be reused, again and again without further downloading. However, an icon's smallness can also be a disadvantage because you have to pack a very specific concept into a fairly small part of the screen. For this reason, your chief concern when designing icons is intuitiveness. Users should be able to look at an icon and almost immediately discern what it means.

The best way to see if your icons are intuitive is to test them with a group of users as you're designing the site. A commonly used test involves presenting users with a set of potential icons and asking them to write down what they think each icon represents. If you find that most users interpret an icon the same way, you can feel good about using that icon to represent the idea they say it does. If there's no clear interpretation of an icon, you should scrap it or send it back to the drawing board.

Once you have chosen your icons, be sure to use them consistently. This helps to reinforce their meaning with the user and makes navigating your site much less stressful.

Note: If you expect a global audience to visit your site, you also need to consider how your icons will be interpreted by users from cultures different from your own. This typically requires trying out your icons on users from those cultures, if possible.

15.7 TIPS FOR REDUCING FILE SIZE

If you think you have an image file that's too big, don't despair! There are plenty of techniques for bringing the size down. Depending on the makeup of the image and the format you saved it in, you may want to try one of the following:

- *Resize the image:* Larger images take up more disk space because there are more pixels and, hence, more color information that has to be stored. By shrinking the height and width of an image to the smallest they can be, you take a big step toward making the file as small as it can be. If you try to use the WIDTH and HEIGHT attributes of the <IMG> tag to resize the image, you're relying on the browser to do the resizing and you're likely to be disappointed with the results. Additionally, resizing with the browser doesn't save you download time because the original image file still has to be downloaded.

- *Use thumbnails:* Thumbnails are very small versions of an image, usually a photograph. Because they're smaller, their file sizes are smaller too. Store

GIFs as JPEGs. JPEG compression works best on images with lots of color gradation. If you have a GIF file that fits this description, try saving it as a JPEG to see if that makes the file any smaller.

- *Increase the compression ratio:* If you're working with a JPEG, you can resave it at a higher compression ratio to shrink the file size. But, don't forget the trade-off: higher compression reduces the quality of the image.
- *Reduce the color depth:* Color depth is another way to express how many colors can be stored by a format. A GIF image has a color depth of 8 bits (256 colors)--but what if there are fewer than 256 colors in the image? In this case, you can reduce the color depth to a smaller number of bits per pixel. With less information to store per pixel, the resulting file will be smaller.
- *Adjust contrast levels in the image:* Contrast refers to the brightness of objects in the image relative to one another. Most popular graphics programs offer retouching options like gamma correction and highlight/midtone/shadow that change contrast within an image. By tweaking these values, you can usually bring down your file size.
- *Suppress dithering:* Dithering refers to the use of colors in an existing color palette to approximate colors that are not in the palette. Dithering tends to increase file size in GIFs because the GIF compression scheme is less efficient, when adjacent pixels are painted with different colors. Disabling dithering will make pixels that are more adjacent, have the same color so the compression can better shrink the file.

15.8 WORKING WITH SCANNED IMAGES

It's not always necessary to create your own graphics. In fact, it's very often convenient to scan something in (if you have access to a scanner) or use an image that someone else has already scanned in. Either approach is perfectly valid. No one will ever expect you to create all of your own images. When you do use a scanned image though, you should make sure that it really contributes to the message you're trying to convey in your document and that you're not just using it for the sake of using it.

Note: Some people will let you use images that they scanned as long as you give them credit in your document. Make sure you acknowledge the sources of your scanned images.

When to Use Them and Where to Get Them

If you do have a flatbed scanner, making your own scanned images is a simple task. You can use the software that came with the scanner, or you can use a program like Photoshop or Paint Shop Pro. If you're looking for existing scanned images, you can try any of the following sources:

- *Graphics service bureaus*: A graphics service house may have existing images you can use on a royalty basis. It can also probably scan images at a higher quality that you could on a desktop scanner.
- *Stock photo and clip art CD-ROMs:* Many companies sell CD-ROMs with stock photos and/or simple line art you can use. You usually have to acknowledge the producer of the CD in your document as the source of the images.

Manipulating Scanned Images

Scanned images invariably need some kind of touch-up done on them so they are a truer representation of the original. By zooming in on the scanned image in an editor, you can usually see imperfections along the edges of objects and in the coloring of pixels. Be sure to give your scan a good "once over" in this way so it can look its best in your document. (Most scanners come with some kind of image touchup software, like Adobe Photoshop.)

15.9 USEFUL GRAPHICS TOOLS

Throughout this chapter, reference has been made too many different manipulations and edits, you can make to an image. Now it's time to look at some of the programs you can use to make these modifications.

Some of the following image editing programs:

- Lview Pro
- Paint Shop Pro
- Adobe Photoshop
- Microsoft Image Composer
- GIF Construction Set

Each of these is a great graphics program in its own right. You should consider each one and then select the one that meets your needs and is within your budget.

EXERCISE

Objective Type Questions

1. Which image file format would you use for compressed photographs?

   (A) .jpg (B) .bmp

   (C) .gif (D) .cmp

   (E) .img

2. When doing image processing

   (A) the first step is compression

   (B) the last step is compression

   (C) it does not matter whether you do compression first or last

   (D) this is a trick question because one cannot compress images

3. Which of the following is not a good choice for a Web page menu of commands?

   (A) Java applet (B) QuickTime video

   (C) Animated GIF file (D) None of the above

4. Which of the following is never used as meaning of PNG acronym?

   (A) PNG's Not GIF

   (B) Proctor 'N' Gamble

   (C) Portable Network Graphics

   (D) None of the above

5. Which Component is not a part of multimedia?

   (A) Camera (B) Music player

   (C) Computer (D) Blank page

6. Which is the multimedia software?

   (A) MAYA (B) Autocad

   (C) Flash (D) Windows XP

7. What is MP-3?

   (A) A sound player on Windows 9x platform

   (B) New multimedia content on the Web

   (C) Format for compressed sound files

   (D) Graphics presentation software

8. Which of the following utilities provides encryption facility?
   (A) Pretty Good Privacy (B) Win-secure-It
   (C) Both (D) None
9. Which of the following is a file/data compression technique?
   (A) Huffman Compression (B) Shannon-Fano Coding
   (C) Lempel-Ziv-Welch (D) All of the above
   (E) None of the above
10. What is MPEG related to?
    (A) Method of audio-video compression
    (B) Multimedia presentations
    (C) Realistic game play
    (D) E-commerce
11. Give the Organization which goal is not to make multimedia things.
    (A) Reliance (B) EA sports
    (C) SEGA (D) DISNEY
12. When You take a picture with the digital camera you create
    (A) a gif file (B) a jpg or jpeg file
    (C) a bitmap or bmp (D) a black or white etching
13. Which program you use to create multimedia presentation?
    (A) Word processing (B) Database
    (C) Powerpoint (D) Spreadsheet
14. When using sound in a website you should
    (A) always make it loop continuously so it does not stop
    (B) always mute it so the person looking at the site cannot hear it.
    (C) give the person viewing your site the option of turning it on or off.
    (D) make it sound real loud so the viewer can really enjoy it.
15. Which of the following statements is false?
    (A) JPEG files cannot be animated like GIF files
    (B) GIF files are commonly used for animation
    (C) JPG files are easy for animation when they contain less than 256 colors
    (D) None of the above

16. What is the most common way animations are used on the Web?

(A) Menu chbices (B) Advertising banners

(C) Games (D) All of the above

17. Which company developed QuickTime movie format?

(A) Microsoft (B) Apple

(C) Sun (D) Oracle

18. There are _____color names recognized by all version of HTML.

(A) 6 (B) 8

(C) 256 (D) 16

19. _____refers to the way the GIF file is saved by the graphics software.

(A) Dithering

(B) Interlacing

(C) Balancing

20. Which of the following would require lossless compression?

(A) text data (B) video data

(C) image data (D) audio data

(E) none of the above--none require lossless compression

Review & Discussion Questions

1. How graphics images are stored in Computer?
2. What is Bitmap Graphics? How Bitmap images are stored?
3. List out the different types of Bitmap images.
4. What is Vector Graphics? How it works? List out the files formats with example.
5. What do you mean by web graphics format? Explain any three graphics formats with example.
6. Define GIF. Explain different types of GIF.
7. Define JPEG. What is the specialty of using JPEG file in Internet?
8. Define PNG. Why now days people are using PNG file format in Internet?
9. How can you reduce image size in Internet? Give example.
10. List out the graphics tools used for image editing.
11. Give the full forms and a difference between .DAT and a .GIF file with respect to multimedia.
12. Give two differences between AVI and MPEG file formats.